IMAGES
of America

NEWPORT

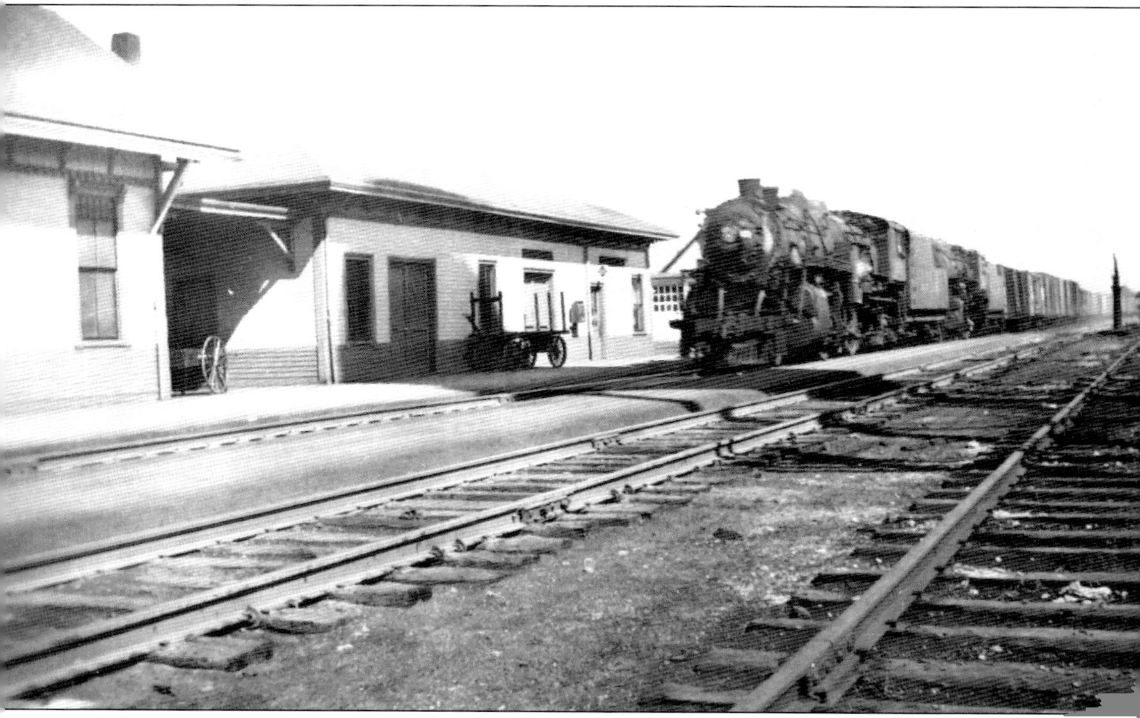

The dog on the cover image may be Ted, who belonged to baggage master Everet Soule. Ted was well known to travelers, as he worked at the Newport Junction for more than 12 years, purportedly even transporting papers to and from the freight office. Ted was struck by a train in the early 1920s but survived and returned to work. (Photograph by Sid Smith; courtesy of Maude Smith.)

On the Cover: The Newport depot was once a bustling destination on Railroad Avenue. Newport was the junction for several Maine Central Railroad lines. The crewmembers pictured here are Ross Gilman, unidentified, Warren Hubbard, Erwin Pushor, agent George Plummer, Ray Faulkner, unidentified, Will Crocker, and two more unidentified men. (Courtesy of the Newport Cultural Center.)

IMAGES
of America

NEWPORT

Leigh Hallett with the
Newport Cultural Center

ARCADIA
PUBLISHING

ISBN 978-0-7385-9160-5

Published by Arcadia Publishing
Charleston, South Carolina

Printed in the United States of America

Library of Congress Control Number: 2011941028

For all general information, please contact Arcadia Publishing:
Telephone 843-853-2070
Fax 843-853-0044
E-mail sales@arcadiapublishing.com
For customer service and orders:
Toll-Free 1-888-313-2665

Visit us on the Internet at www.arcadiapublishing.com

This book is dedicated to Omar Perry, a good neighbor and kind man, whose generous bequests led to the creation of the Newport Cultural Center.

Contents

ACKNOWLEDGMENTS

Over its 50-year history, the Newport Historical Society assembled a fine collection of old photographs and documents about the town of Newport. Many of those items became part of the collection of the Newport Cultural Center (NCC), which formed when the Newport Public Library merged with the Newport Historical Society in 2005. I am grateful to the people who gathered those documents and for their decades of devotion to preserving the history of Newport.

The citizens of Newport deserve credit for the existence of the Newport Cultural Center; not only did they come up with the idea for a new kind of facility, they raised over $1 million to build it. Newport town manager Jim Ricker was an ardent advocate for the project from its inception. The creation of the NCC was also supported by area businesses and organizations. Goody Gilman was particularly instrumental in making the Newport Cultural Center possible and continues to provide cheerful support for all sorts of our endeavors. Greg Lovley, a local businessman and history enthusiast, has been tremendously supportive of the NCC. Because so many individuals worked together, Newport now has a safe, secure, and beautiful structure in which to preserve its cultural heritage. It has made the creation of this book not only possible, but also pleasurable.

Several Newport natives provided vital assistance and support, especially David Hall, Sharon Hopkins, Steve Rowe, Goody Gilman, Dale Carsley, Maude Smith, Barbara Fletcher, and Dody Duplisea. My husband, Winn Price, was not only forbearing, but provided proofreading services as well.

Unless otherwise noted, all photographs are from the Newport Cultural Center, whose archives include the former Newport Historical Society's collection as well as collections assembled by local history lovers, such as Ronald Plummer and the late Kristi Hamilton. Paul Giguere of the Maine Department of Transportation (MaineDOT) and Kevin Johnson, photo archivist for the Penobscot Marine Museum (PMM), both generously provided help with images from their collections.

Introduction

The town of Newport is nestled in the Sebasticook Valley of Central Maine and surrounds the 6,000-acre lake known as Lake Sebasticook. North Newport and East Newport are important and historic parts of the community, each located on their respective sides of the lake.

Thousands of years ago, Native Americans frequented the Sebasticook Valley, a portage between the Sebasticook and Kennebec Rivers. One of the oldest carbon-dated archaeological sites in North America is a fish weir in the Sebasticook Lake. Protected under mud for millennia, the site has provided insight into tribal culture in the area.

In the late 18th century, surveyors roughly mapped out the area around the Great East Pond, as Sebasticook Lake was then called. Settlers soon followed, especially favoring both the north side of the lake and around the lake's outlet at the East Branch of the Sebasticook River. The latter area is where the village developed, and the town incorporated on June 14, 1814, as the 208th town in the District of Maine. (Until 1820, Maine was part of Massachusetts.) The lake provided bountiful fishing to the early settlers, and the slopes around the lake were well suited for agriculture. Still, it was a frontier town and was set amid dense forests that inhibited travel.

A new phase of local history began when the railroad came to Newport in 1855. Eventually, the town became an important junction between two lines of the Maine Central Railroad. Improved mobility of people and goods dramatically changed the way of life in the town. Factories were built along the railroad tracks, producing wool fiber, wool fabrics, and canned milk. These products were made for export, even while trains brought in carloads of the products townsfolk wished to purchase in the village shops.

The Maine Central Railroad also brought visitors to Newport, drawn by the beautiful Sebasticook Lake. In the 1860s, the Grand Army of the Republic purchased the peninsula it called Camp Benson and began outfitting the camp with recreational amenities. Newport was an easy train trip from other Central Maine towns and also began attracting visitors from Portland and Boston. Enterprising locals opened inns and boardinghouses. Newport's Board of Trade advertised the town as "Maine's Delightful Inland Resort." The lake was reported to be unparalleled in plentitude of fish. By the end of the 1800s, there were multiple charter boat businesses ferrying visitors to the inns, fishing spots, and recreational venues around the lake. Soon, fine vacation homes and charming cottages were built around the lake.

Unfortunately, the industrial age took a heavy toll on Sebasticook Lake. By the mid-20th century, the once-pristine lake was polluted by the town dump, by run-off from the farms around its perimeter, and by residential and industrial sewage flowing down the East Branch of the Sebasticook River. In the early 1960s, the lake was deemed too polluted for swimming, and many of the inns and camps around the perimeter were empty all summer. The Newport Woman's Club spearheaded the effort to reverse the decline of the lake. Over 1,700 townspeople signed a petition requesting that the state legislature pass LD 1143, a law to reclassify the East Branch of the Sebasticook River prohibiting its use for industrial waste and sewage. Sponsored by local representative Seth Bradstreet and supported by former governor (and Newport native) Lewis Barrows, the bill passed in 1965. Thanks to the rigorous efforts of concerned citizens in the 1960s, Newport once again has an attractive lake that draws visitors to the area.

The 1960s was a decade of turmoil in the town. Whether to establish a consolidated school district with other area towns was a contentious issue. Eventually the Nokomis Regional High School was built, and the old high school on Elm Street became the grade school. The new school was built outside of town and was no longer visible or within walking distance for most Newport residents.

Similarly, the new freeway, I-95, drew attention away from downtown Newport. The town was fortunate to be located so near the new artery, but it was a double-edged sword. Travelers who had previously taken state roads through town (Route 100 was the main road to Bangor and Route 2 the main path to Skowhegan) soon bypassed towns in favor of the new freeway. By the 1970s, downtown clothing and food shops, restaurants, and hotels were struggling to stay in business. In fact, many of Newport's thriving new businesses were built adjacent to the highway, in a formerly rural area known as the Triangle. Located at the hub of so many major roads (including Route 7, the gateway to the Moosehead Lake region), Newport has become something of a junction again, as it had been in the railroad days. Alas, in 2012, motorists may refuel and dine near the interstate exit, missing the town itself and its large lake.

For Newport's residents, though, there were many improvements around the end of the 20th century and beginning of the 21st. The removal of the lower dam at Main Street meant that the river basin was no longer flooded year-round. In the 1990s, the town took on an award-winning project to restore the river to a more natural course, as it would have been before the first dams had been built 160 years prior. The winding course of the restored riverbed is not only more attractive but is also more hospitable to wildlife. Great blue herons can often be seen wading in the meandering waters of the East Branch of the Sebasticook River as it passes through town.

In 2009, the Newport Cultural Center opened, combining collections from the former public library and the historical society. The facility also houses historical records and artifacts and is a venue for the arts. Located on Main Street, the building was designed to recall the historic architecture the 19th century. Two years later, a new river walkway was built, allowing pedestrians to stroll along the water between Main and Center Streets. In 2011, the swim front on the American Legion's four-acre property in the cove was restored by the town to encourage people to take advantage of the revitalized lake. The tennis courts were completely rebuilt as well. A modern boat landing with parking amenities also draws people to the area.

The appearance of Newport has changed dramatically over its 200-year history. Fortunately, beautiful reminders of a bygone era exist in the residential structures around the town. Although there is relatively little industry in the town today, a diversified economy and larger towns nearby make it possible for many people to call Newport home. Sebasticook Lake has been restored to its natural beauty and is once again a destination for boating, fishing, and swimming. After two centuries of growth, Newport remains a town blessed by a central location and abundant historic and natural charm.

One

Sebasticook Lake

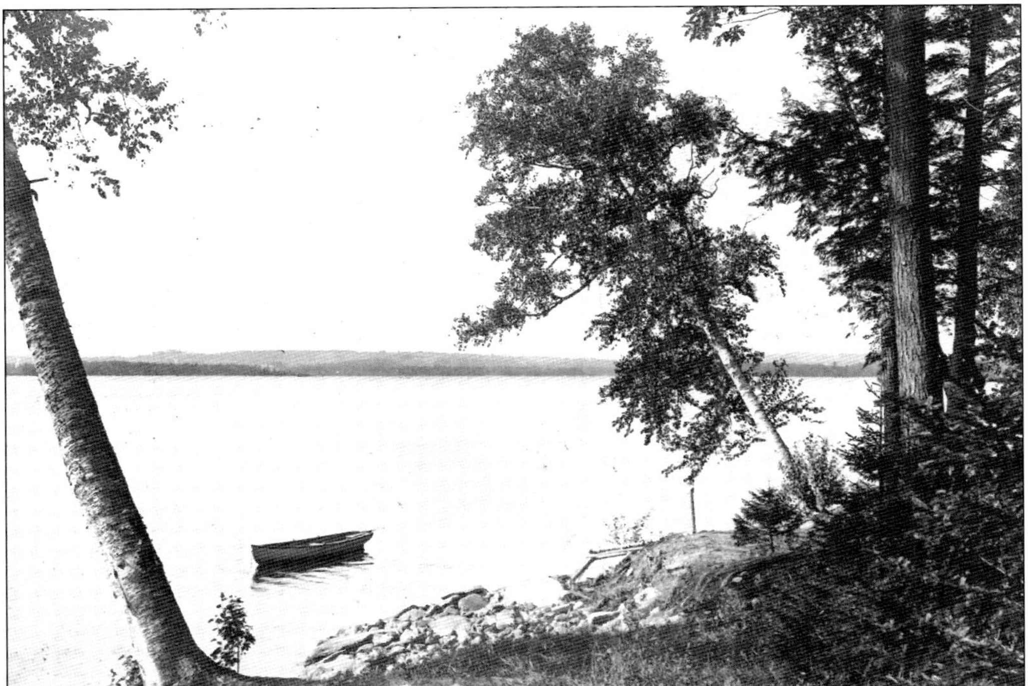

Long before the arrival of the first white settlers in Central Maine, Native Americans were fishing in Sebasticook Lake and navigating its waters in canoes. In 1991, two amateur archaeologists made the startling discovery of the remains of a wooden fish weir on the north shore of the lake. Later, a team of archaeologists from the University of Maine at Farmington studied the site, and carbon dating revealed that it dated back to nearly 4000 BCE.

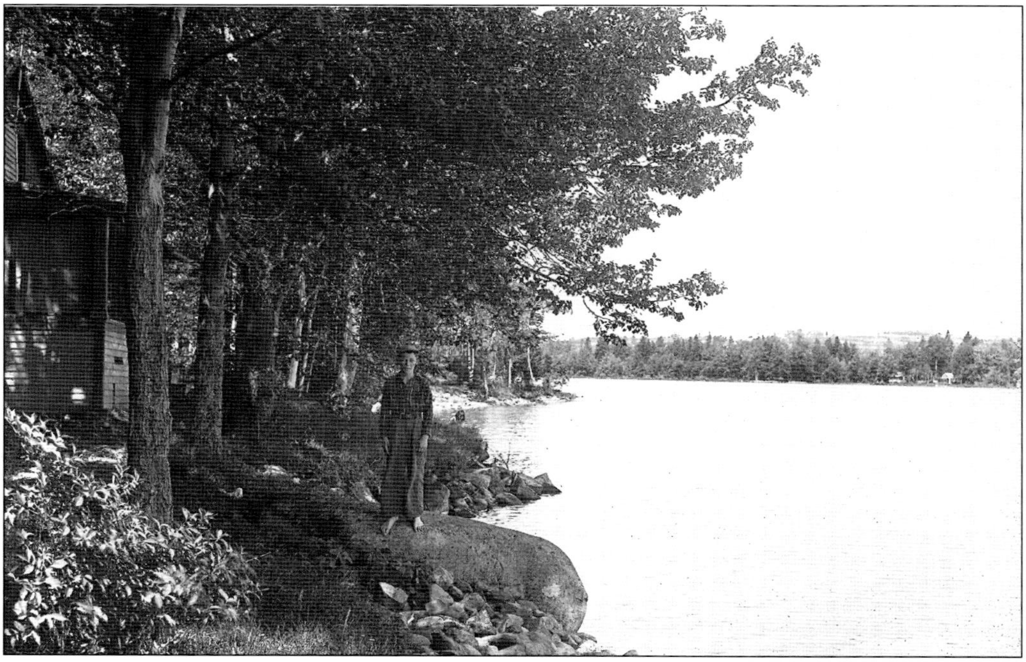

Dr. E.W. Trueworthy maintained a large summer home on a hill overlooking the lake and cherished his time in his Newport. He described the lake as "a beautiful sheet of water surrounded in the main by high land, with rocky shores or sandy beaches . . . For its size there is no better fishing lake in New England." The lake was famous for its fish, especially white perch and black bass. (Courtesy of the PMM.)

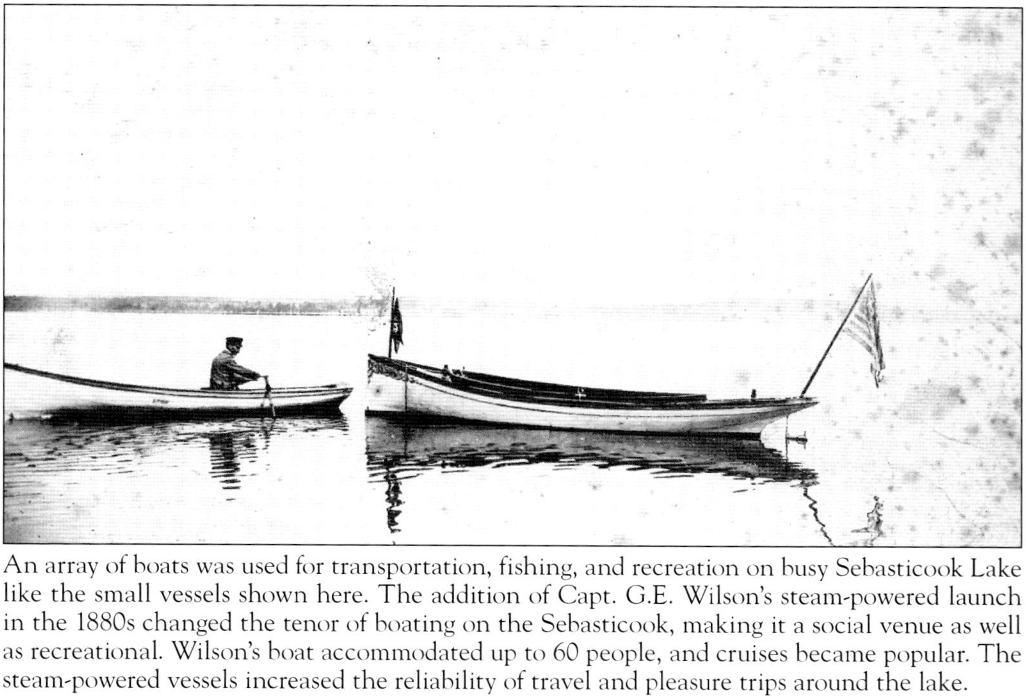

An array of boats was used for transportation, fishing, and recreation on busy Sebasticook Lake like the small vessels shown here. The addition of Capt. G.E. Wilson's steam-powered launch in the 1880s changed the tenor of boating on the Sebasticook, making it a social venue as well as recreational. Wilson's boat accommodated up to 60 people, and cruises became popular. The steam-powered vessels increased the reliability of travel and pleasure trips around the lake.

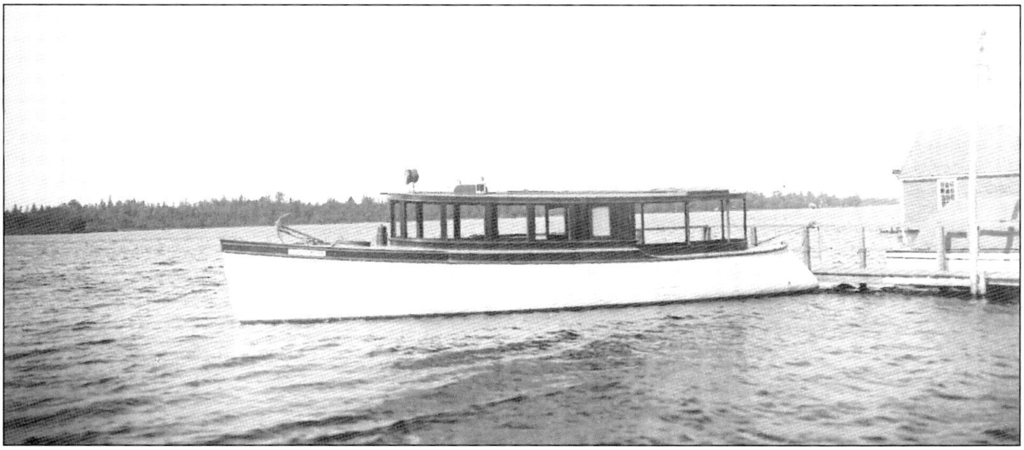

The *Totem* was built by master carpenter and machinist Homer Miles, who constructed the boat and its smaller sister, the *Madeline,* in a shop behind his Water Street home. Miles named the smaller boat after his daughter and with it competed in a three-mile motorboat race on Sebasticook Lake in 1912. He and the *Madeline* took home the first-place silver trophy, which is still in the possession of his descendants.

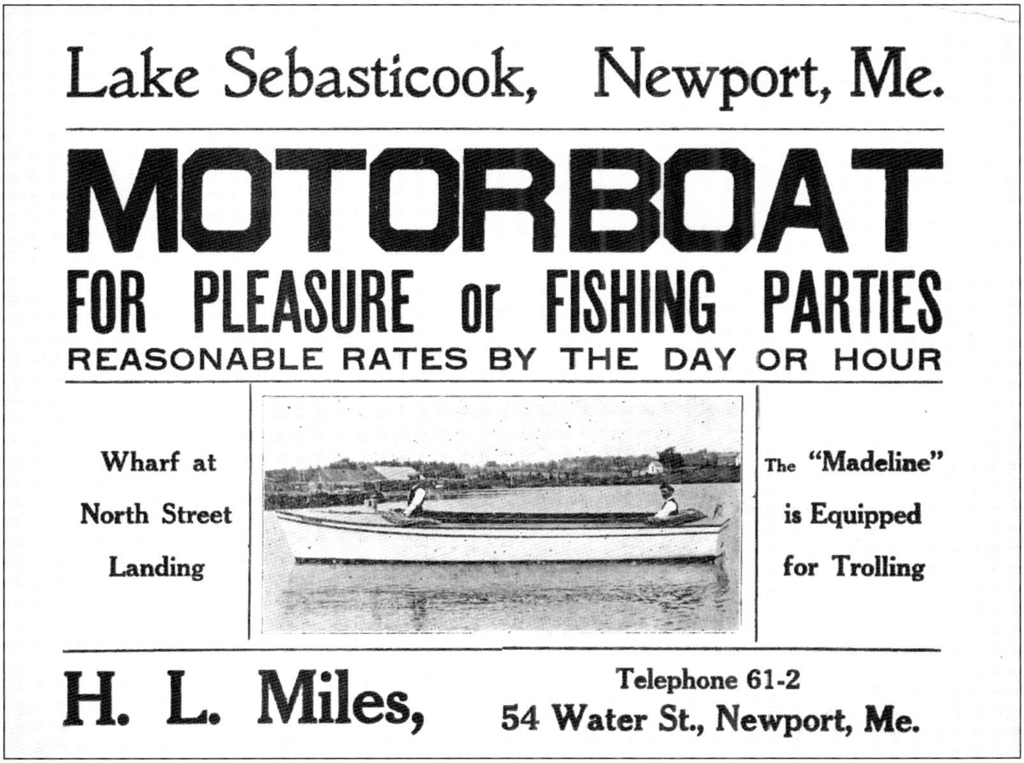

Homer Miles used his boat, the *Madeline*, which could accommodate up to 16 people, to run a charter service and a ferry to Camp Benson. The motorboat offered an appealing mode of travel for reaching recreational facilities at Camp Benson or for visiting family and friends on distant shores of the lake. Fishing was also popular, and the *Madeline* was outfitted for trolling. Homer's boats were moored at a wharf at the end of Water Street.

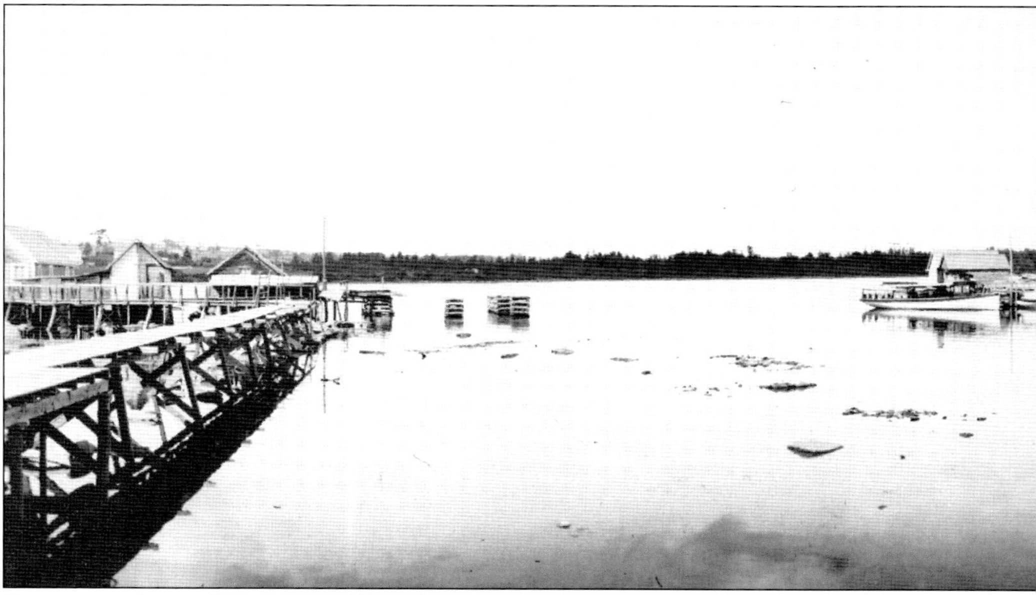

Current residents of Newport will hardly recognize this scene, built up as it is with wharves and boathouses. Taken at the end of Water Street, this image shows Philbrick's wharf at left and the dam at right. The land in the distance is where the Legion Hall and swim front are now located. Also in the distance, Wilson's steamer *Norita* is tied up. By 1920, there were 20 to 30 charter boats operating on the lake. Located several blocks from the train station, this area was where

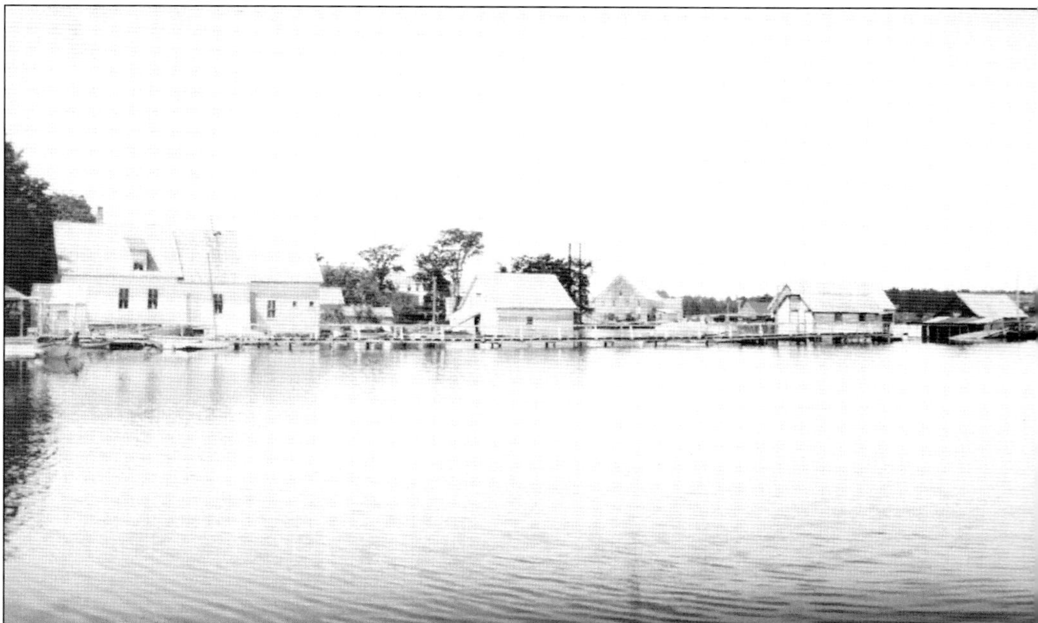

The steamer *Norita* was tied up at a wharf at the end of Water Street, where her owner, Captain Wilson, lived (where the American Legion Hall is currently located). The *Norita* could hold up to 60 passengers and was often used to ferry people across the lake to Camp Benson or on pleasure cruises around the lake. Vacationers could ride the train to the depot, stroll down Water Street,

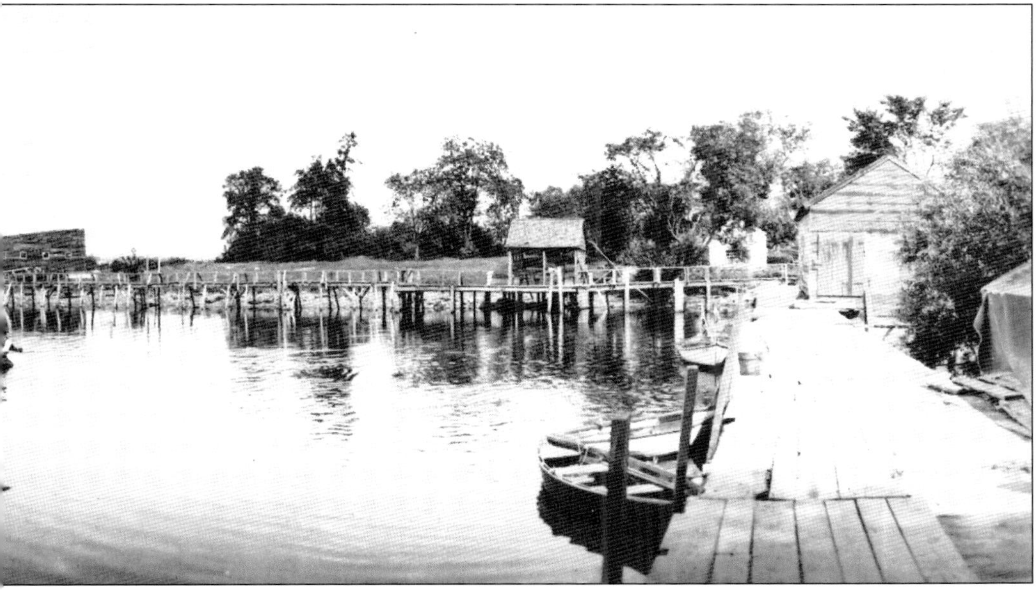

people headed to hire a steamboat or rent a rowboat or canoe. Now there is a modern public boat landing in the cove. By adjusting the dam, the lake is drawn down each fall as part of the maintenance program to keep the water clear. The regular raising and lowering of the lake has proven to be an expensive engineering challenge, but the return of wildlife to the lake and its restoration as a recreational resource make it worthwhile.

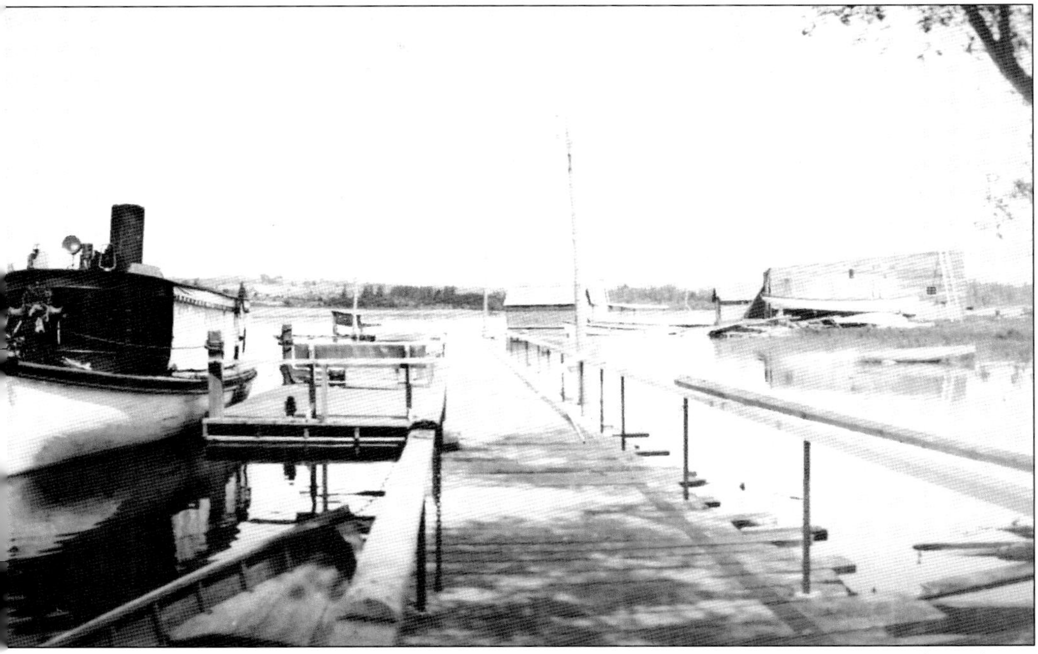

step aboard a steamer, and soon thereafter step out onto the boardwalk at the Pavilion dance hall at Camp Benson. Gray's store and the Brown's home are visible on the far left. Cooper's Mill can also be seen.

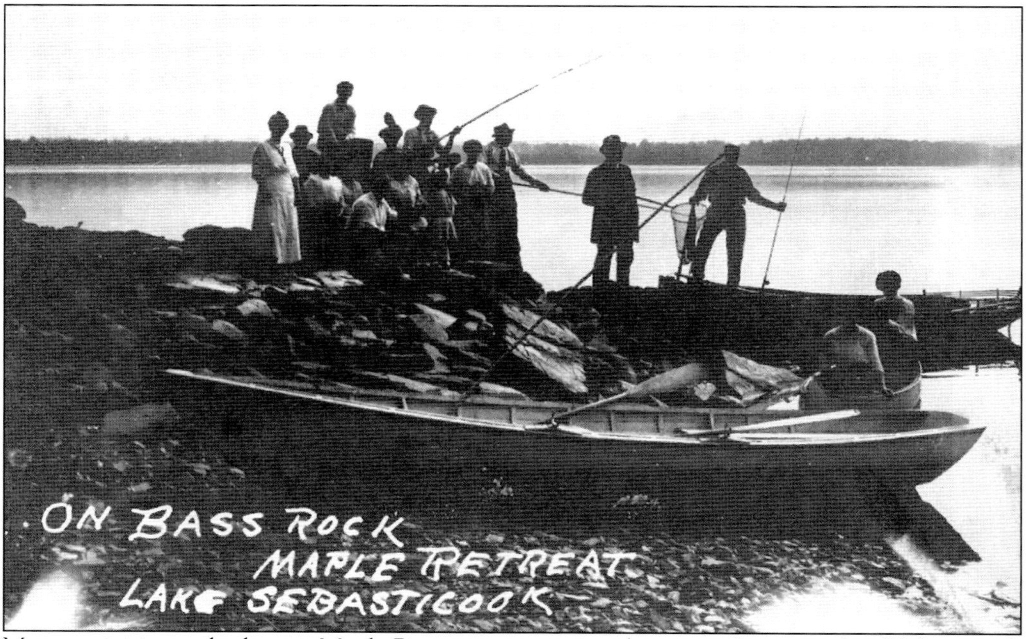

Many activities took place at Maple Retreat, a recreational area on the east side of Sebasticook Lake. It was a picnic site, campground, and also had cottages to rent. Fishing was one of the favorite activities, and the fish were plentiful. Local residents enjoyed the activities there, and many railroad workers and others came up from Massachusetts to spend the summer. (Courtesy of Dody Duplisea.)

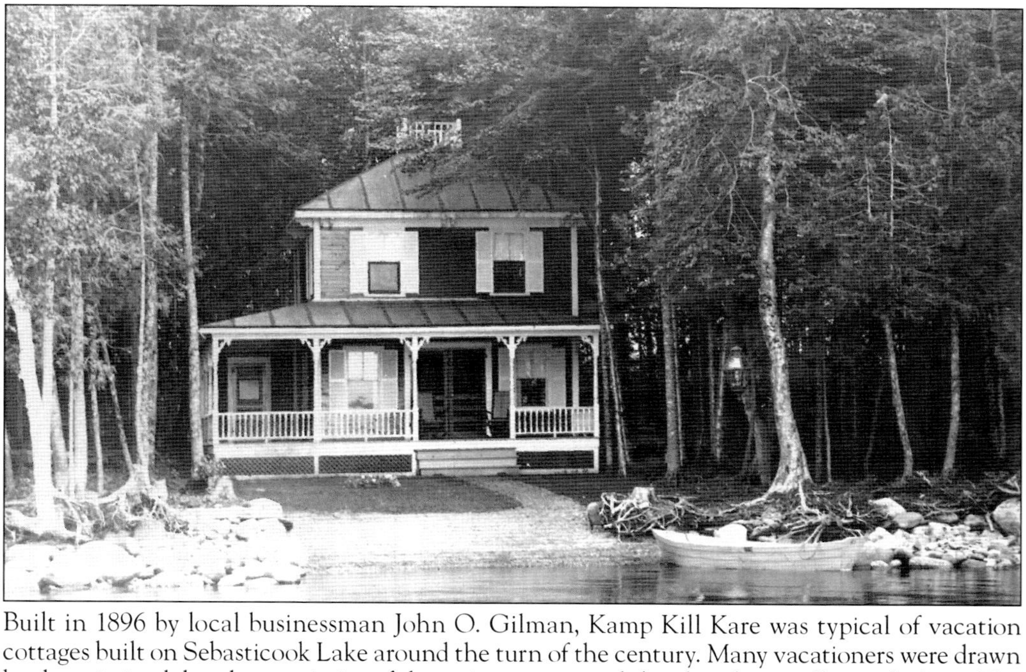

Built in 1896 by local businessman John O. Gilman, Kamp Kill Kare was typical of vacation cottages built on Sebasticook Lake around the turn of the century. Many vacationers were drawn by the pristine lake, the proximity of the train station, and the abundance of boats for hire. The home shown here is still owned by the Gilman family.

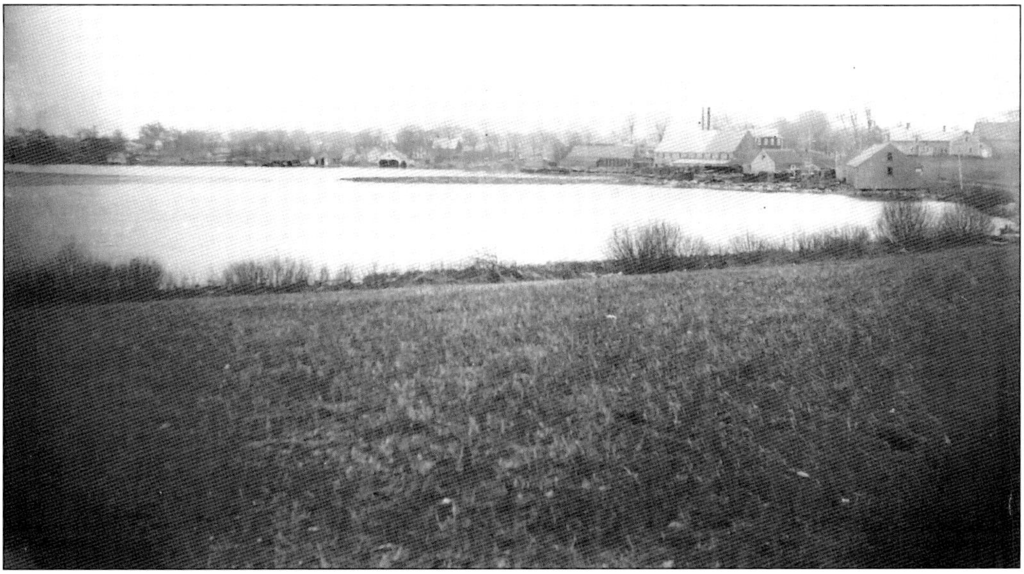

Sebasticook Lake was a vital part of Newport's 19th-century economy. This image shows one of the businesses that relied heavily on the water for transportation. The Cooper Brothers Mill, which was located off High Street in the cove of the lake, used the lake to float in lumber and load it onto carriages that were pulled out of the water by horses.

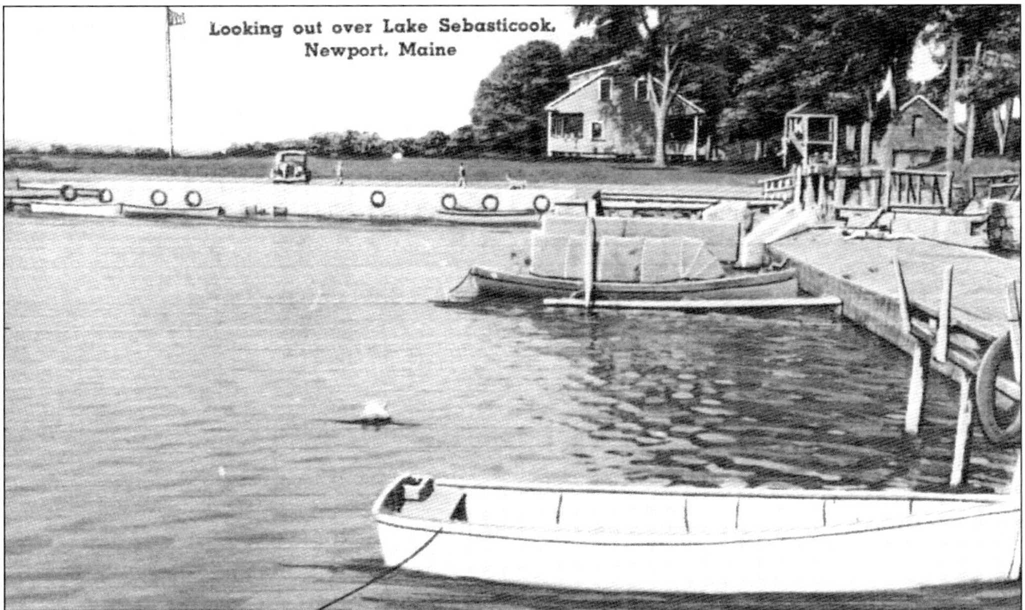

The so-called "upper dam" on North Street has long been used to control the height of the lake's water. At least as far back as 1911, there were disputes between lakeshore residents and the power company that owned the dam over proper maintenance and lake level. A newspaper columnist at the time referred to the imbroglio as "the dam bogey," which was revisited as recently as September 2011 when damage from Hurricane Irene caused a precipitous drop in the lake's level. (Courtesy of Ronald Plummer.)

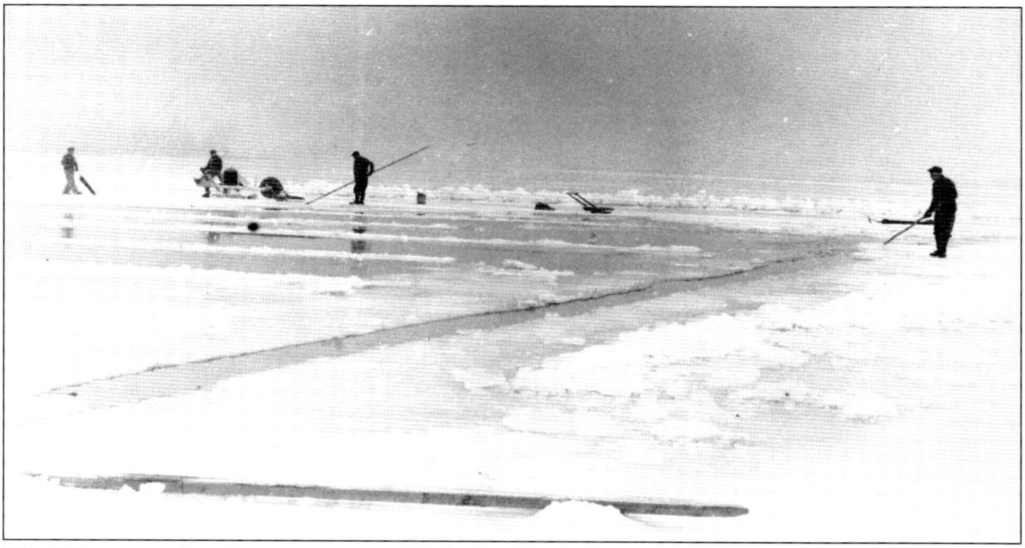

The Sebasticook Ice Company was established in 1889. Crews cut ice from the lake for refrigeration well into the 1940s. Originally using manpower and horsepower exclusively, the men pictured in this 1943 photograph used trucks and conveyor belts to move the massive blocks of ice. The cold, treacherous work resulted in a good supply of ice for Newport and Pittsfield, much of it stored in an icehouse on Sebasticook Street. (Courtesy of the John Dyer family.)

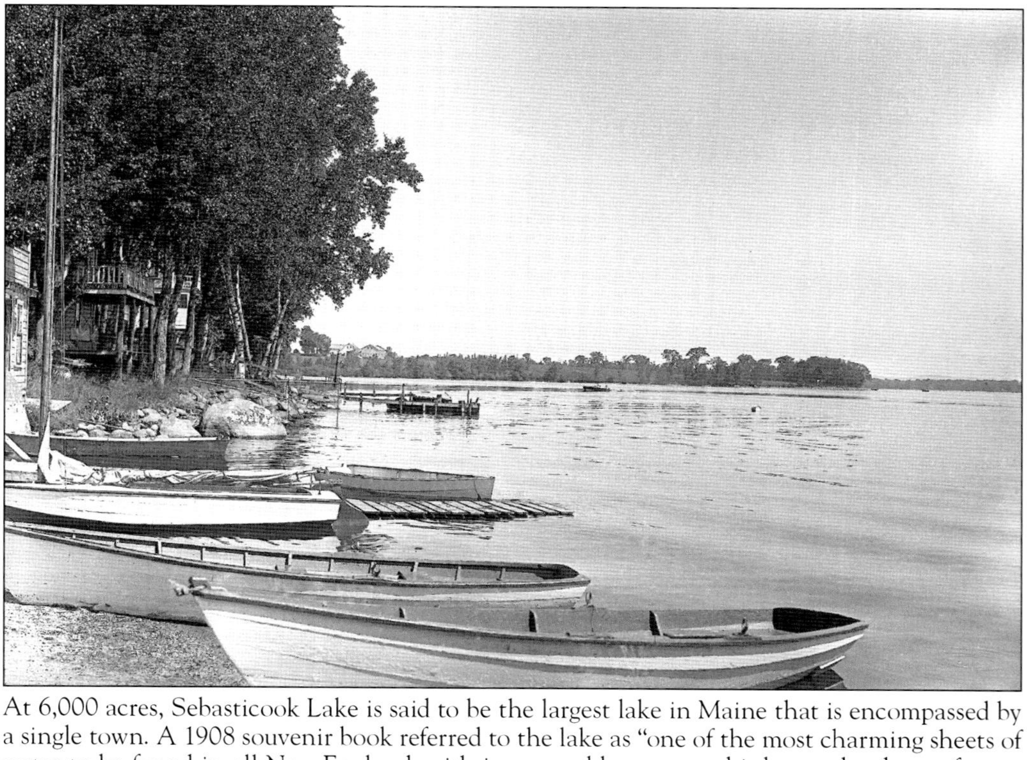

At 6,000 acres, Sebasticook Lake is said to be the largest lake in Maine that is encompassed by a single town. A 1908 souvenir book referred to the lake as "one of the most charming sheets of water to be found in all New England, with innumerable coves and inlets and a shore of more than 20 miles." The lake was renowned for its excellent fishing into the mid-20th century.

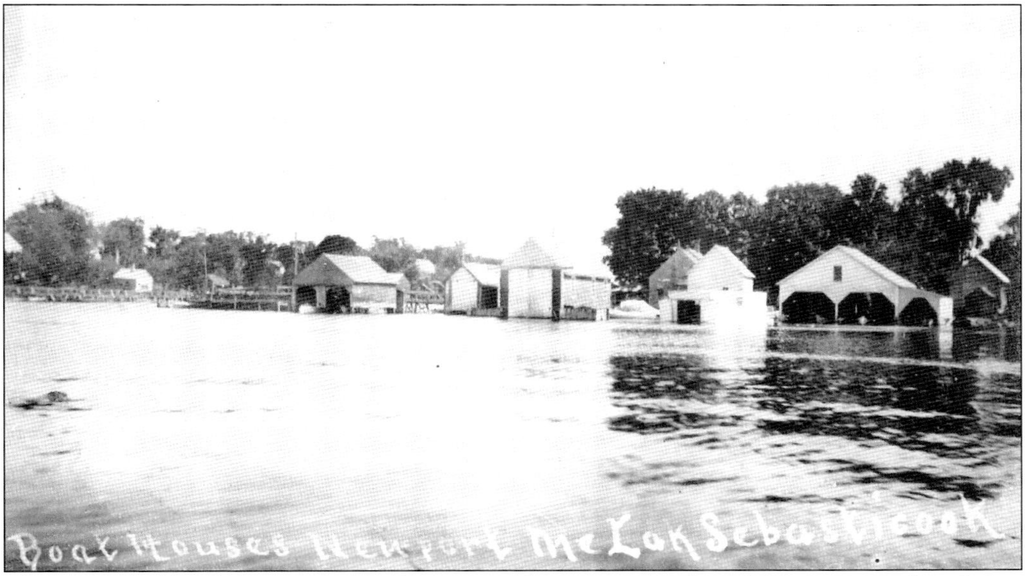

The number of boathouses rimming the cove in this image is striking. Many were used to shelter the charter boats that ferried people around the lake. Fluctuating water levels in the early 1900s made it harder to maintain structures such as these. (Courtesy of Ronald Plummer.)

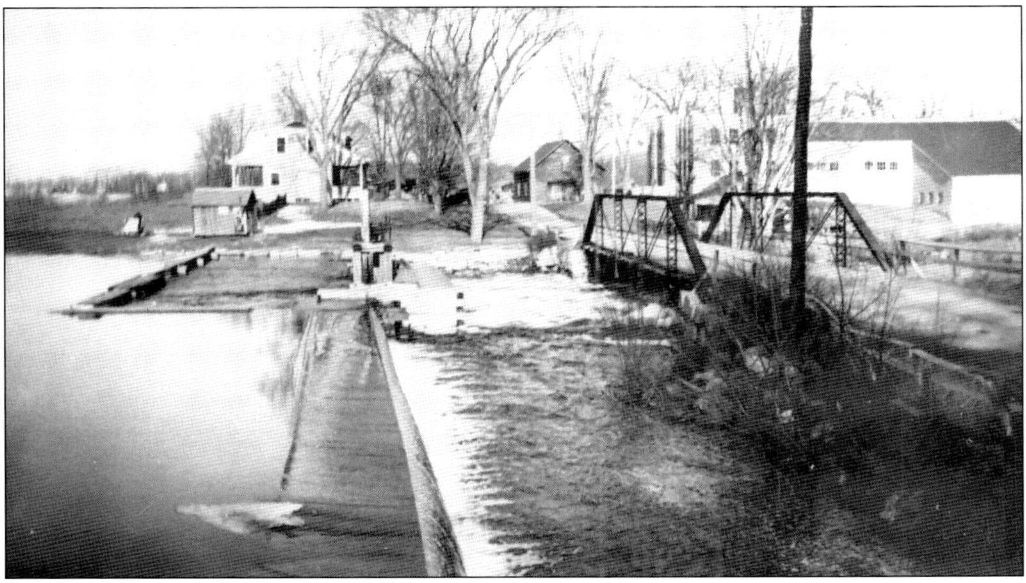

Pictured is the upper dam, with the armory in the background. The American Legion Newport Post 105 formed in 1933. The Legion Hall was built in 1936, where Captain Wilson's home and boathouse had stood before being destroyed by fire. The American Legion makes much of the four-acre property available to the public, including the swim front, which was refurbished by the town in 2011. (Photograph by Sid Smith; courtesy of Maude Smith.)

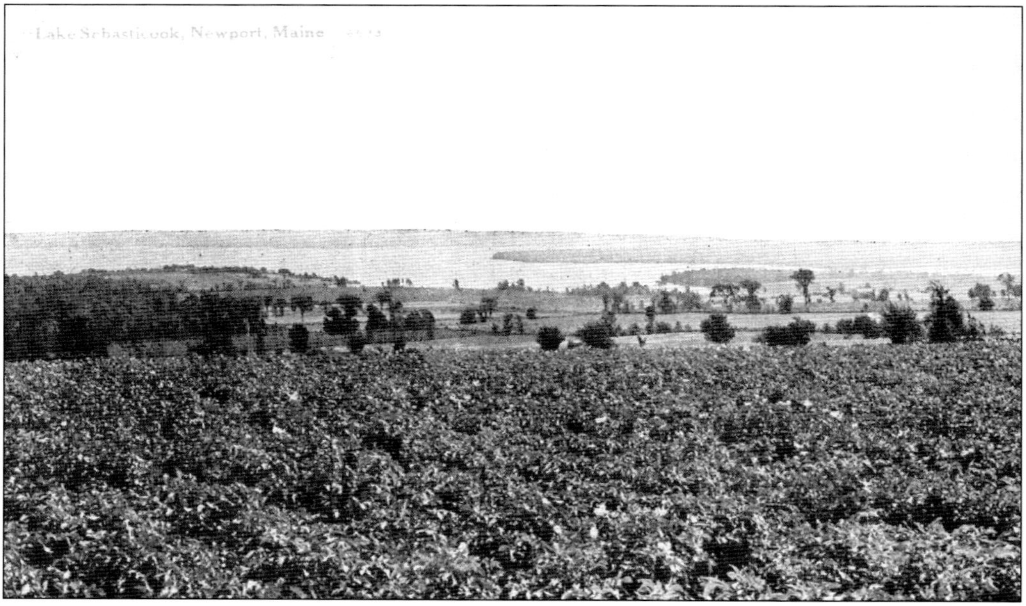

Pollution from the town dump, upriver factories, sewage, and agriculture took a toll on the lake. In 1965, the town selectmen closed the swim front, deeming the water too polluted for safety. Dr. Paul Burke described the lake as "an open catch basin with an open sewer (from the Corinna stream) emptying into it . . . I do not feel the lake is suitable for recreational purposes such as swimming and boating."

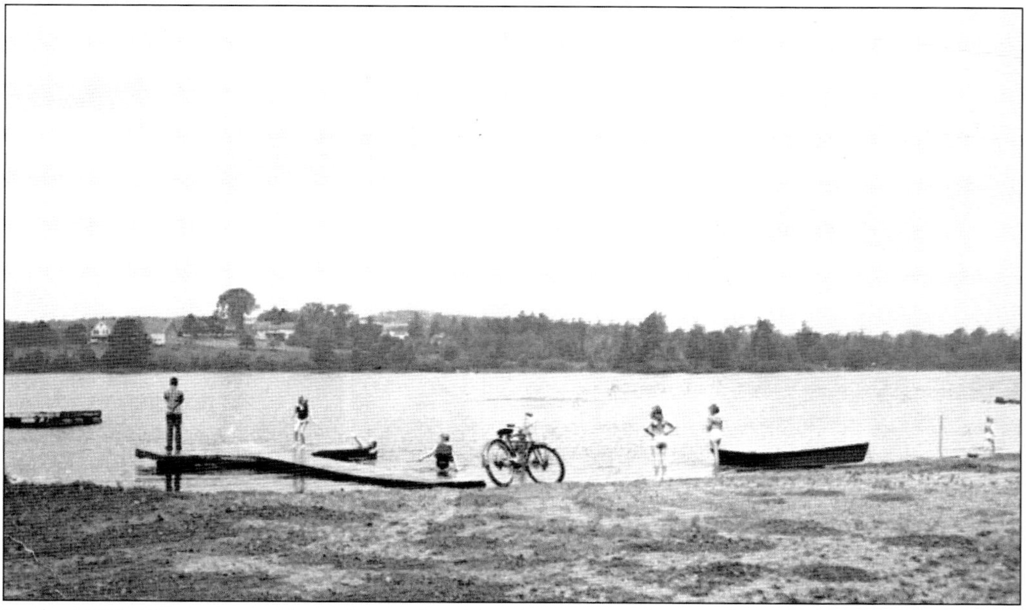

In the 1960s, Newport residents fought hard for the passage of a state law to prohibit sewage from being dumped in the Corinna stream and thereby into Sebasticook Lake. The law was passed, and lake cleanup began. In 1982, the Sebasticook Lake Association formed, an advocacy group that has grown to include 400 members. The swim front (pictured) is once again a popular summer destination and was refurbished in 2011.

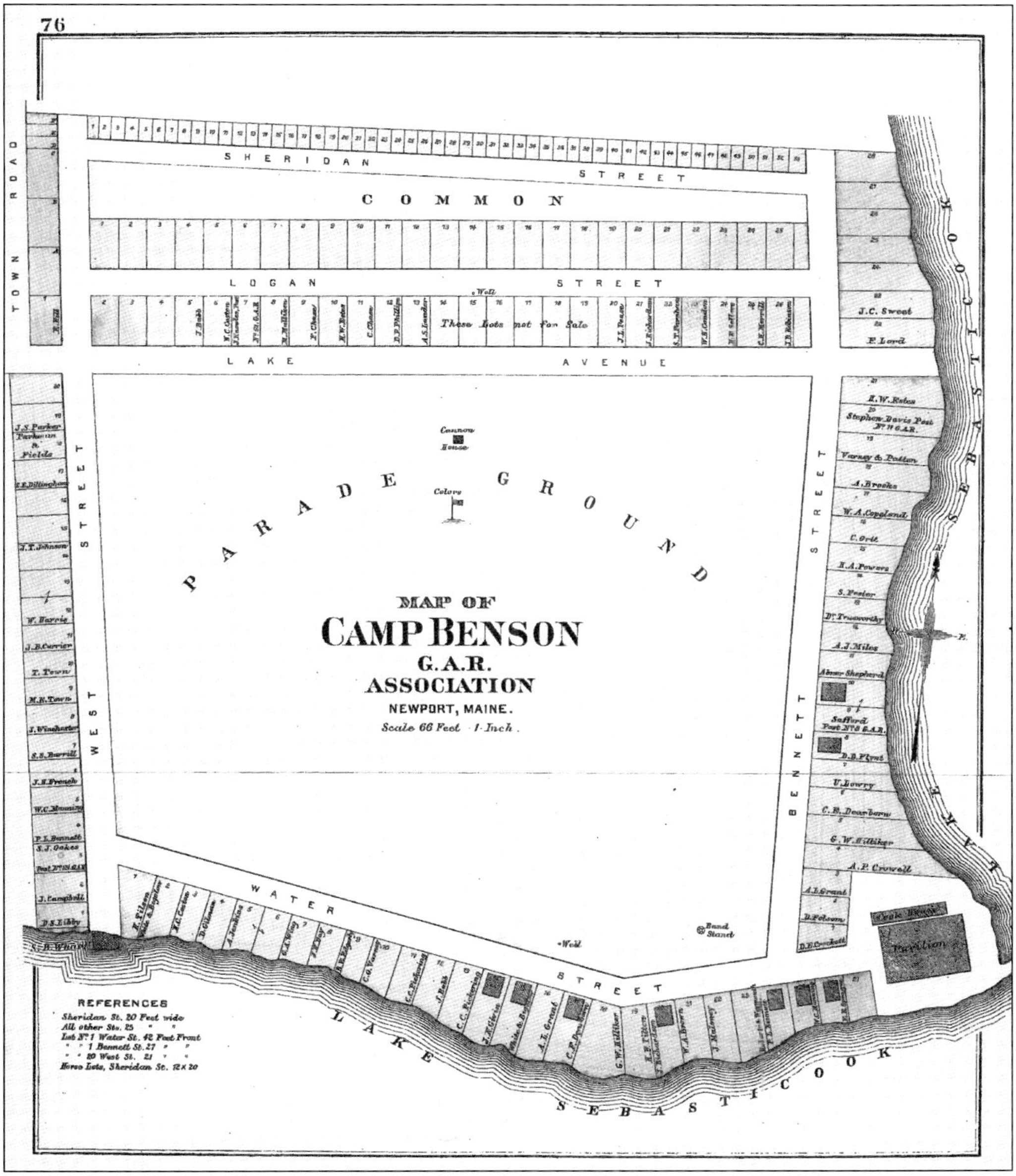

Located just outside of town (heading towards Corinna), Camp Benson is on a peninsula in Lake Sebasticook, opposite the village of Newport. The open land at the center was originally a muster ground in the 1800s. After the Civil War, the H.G. Libby Post No. 118, Department of Maine, Grand Army of the Republic (a fraternal organization of Union veterans founded in 1866), established an association to manage the property. The H.G. Libby Women's Relief Corps, an associated organization, focused on providing support for Civil War veterans. Originally designated for veterans and their families exclusively, the camp gradually became popular with locals and vacationers looking for recreation. At its peak, the camp was a popular resort, with both cottages and camping lots. This map shows the prominent location of the dance hall (the Pavilion) at the tip of the peninsula, with private parcels of land demarcated around the perimeter. The bandstand, well, and cannon house are also noted.

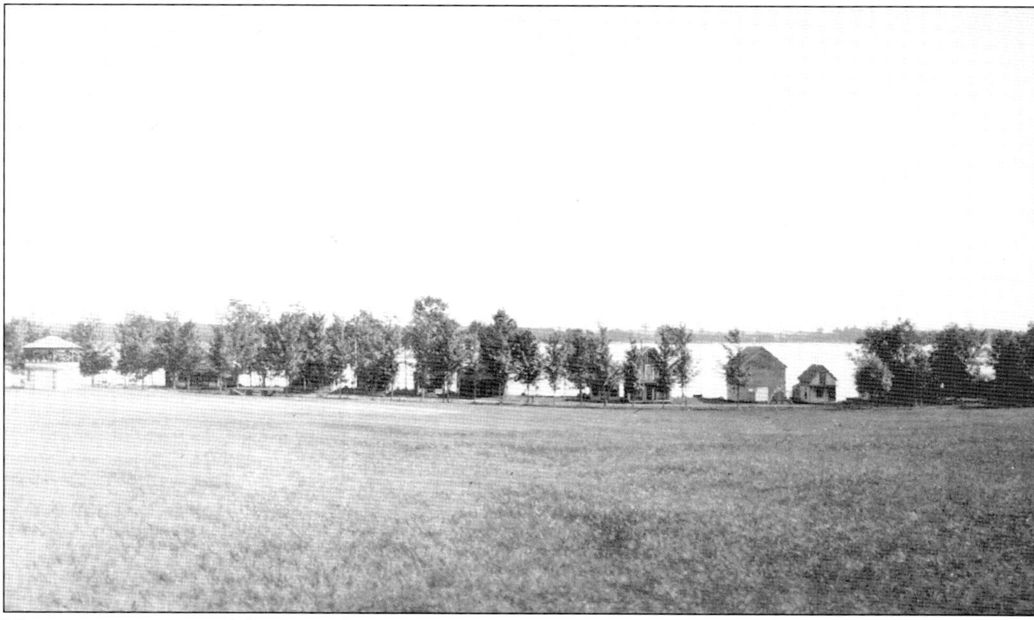

The camp was named for Dr. John Benson, a Newport doctor who served in the Civil War, and the roads were named for Union generals. The central portion of the peninsula remained open

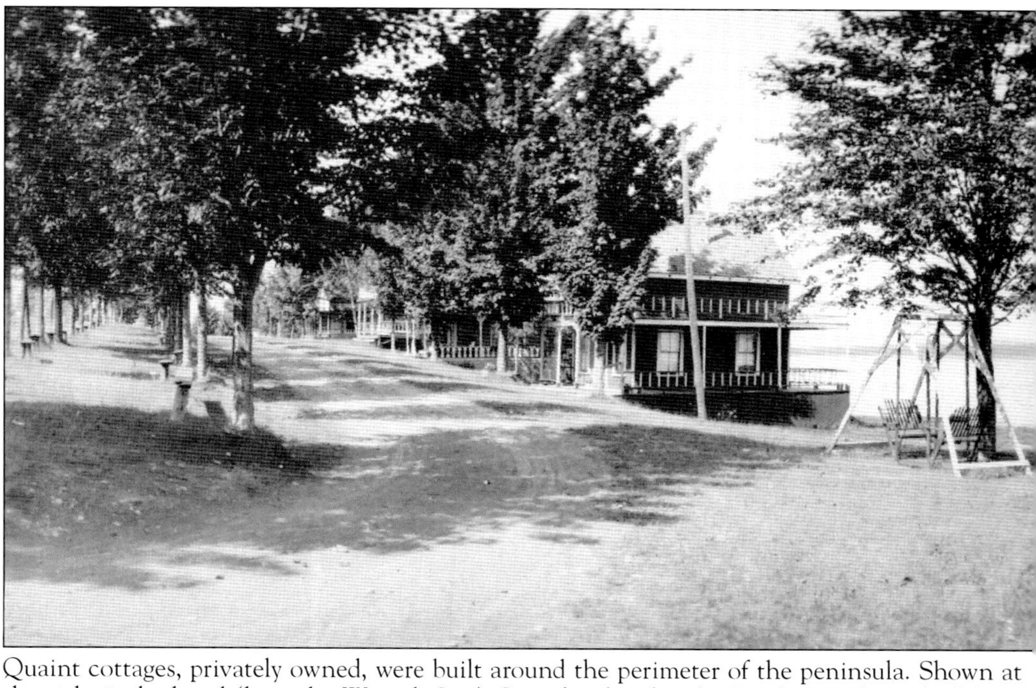

Quaint cottages, privately owned, were built around the perimeter of the peninsula. Shown at the right is the hotel (later the Wayside Inn). Straight ahead is the Pavilion, a dance hall built

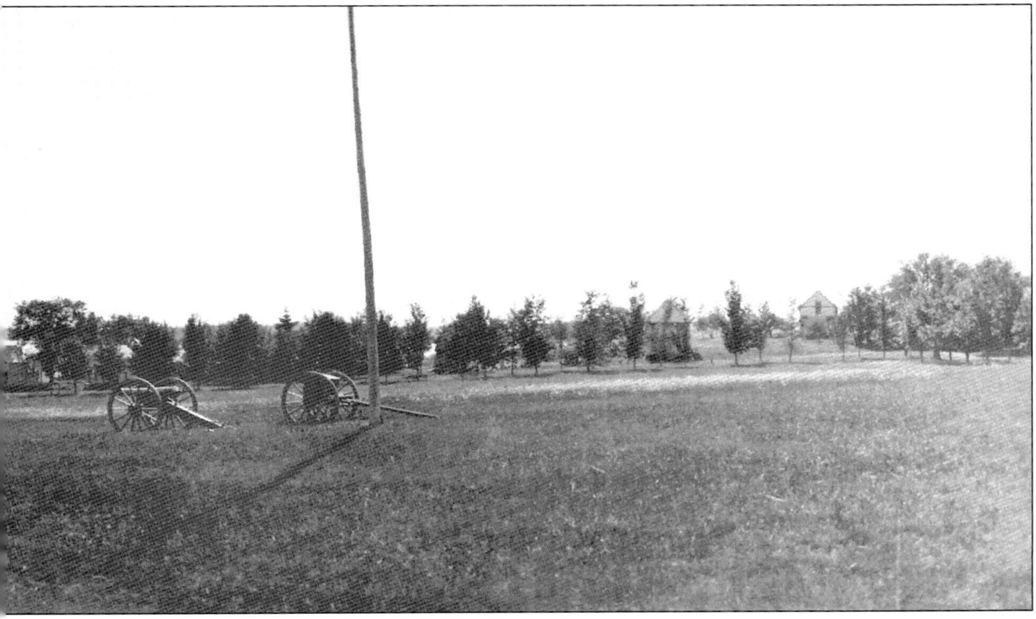

for large gatherings.

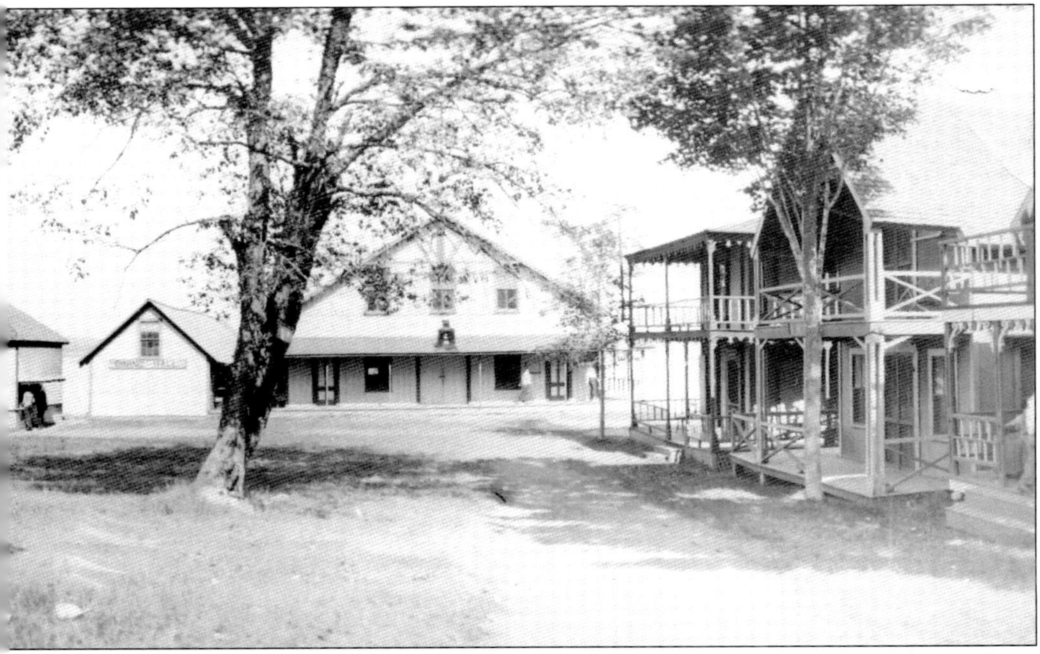

over the lake. Charter boats dropped off passengers at a boardwalk to the right of the Pavilion. To the left of the dance hall are the snack stand and the beach.

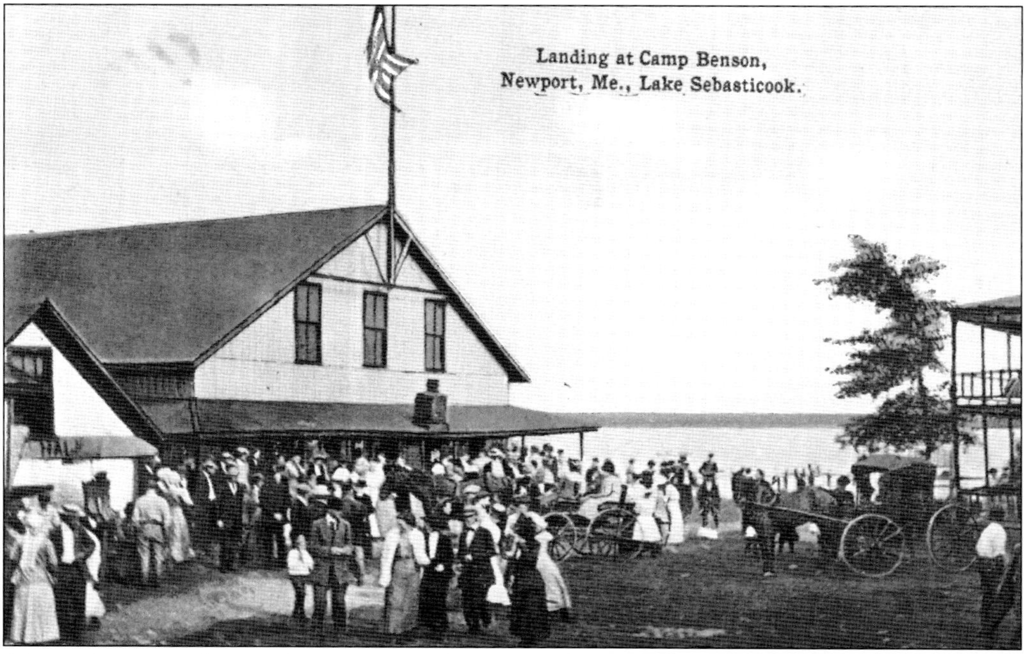

The orchestra at the Pavilion wowed audiences, and a visitor who was quoted in a newspaper at the time declared even Coney Island could not rival the dances held at Camp Benson. The Governor's Day celebration was the highlight of the summer encampment season and featured many special programs and an evening ball. Over the years, many governors attended gala festivities at Camp Benson.

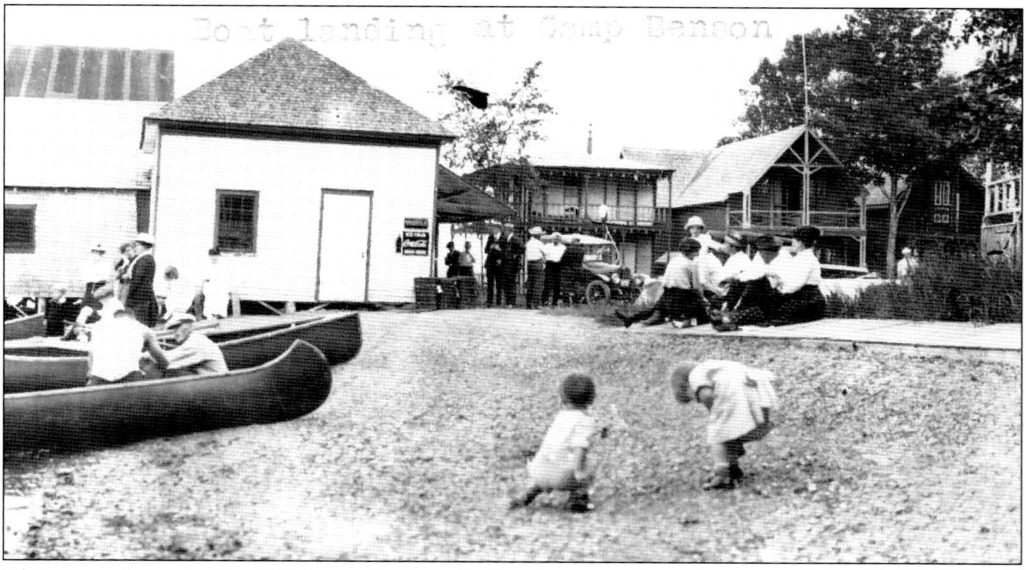

This scene from the late 1800s emphasizes the family atmosphere that prevailed at Camp Benson. Each August, members of the Grand Army of the Republic returned for their annual reunion. It was a time for fellowship among Civil War veterans, and a time to remember those lost. Veterans and their families reconvened each summer for swimming, boating, baseball, dancing, and other wholesome pursuits.

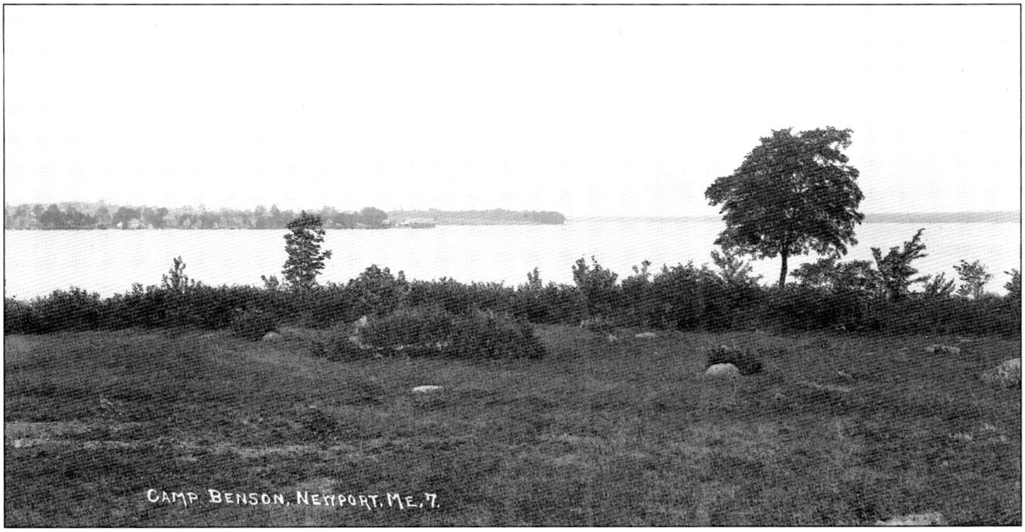

This photograph, likely taken from somewhere along Grove Street, shows the view across the lake to Camp Benson. Near the turn of the 20th century, it was easy to find a boat to ferry one across the water. In the 1960s and 1970s, tourism around the polluted lake drastically declined, but by 2000, the Sebasticook Lake area had again become a lovely place to visit and reside. (Courtesy of the PMM.)

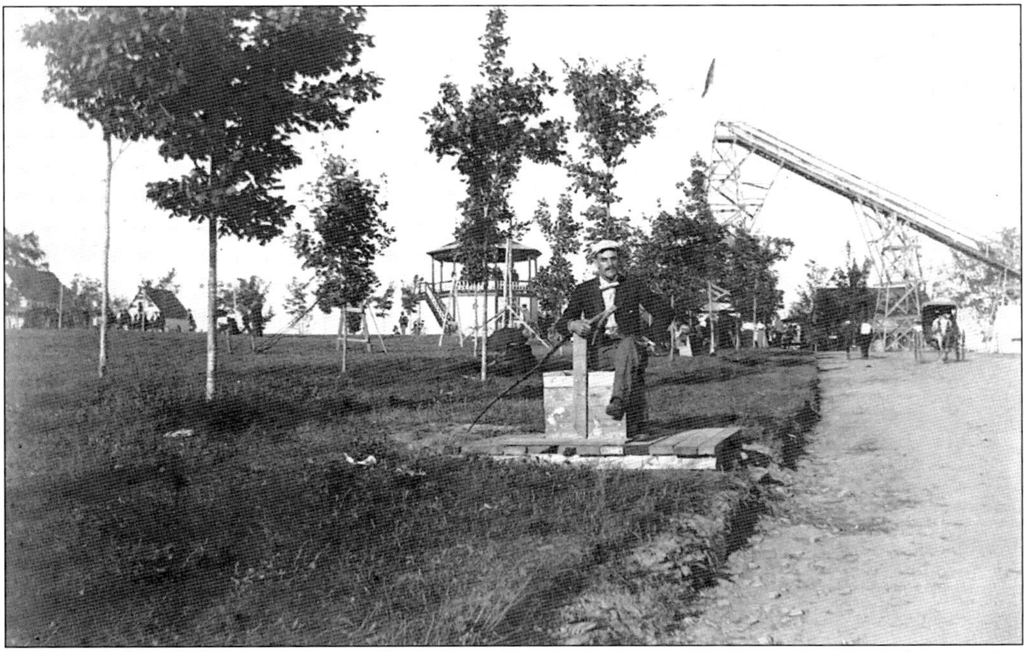

By the early 1900s, Camp Benson had become a popular resort, no longer exclusively for GAR members. Out-of-towners arrived in Newport, "Maine's Delightful Inland Resort," by train to attend events and dances at the site, and others vacationed there. In this photograph, an unidentified man (possibly Homer Miles, owner of the boat *Madeline*) poses seated on the well, with the bandstand and a waterslide in the background. Baseball games were another popular form of entertainment at the resort.

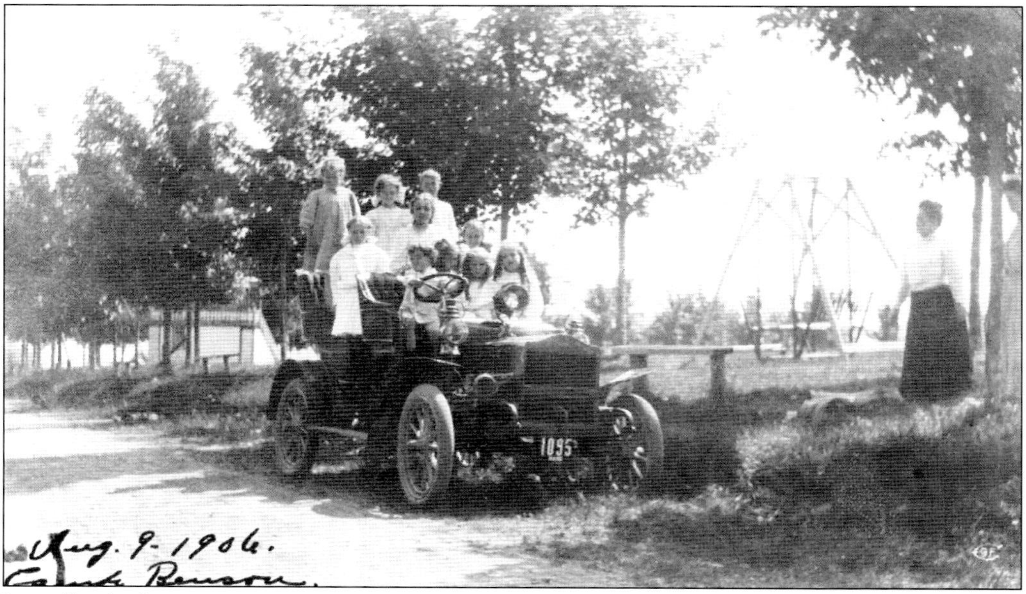

Initially, the best route to Camp Benson was via boat. By 1869, a branch railroad extended as far as Dexter from Newport, and it was possible to take the train to the peninsula. Once a road was built to Camp Benson, families had the option of driving out for the day. Here, an unidentified family poses for a portrait on August 9, 1906.

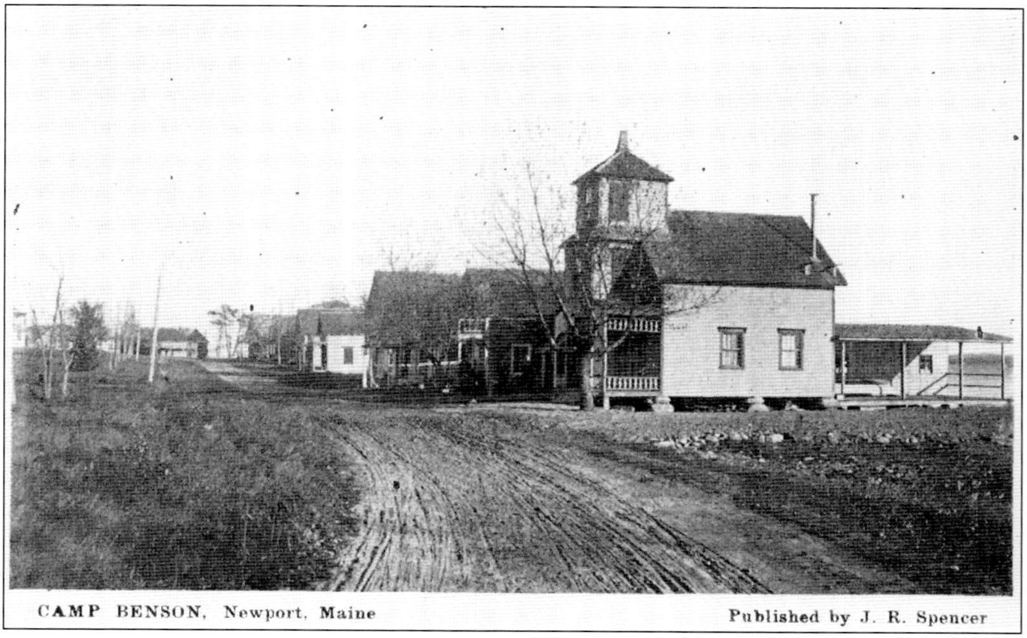

Many of the original cottages were built snugly together, in the Victorian fashion. At Camp Benson, land could only convey to a member of Grand Army of the Republic. Building-use covenants forbade indecent, illegal, irreligious activities of any sort. Many of the original cottages have been lovingly maintained and restored.

Two

Town Life

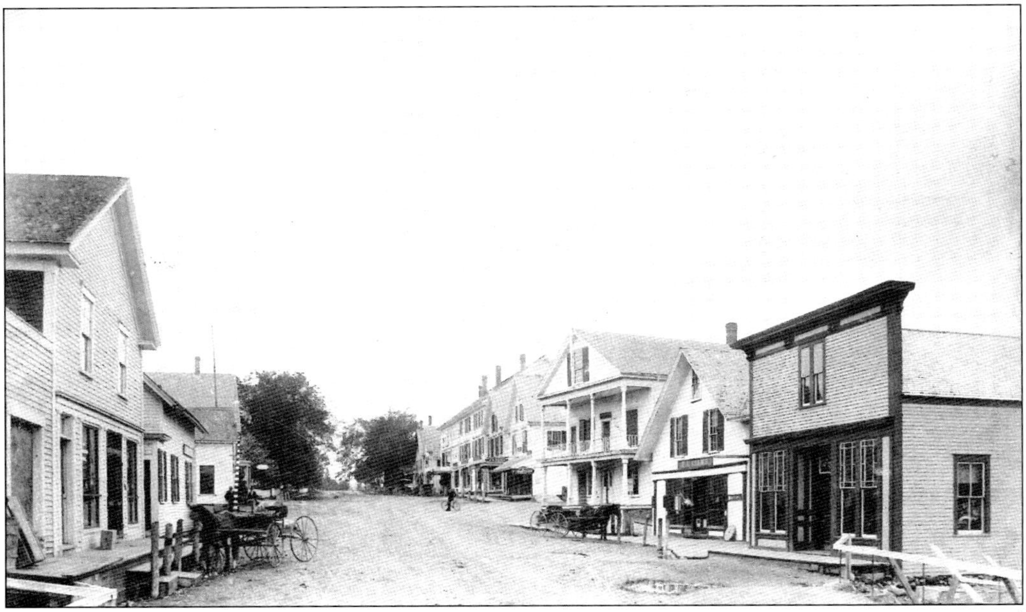

This 1890 photograph features a view of Main Street facing west from the bridge. In the foreground at left is a building that was formerly a hardware store and later the optometry office of Drs. Ralph and John Dyer. (In 2011, the building was razed to make way for the new bridge.) Note the elevated wooden sidewalks, punctuated with hitching posts for the horses.

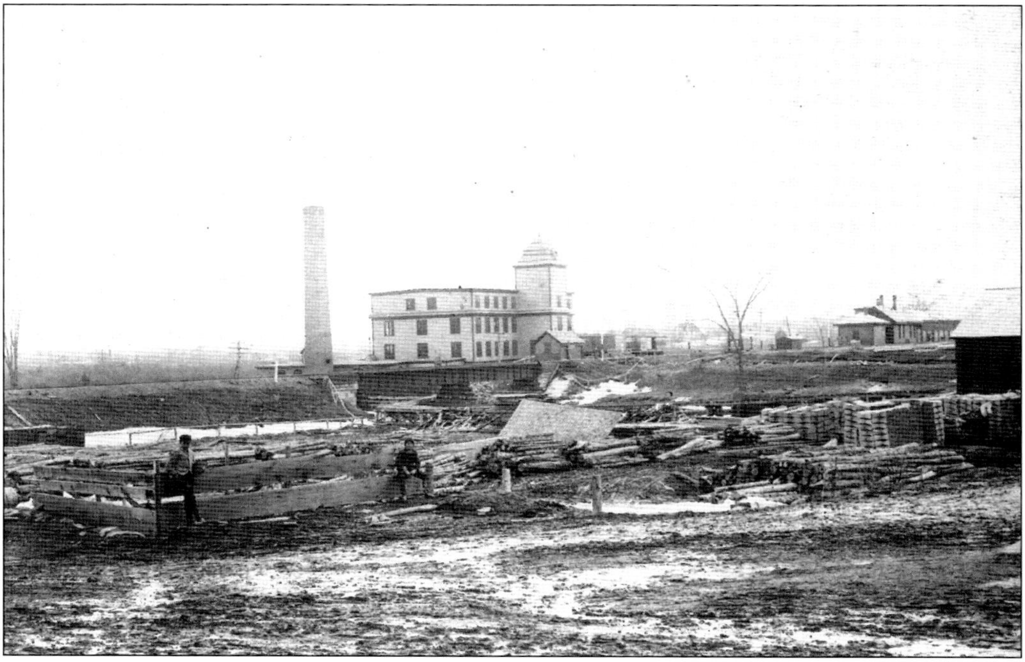

This rather bleak 1890s scene features the view from Elm Street facing the mill. In the foreground, on the west side of the river, is a lumber mill (later the location of various businesses, including Friend and Friend). The train depot can be seen at right in the background.

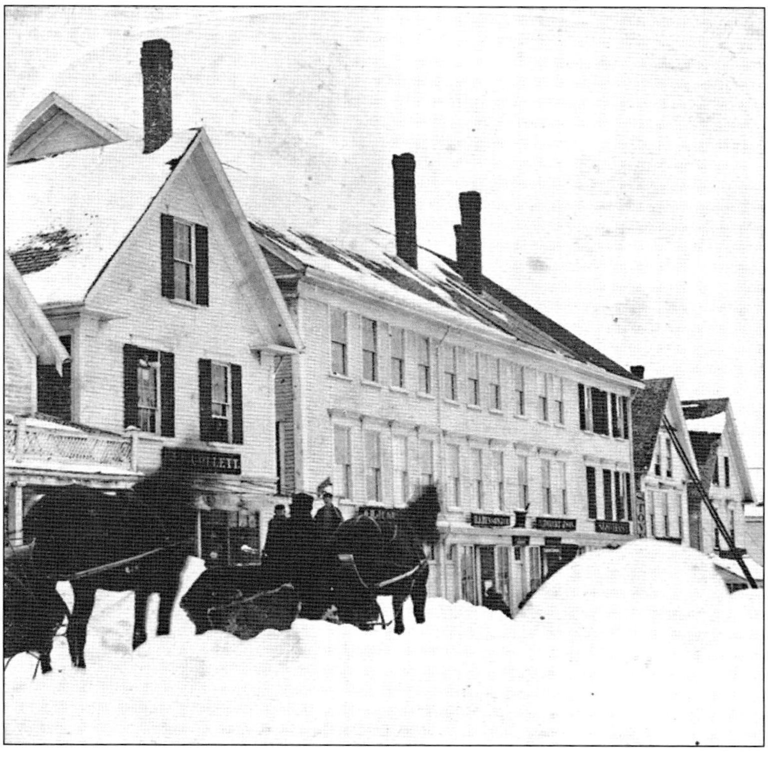

Horses pull sleds down Main Street after a heavy snowstorm in this March 22, 1873, photograph. The two buildings at the far right remain standing today at the corner of Main and Water Streets. The large retail block in the center, the present site of the Newport Cultural Center, burned in 1990. (Courtesy of Goody Gilman.)

This image shows a fine horse and buggy pausing in front of a gracious building located on the corner of Main and Water Streets. Caleb Shaw (brother of Benjamin Shaw, one of the town's earliest settlers) drove the first wheeled vehicle through town in 1818. In 1840, there were still just four wagons in the village. That year, Thomas Dexter established a carriage-making business in town, and others soon followed.

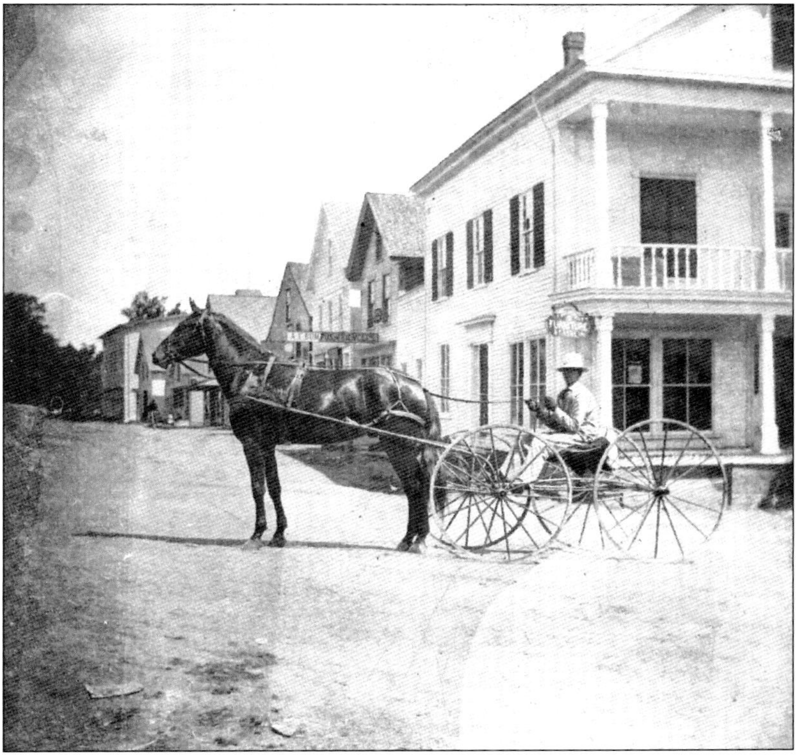

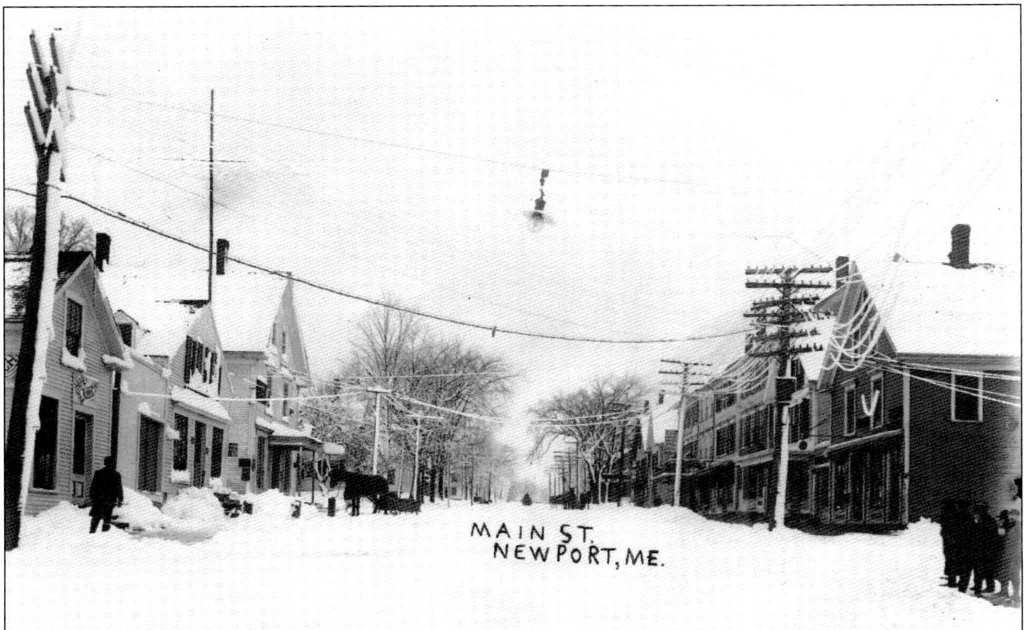

This early-20th-century view of Main Street facing west shows the difficulty a heavy snow presented in the days before snowplows. On the left, a horse is tied to a hitching post, with a sleigh waiting behind. Note the single electric light hanging over the roadway.

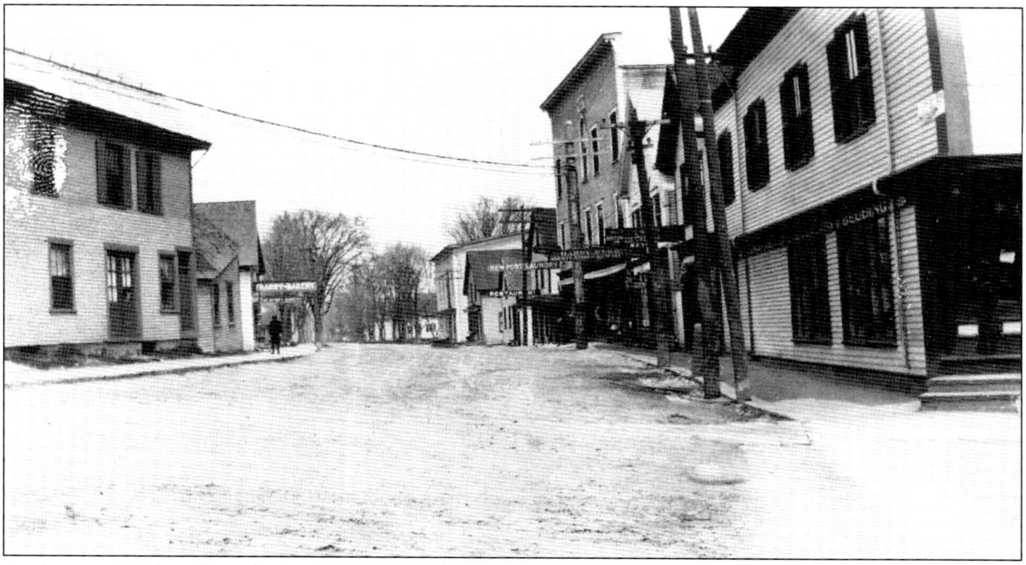

Arthur and John Croxford constructed the Croxford building in 1902, the second structure on the right. It featured running water and electricity. Arthur's grocery store was on the ground floor, along with a hat shop and the Newport Laundry. Dr. Benson's medical office and Dr. B.G. Croxford's dental office were located on the second floor. The Masons' Meridian Splendor Lodge No. 49 occupied the third floor. (Courtesy of the Hall family.)

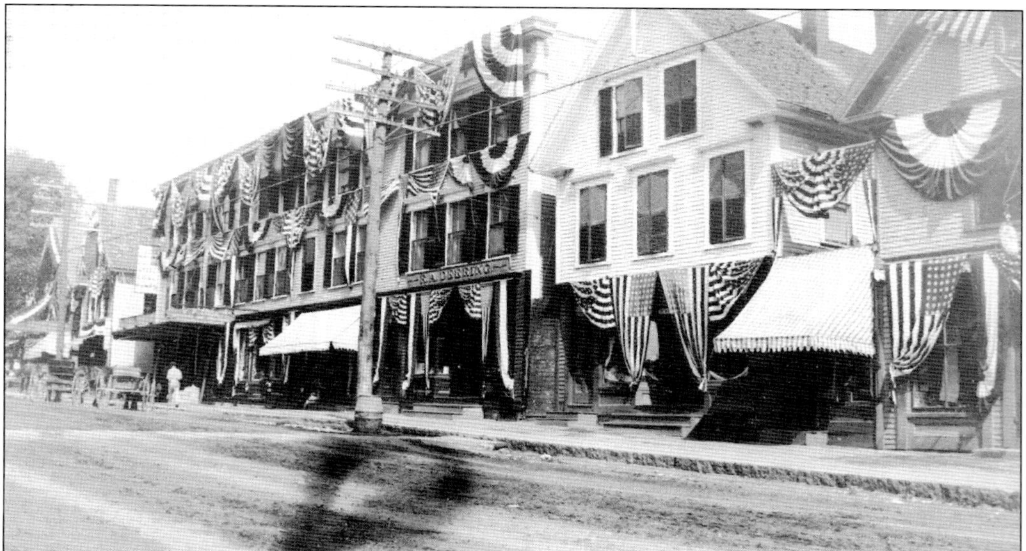

The Newport Light and Power Co. was founded in 1901 by C.E. Smith and C.O. Sturtevant. By 1902, they had an operating electrical plant and began supplying power to the town and its businesses. By 1908, most of the businesses and public buildings had electric lights and many homes did as well. That year the town paid $566 in electric bills for the streetlights. (Courtesy of the Hall family.)

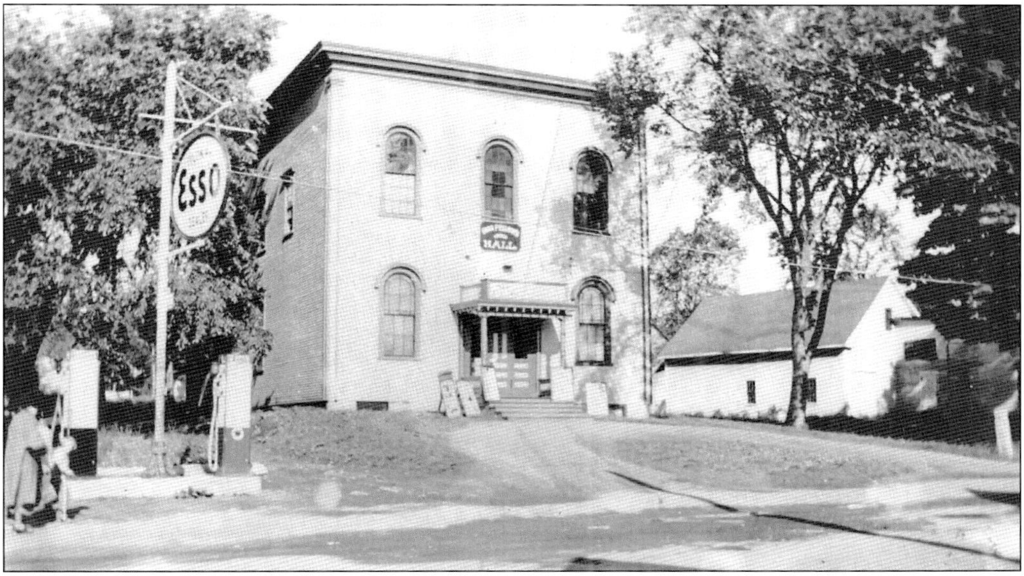

The Newport Playhouse was located on Water Street (the current site of the Maine District Court). The Independent Order of Odd Fellows utilized the top floor of the building, and the movie hall occupied the ground floor. Later, it became the first home of Gilman Electric. This photograph from the 1920s shows Esso gas pumps, in an era when increasing demand meant pumps were positioned on sidewalks and near the roadways.

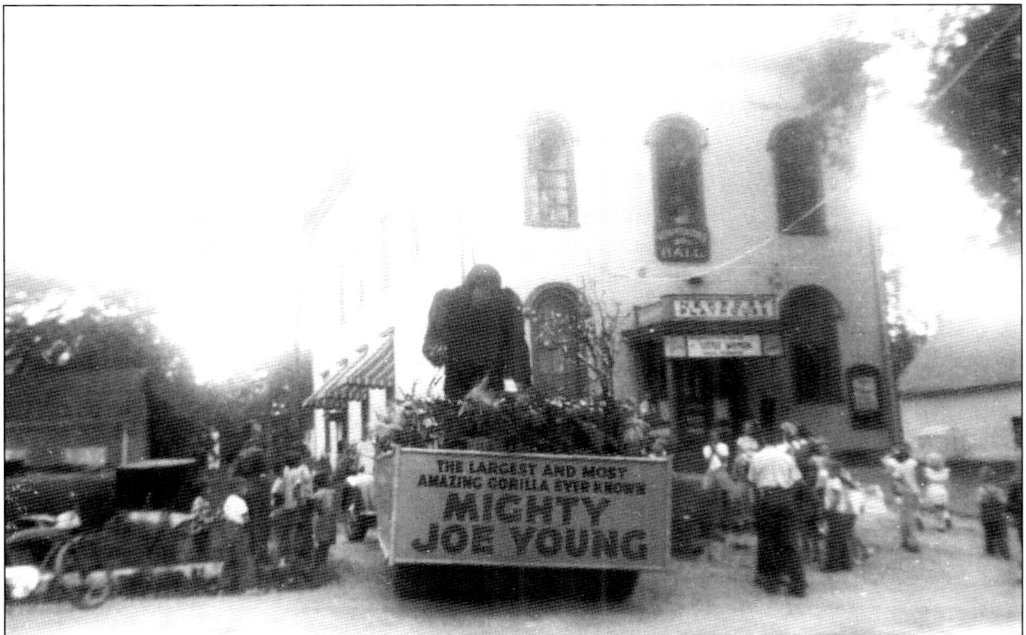

Taken about 1949, this image shows the Newport Playhouse on Water Street. The building was used in many capacities but eventually fell into disrepair. It was torn down in 1978 after it collapsed under the weight of snow. When this photograph was taken, the movie *Mighty Joe Young* was featured and a likeness of the famous gorilla could be seen out front. (Courtesy of Dale Carsley.)

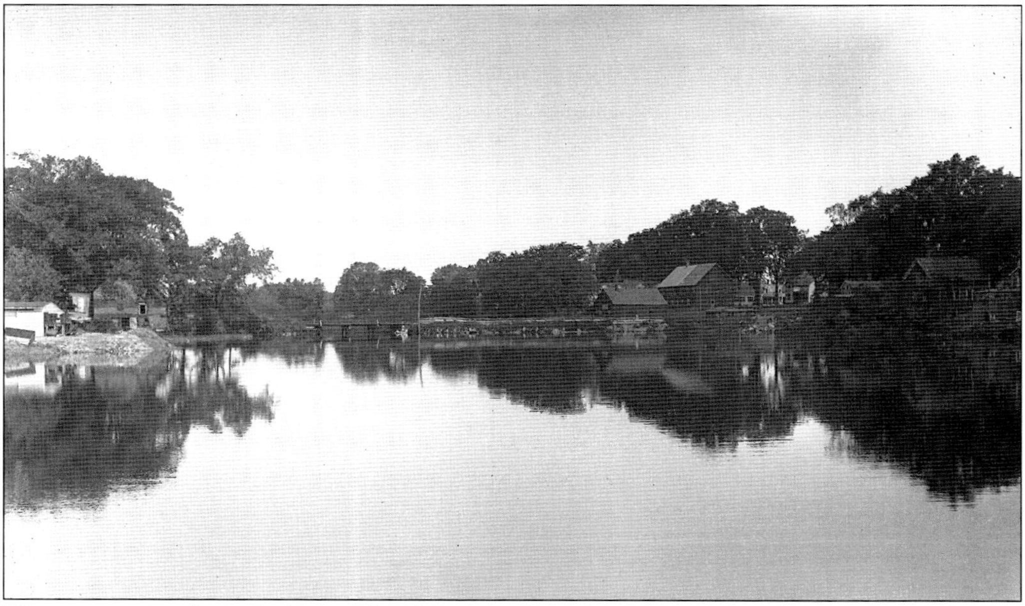

The river passes through the middle of town, and it has long been crossed by three bridges and a trestle. Previously, there was a dam south of Main Street, which flooded the river basin toward the lake. After the dam was removed in the 1990s, the town began a project to restore the river to a more natural course. In 2011, a walking path was created along the river. (Courtesy of the PMM.)

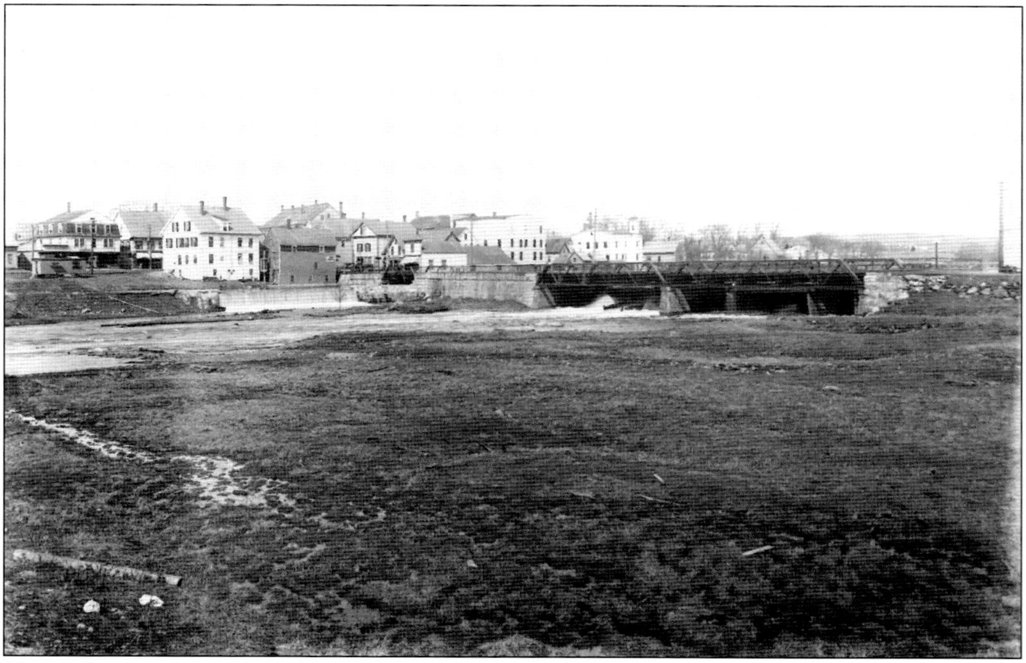

Shown here is the view from Elm Street facing west toward town. The falls and the mill flume are visible below Mill Street, on the left. The little building shaped like a caboose on the far left is the C.F. Huff Photographic Saloon, which was moved to Skowhegan in 1906.

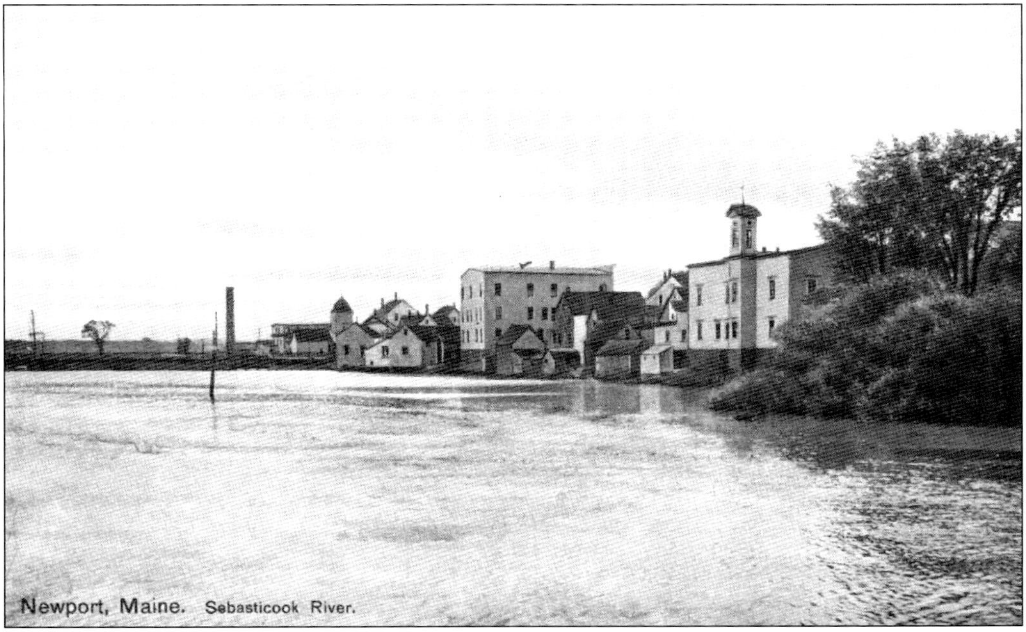

This photograph was taken from the middle bridge (now Center Street bridge) and shows the river side of Water Street. In the 19th century, many businesses were situated on the street, including a tannery, a blacksmith, and a potash plant. The dominant structure in the center is the Croxford building, which remains today.

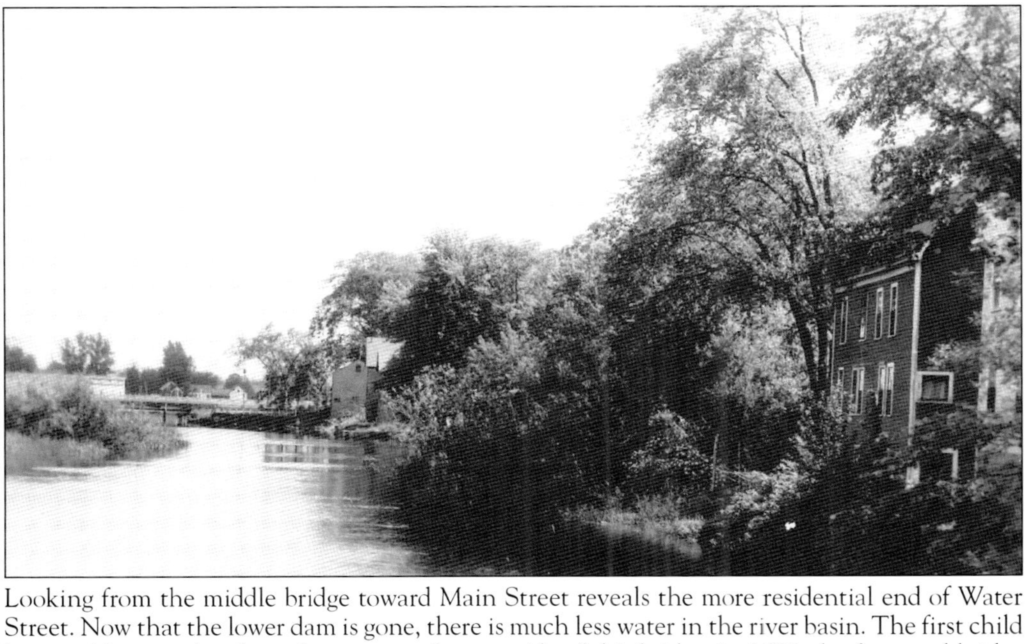

Looking from the middle bridge toward Main Street reveals the more residential end of Water Street. Now that the lower dam is gone, there is much less water in the river basin. The first child born in Newport lived in a house near the east side of this bridge. In 1897, the first steel bridge was installed at a cost exceeding $13,000, which included site preparation and installation.

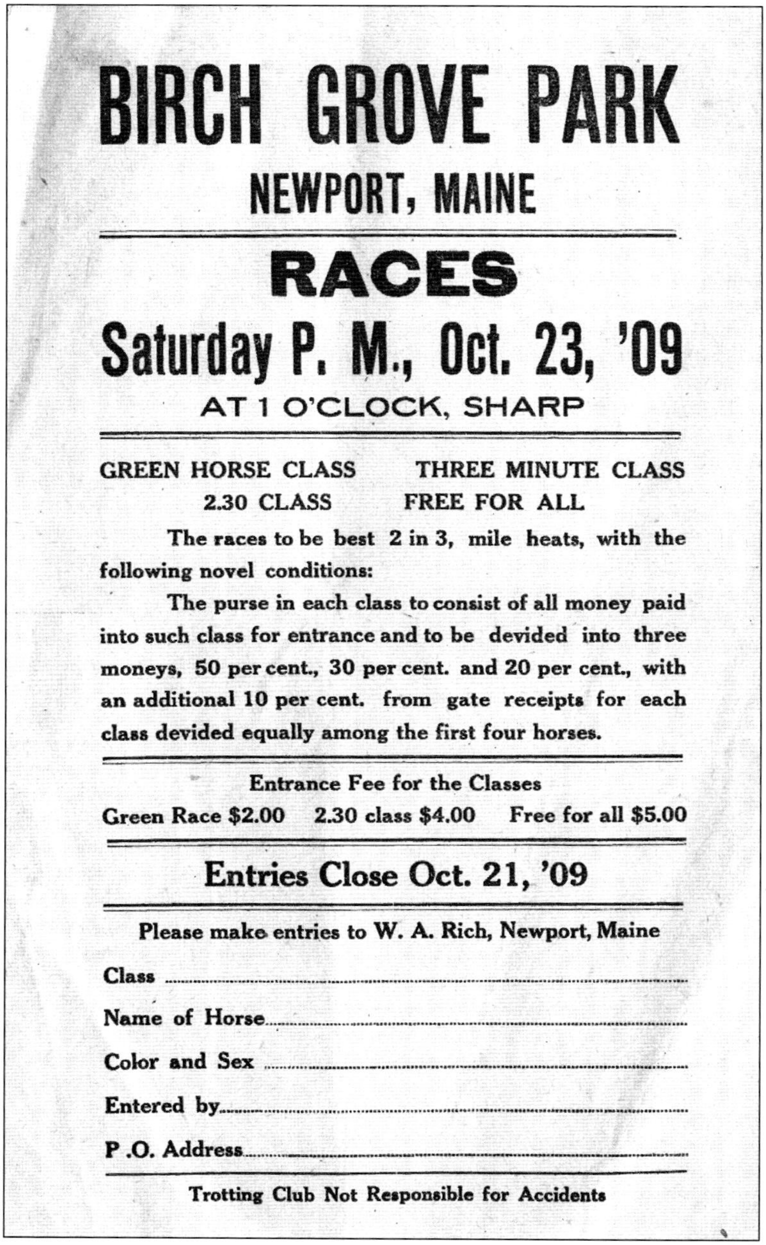

BIRCH GROVE PARK

NEWPORT, MAINE

RACES

Saturday P. M., Oct. 23, '09

AT 1 O'CLOCK, SHARP

GREEN HORSE CLASS THREE MINUTE CLASS

2.30 CLASS FREE FOR ALL

The races to be best 2 in 3, mile heats, with the following novel conditions:

The purse in each class to consist of all money paid into such class for entrance and to be devided into three moneys, 50 per cent., 30 per cent. and 20 per cent., with an additional 10 per cent. from gate receipts for each class devided equally among the first four horses.

Entrance Fee for the Classes

Green Race $2.00 2.30 class $4.00 Free for all $5.00

Entries Close Oct. 21, '09

Please make entries to W. A. Rich, Newport, Maine

Class ....

Name of Horse..........

Color and Sex ....

Entered by..........

P .O. Address..........

Trotting Club Not Responsible for Accidents

The Birch Grove Trotting Park was located at the end of Park Avenue, near the lake. The property is now privately owned, but the outline of the horse racetrack can still be seen. In the early 1900s, it was also popular to race horses up Elm Street between North and Main Streets. Competitors arrived from other towns, and some Saturdays hundreds of people turned out to watch the races. By 1905, automobiles were already posing a threat to horse traffic in town, however. The newspapers reported distressing instances of horses and passengers being injured when speeding automobiles startled horses on local roads. A reporter at the time noted, "A good deal of trouble might be avoided if the chauffeur of an automobile would take a little precaution in passing through a town or village instead of dashing madly along as though the whole earth was theirs."

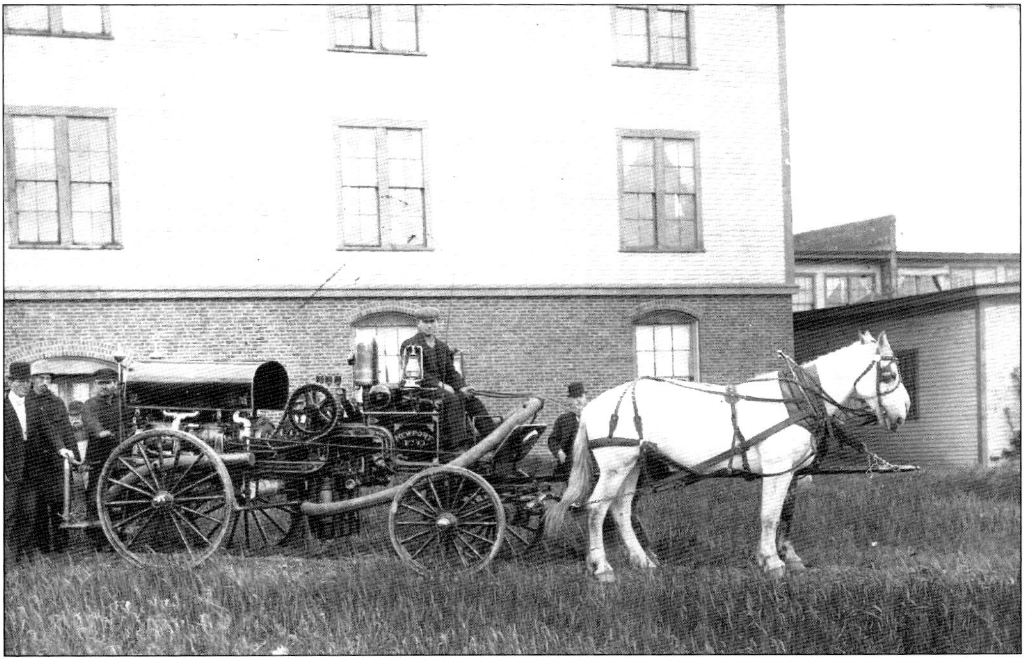

In the early 1900s, the Newport Fire Department played a major role in the Fourth of July celebrations at Camp Benson; it was the department's important fundraising event. This photograph from the 1910s shows Newport's fire wagon, driven by Frank Williams. Local businessman Ellis Jones stands behind the horse. The equine members of the fire team were housed in a barn at the north end of Water Street.

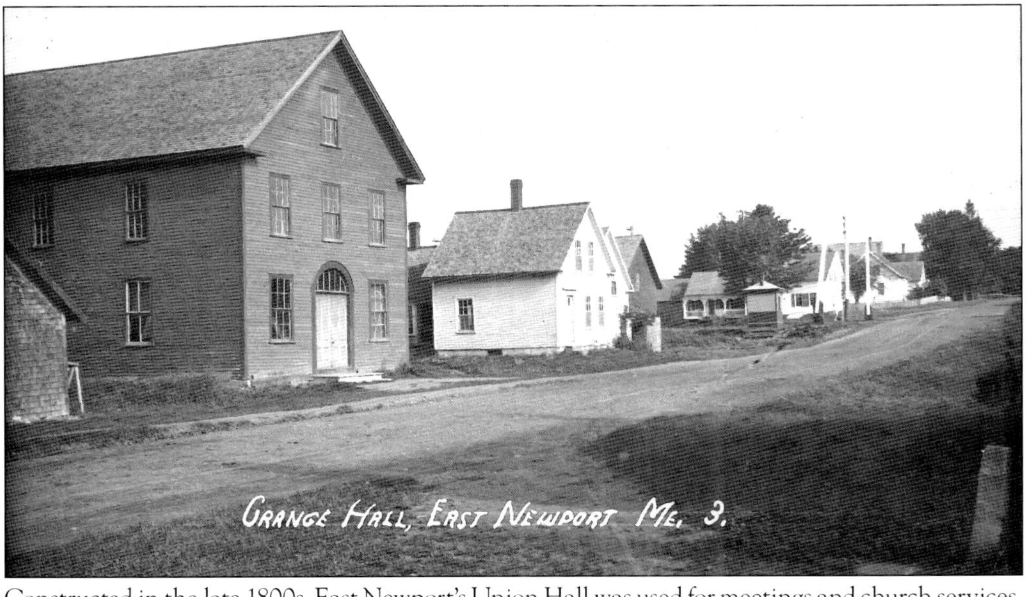

Constructed in the late 1800s, East Newport's Union Hall was used for meetings and church services. The meeting hall and stage were downstairs, and the dining room and kitchen (with no running water) were upstairs. The Eastville Grange was organized in 1904. At one time the building also was used for high school classes. The building is now vacant. (Courtesy of the PMM.)

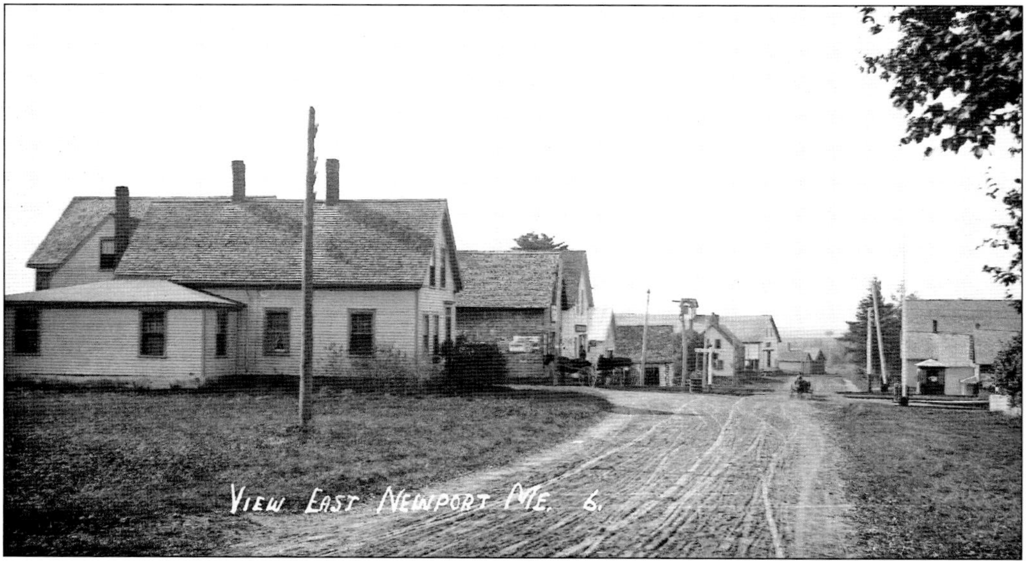

In the early 20th century, stagecoaches ran twice a day to and from both Plymouth and Dixmont to East Newport, where a train depot and village shops were located. For a time, Dow and Paine operated a potato-shipping business out of two barns in East Newport, one of which was later converted to a woolen mill. (Courtesy of the PMM.)

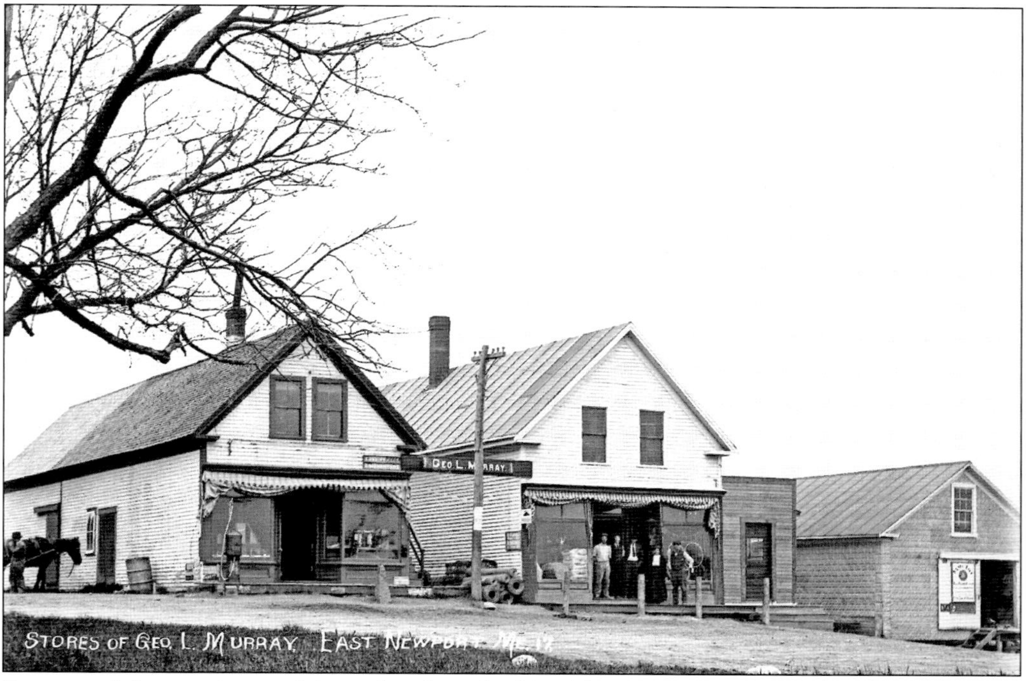

Because of the proximity of the railroad tracks, East Newport was not as isolated as one might expect. Murray's store, located on the site of today's East Newport store, also served as the local post office. The proprietor also bought and sold pulpwood. Passengers could board trains to quickly travel to area towns, such as Carmel and Bangor to the east and Newport and Pittsfield to the west. (Courtesy of the PMM.)

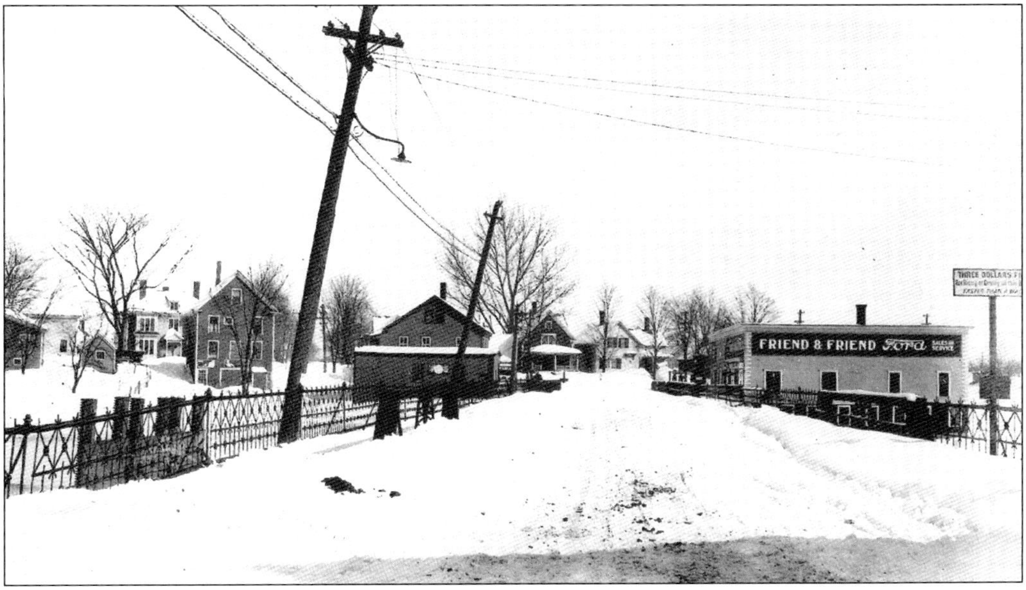

The wooden Main Street bridge was destroyed by fire in 1879 and again in 1900. (The mills associated with the dam in that area posed particular fire hazards.) A steel bridge crossed the Sebasticook River until 1930. The sign on the right reads, "THREE DOLLARS FINE for riding or driving on this bridge *FASTER THAN A WALK*." (Courtesy of MaineDOT.)

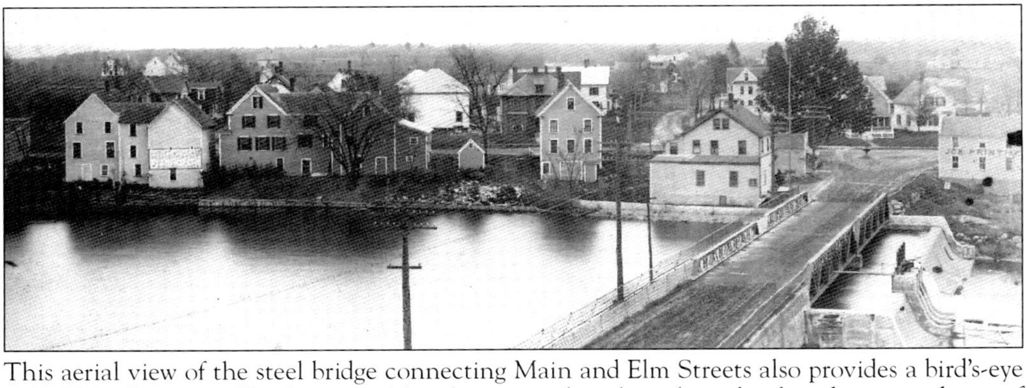

This aerial view of the steel bridge connecting Main and Elm Streets also provides a bird's-eye view of residences on Elm Street and farmhouses in the relatively undeveloped area northeast of Elm Street. Note the watering trough at the intersection of Main and Elm Streets. To the right of the east end of the bridge is the Arthur Lander building (a print shop).

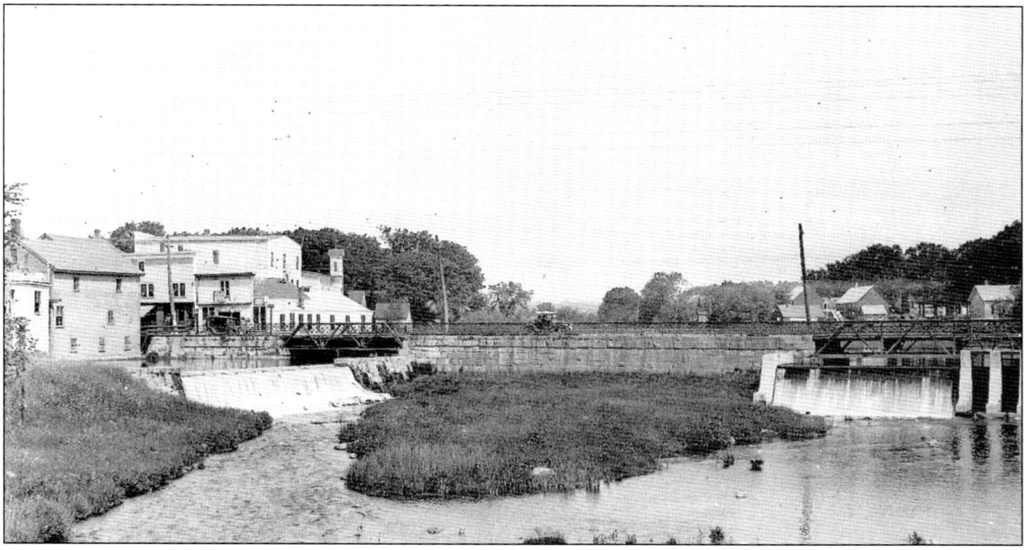

This upriver view shows the dam used to power the wool mill. Rights to dam the river were established by a group of early businessmen, who incorporated as the Newport Mill Dam and Manufacturing Company in 1836. The site was used to generate power for sawmills and gristmills. The dam visible in this photograph generated power for the woolen mill and cost $31,000 to construct. (Courtesy of MaineDOT.)

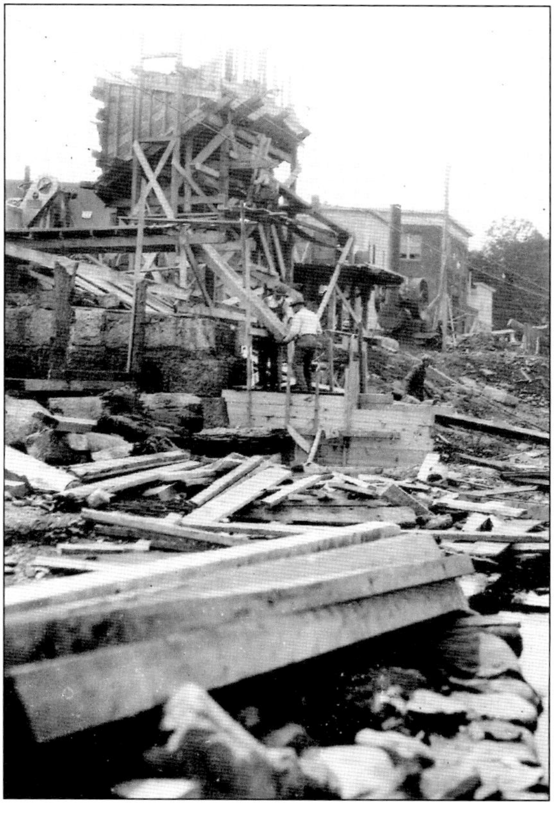

In 1931, a 370-foot cement bridge that cost $41,000 was constructed over the river, connecting Main Street and Elm Street. The Honorable Lewis O. Barrows, a Newport businessman and future governor, convinced state highway commissioners to examine the old bridge, which was determined to have been standing only "by grace of God and force of habit." The cumbersome wood scaffold used for bridge construction is shown. (Courtesy of MaineDOT.)

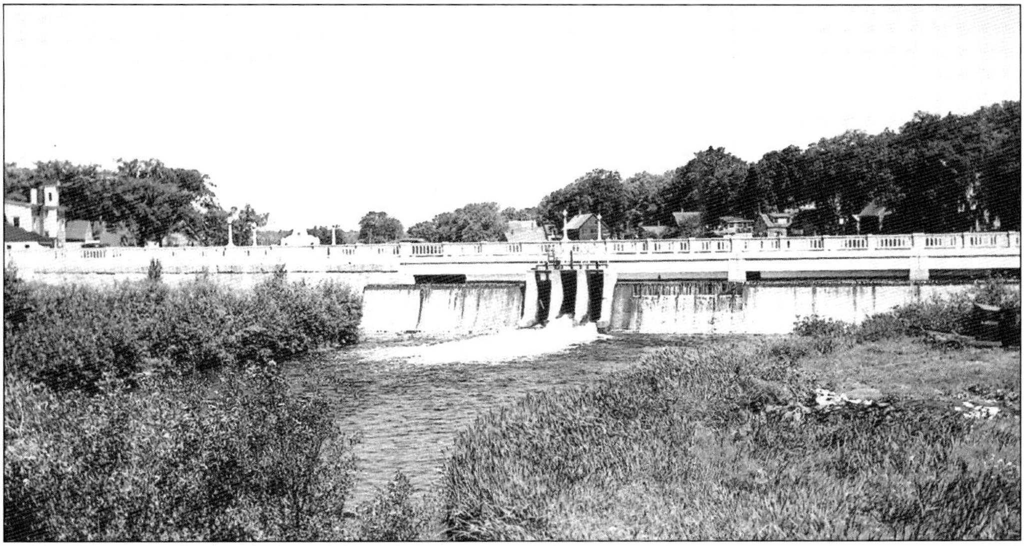

Throughout the 19th century, the area around the lower Main Street bridge was one of varied and bustling industry. In 1838, Mark Fisher and Joseph Southwick built the largest tannery in the state on the Elm Street side of the river near the bridge. The former gained renown for patenting a technique for welding cast iron to cast steel. (Courtesy of MaineDOT.)

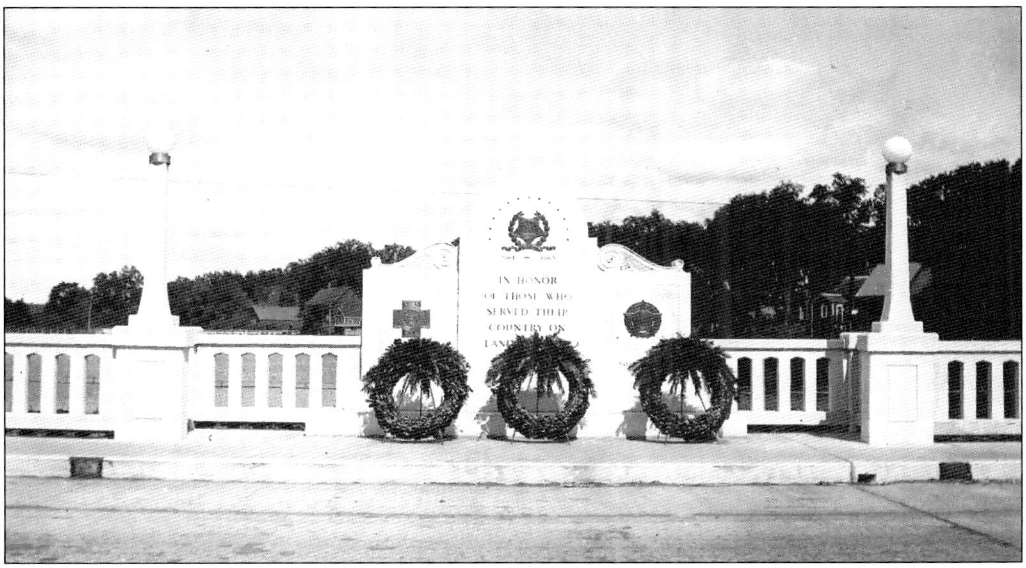

A war memorial was dedicated by Gov. William Gardiner when the cement bridge was installed in 1931. The new monument honored Newport soldiers who fell serving their country in the Civil War, Spanish-American War, and World War I. Funds for the $4,000 monument were raised by the H.G. Libby Women's Relief Corps, a charitable organization associated with the Grand Army of the Republic. (Courtesy of MaineDOT.)

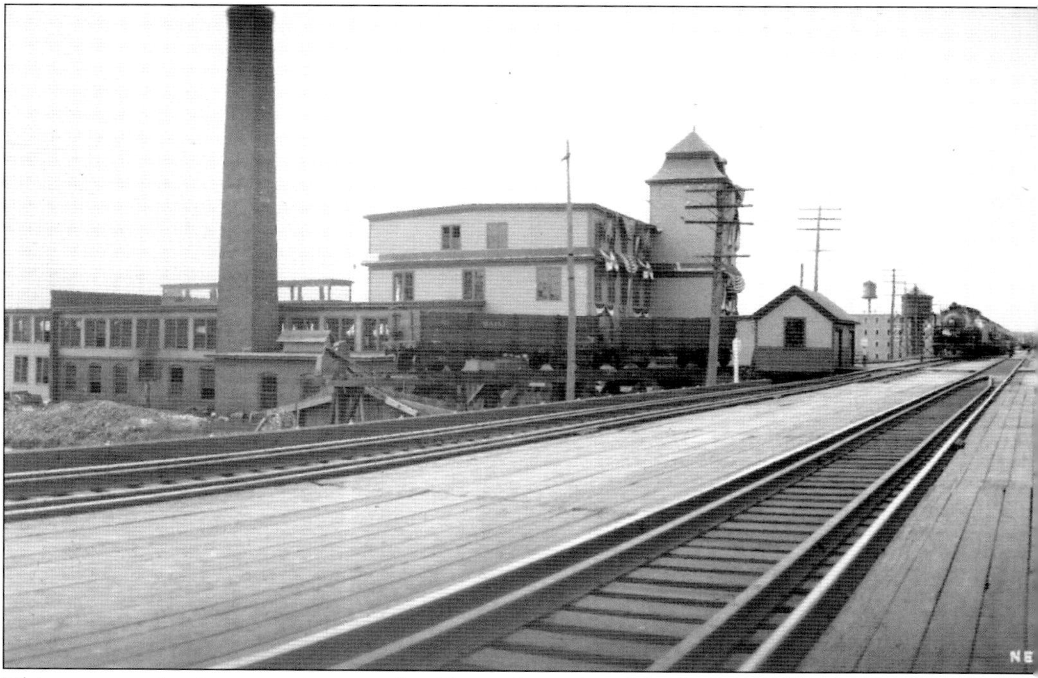

This panoramic view was photographed from the railroad bridge over the East Branch of the Sebasticook River, just below the Main Street bridge. It presents an interesting view of the town, as an approaching rail traveler might have seen it in the early 1900s. The Newport Woolen Mill

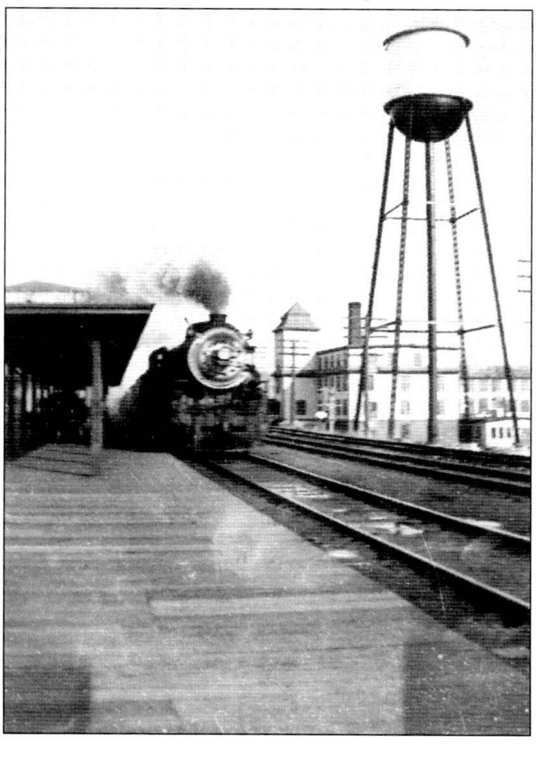

This snapshot from the late 1950s captures three of Newport's most recognizable landmarks at the time: the train depot, the water tower, and the woolen mill in the background. The last steam engine passed through Newport on June 13, 1954. The event was commemorated with a special gathering of the Maine Obsolete Automobile League. Townsfolk gathered at the platform to mark the final passing of "Old 470."

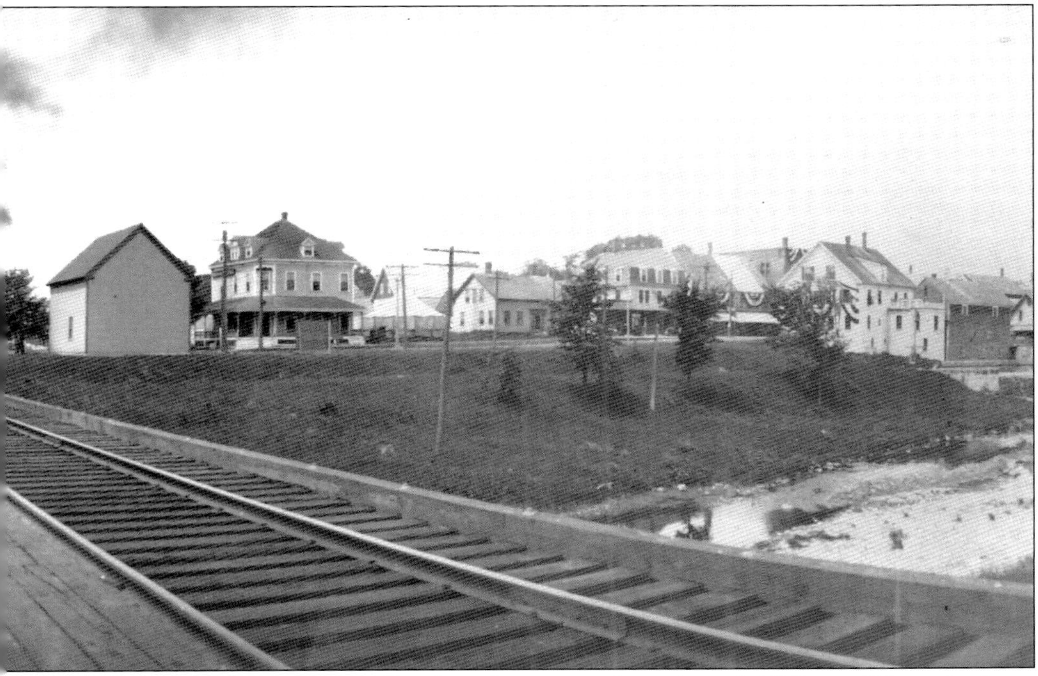

is on the left, and the Sebasticook Hotel can be seen on the right on Mill Street. The train depot is obscured by the steam engine belching smoke.

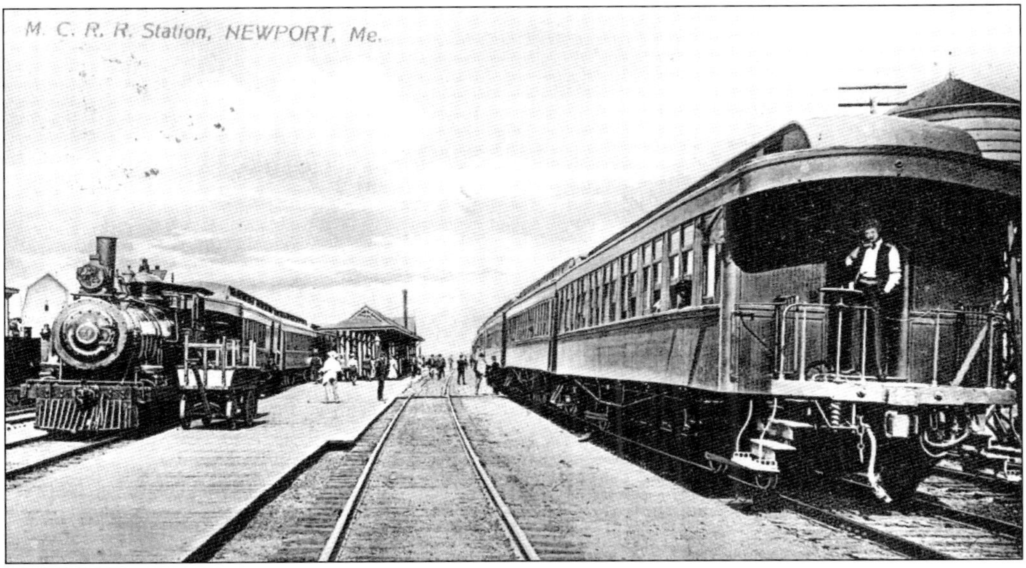

Newport was the junction of the Maine Central Railroad, with trains heading north to Corinna, Dexter, Dover, and the Moosehead region. Passengers could ride to Bangor, Bar Harbor, Waterville, Portland, and the Maritime Provinces. On board, they could purchase food, gum, newspapers, and magazines. The Maine Central Railroad ceased passenger service on Labor Day in 1960. This c. 1905 photograph illustrates how busy the passenger service was at the Newport depot. (Courtesy of Ronald Plummer.)

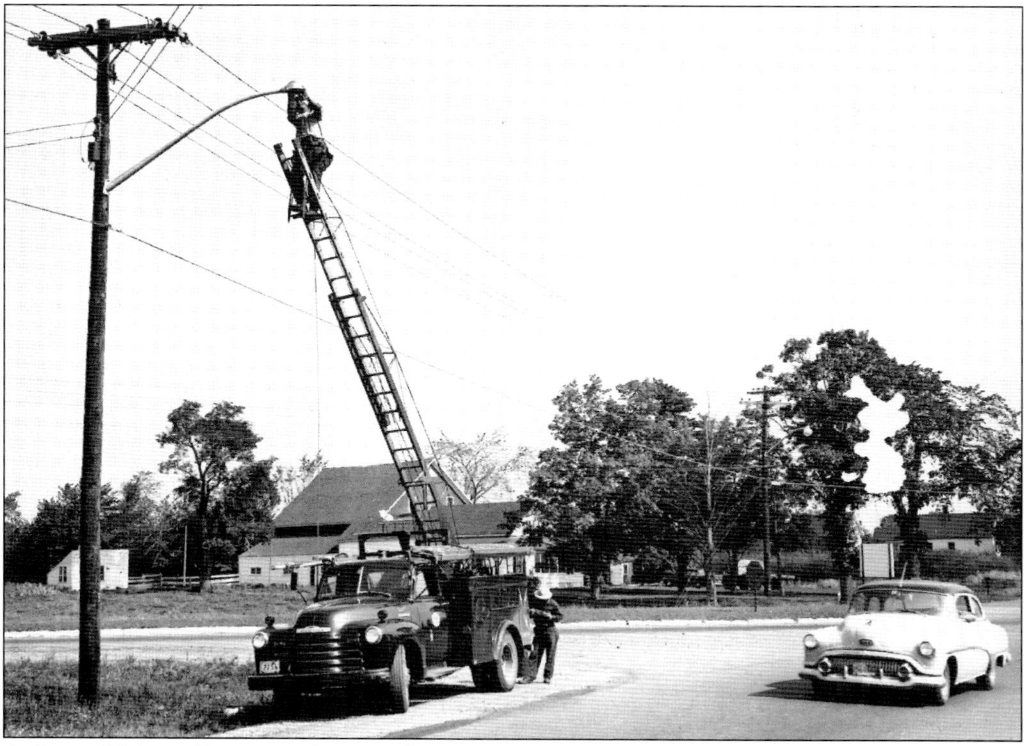

A Central Maine Power employee is shown installing a new mercury light fixture to illuminate the intersection of Routes 100 and 2. The Andrew Towle farm is in the background. Traffic lights were first installed at this busy intersection in 1989. (Courtesy of MaineDOT.)

Newport's library was incorporated in 1899 and was open two afternoons per week in the town hall. There were traveling libraries in North and East Newport. The consolidated Newport Public Library was established in 1924, and land for a building was purchased in 1937. The library pictured here opened in 1954 with 8,000 books and operated at that location until 2009, when the collection was moved to the Newport Cultural Center.

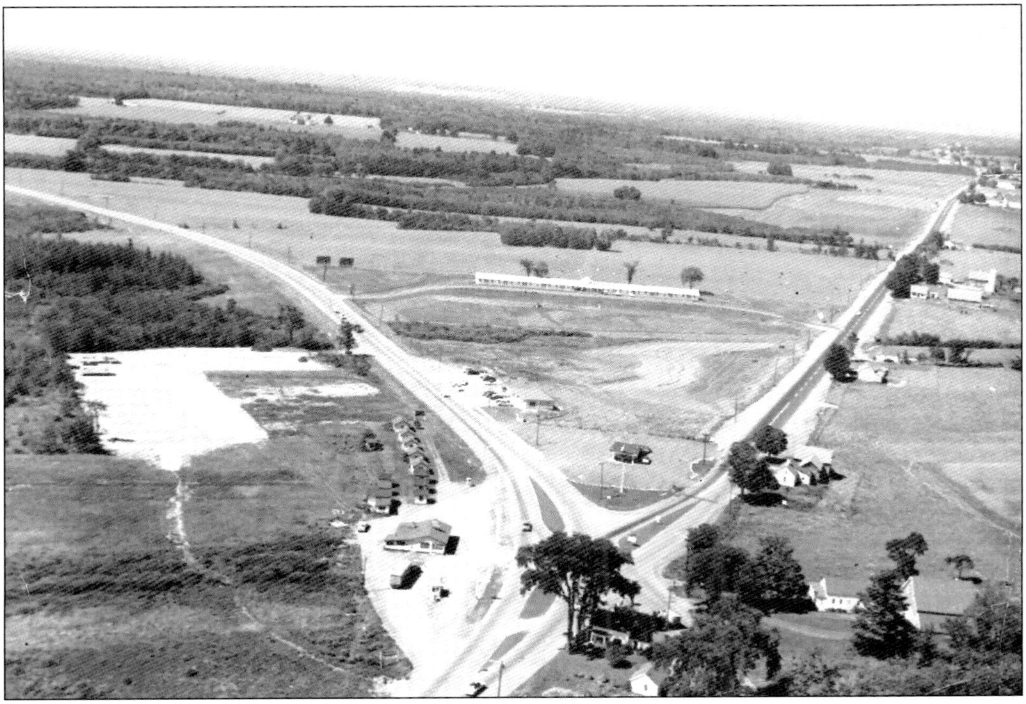

This view of the Triangle intersection is from about 1950. On the left are the Oakes Cabins. The former Clark's Motel, now Lovley's Motel, sits between Routes 100 and 2. The Andrew Towle farm in the lower right is now the site of Bud's Shop 'n Save. The rural nature of this area changed dramatically when Interstate 95 was constructed in the 1960s. The interstate between Pittsfield and Newport opened in 1964.

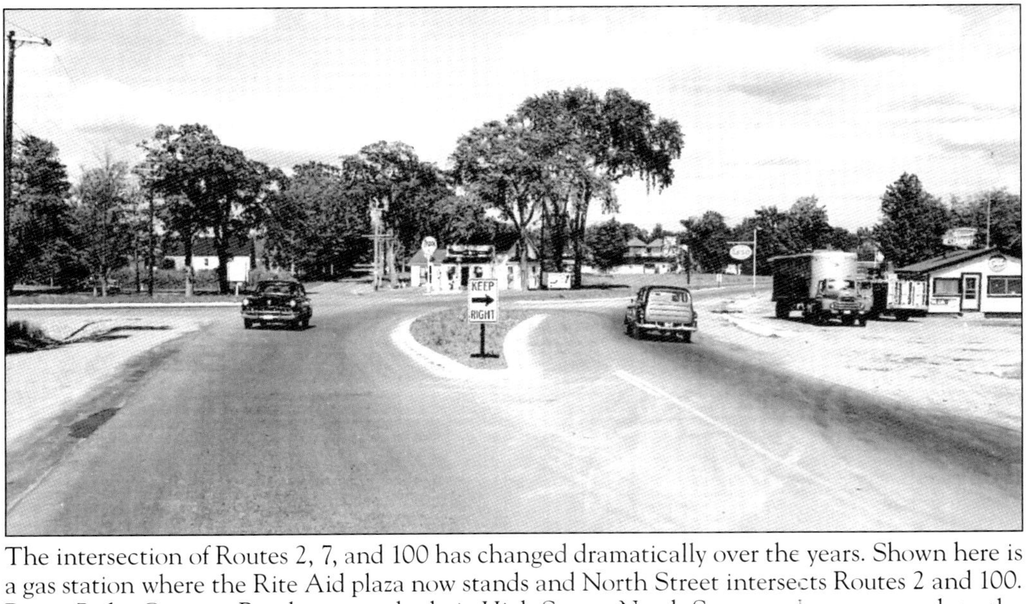

The intersection of Routes 2, 7, and 100 has changed dramatically over the years. Shown here is a gas station where the Rite Aid plaza now stands and North Street intersects Routes 2 and 100. Route 7, the Corinna Road, was reached via High Street. North Street no longer extends to the Triangle intersection. (Courtesy of MaineDOT.)

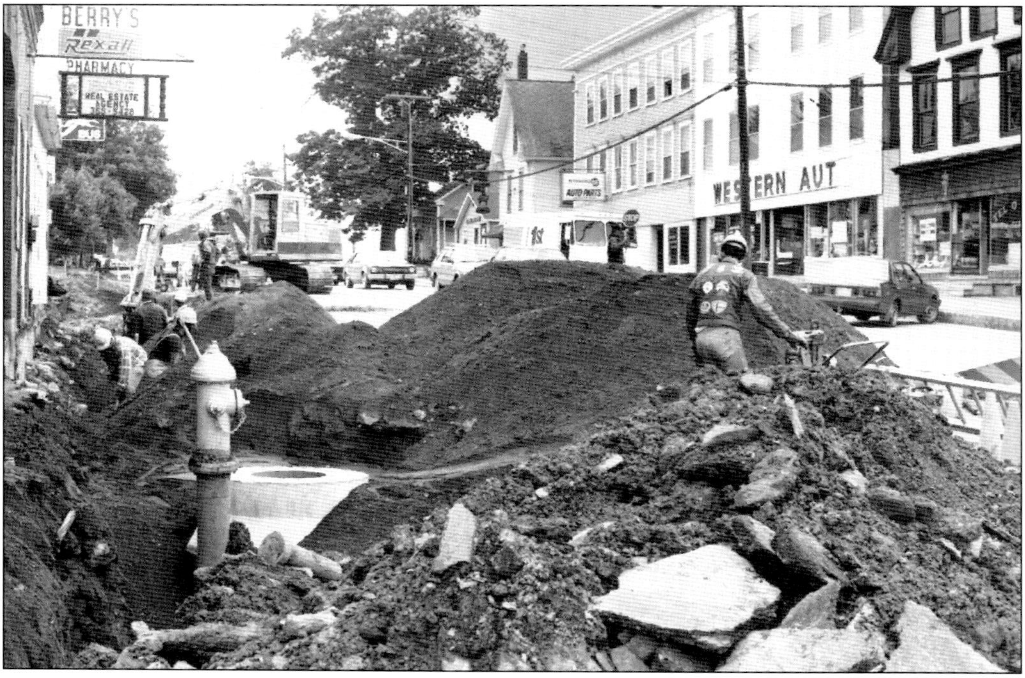

By 1900, a sewer line with manholes had been installed on Main Street. By the 1970s, traffic was being drawn away from downtown Newport by the interstate. This photograph shows a downtown pharmacy, bus stop, and other retail establishments. The large oak in the center background still stands and is one of Newport's finest old trees. (Courtesy of the *Bangor Daily News*.)

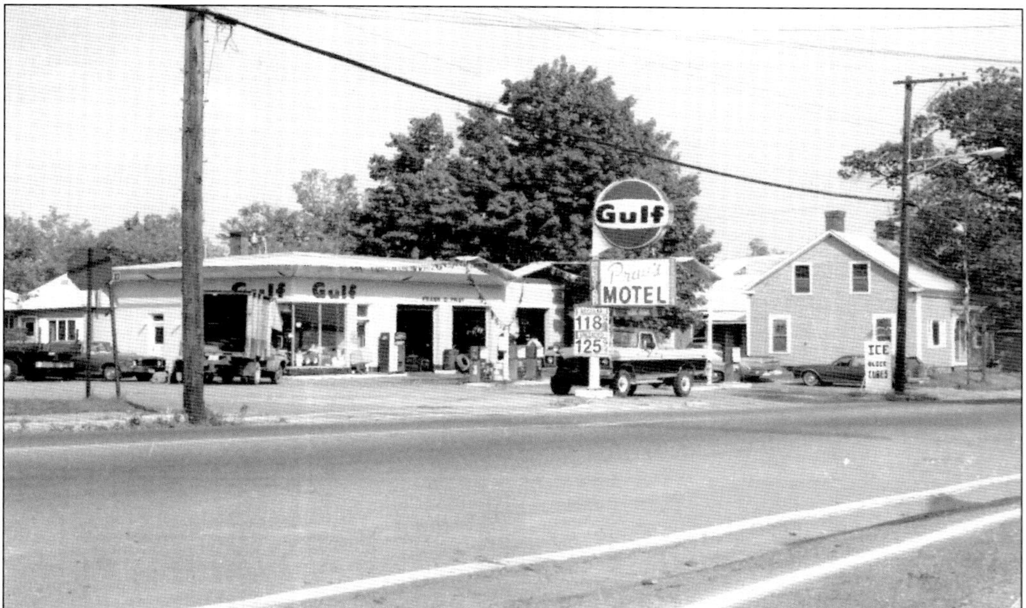

By the mid-20th century, Newport's downtown was characterized by automotive businesses. Gas stations and garages had replaced many of the old homes. Pray's Motel and garage, shown here in the 1970s, was built on the site where Dr. Oscar Emerson's large home once stood.

Three

Homes and Neighborhoods

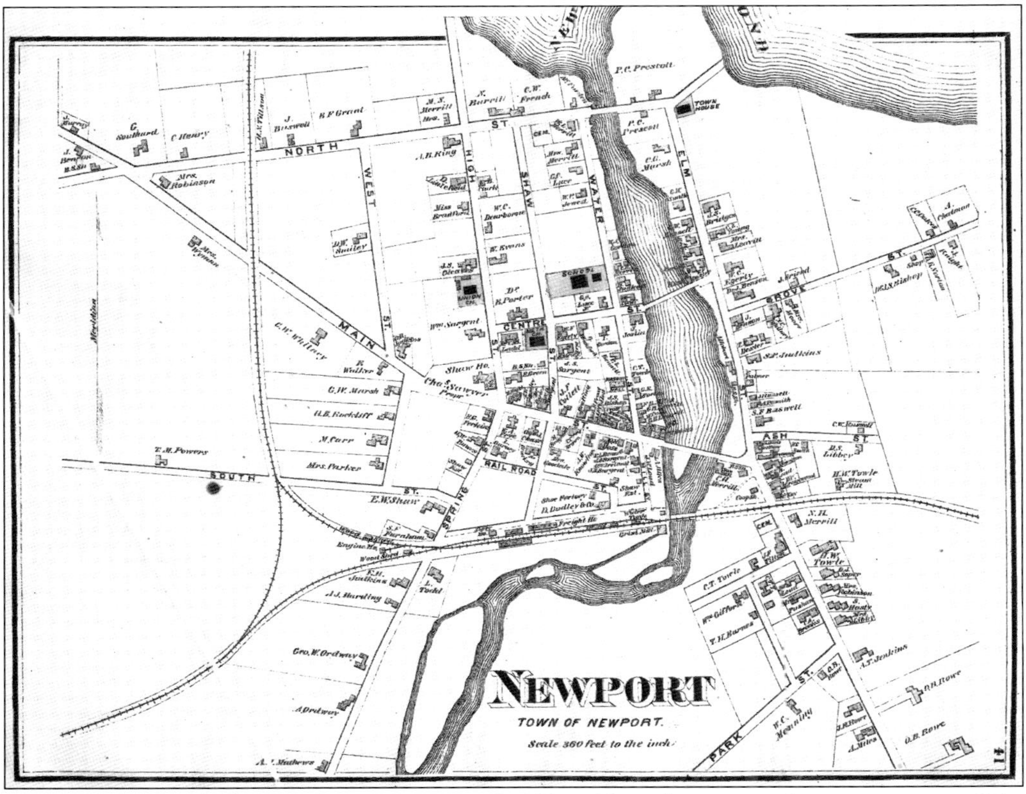

This map depicts the layout of Newport around 1875 and lists the names of property owners. The juncture of the railroad lines is clear, as is the former width of the river above the dam. The detailed information about property ownership is invaluable for those interested in local history.

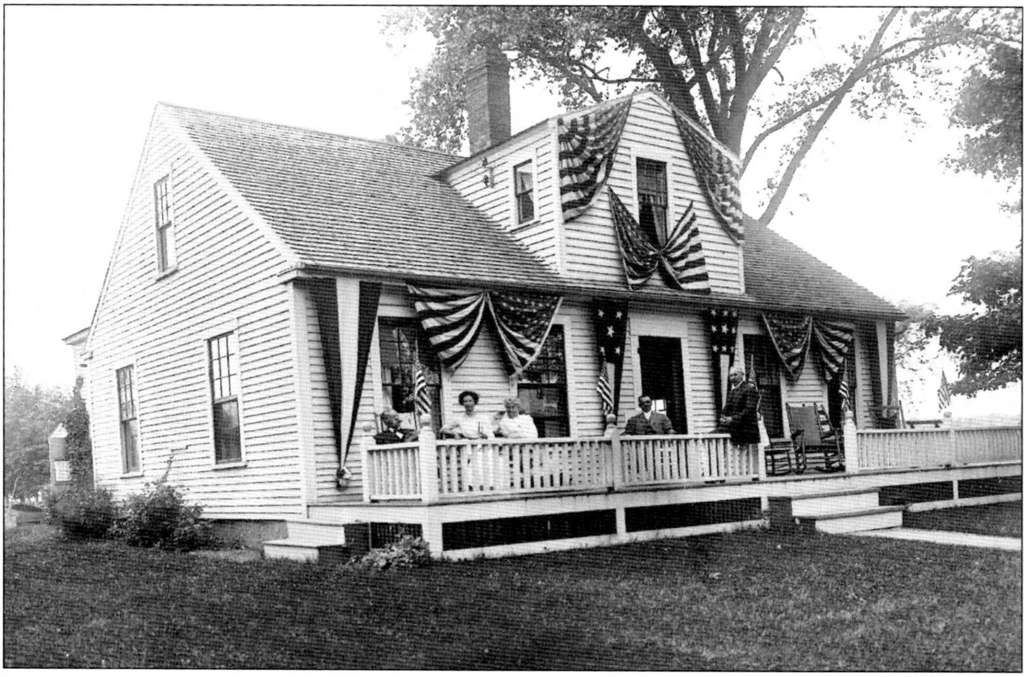

Built before 1810, this residence at the corner of High and North Streets is considered by many to be the oldest existing frame house in Newport. It was built for Benjamin Shaw, who had recently moved from New Hampshire, and records indicate that 'Squire Shaw's home was the location of the first town meeting.

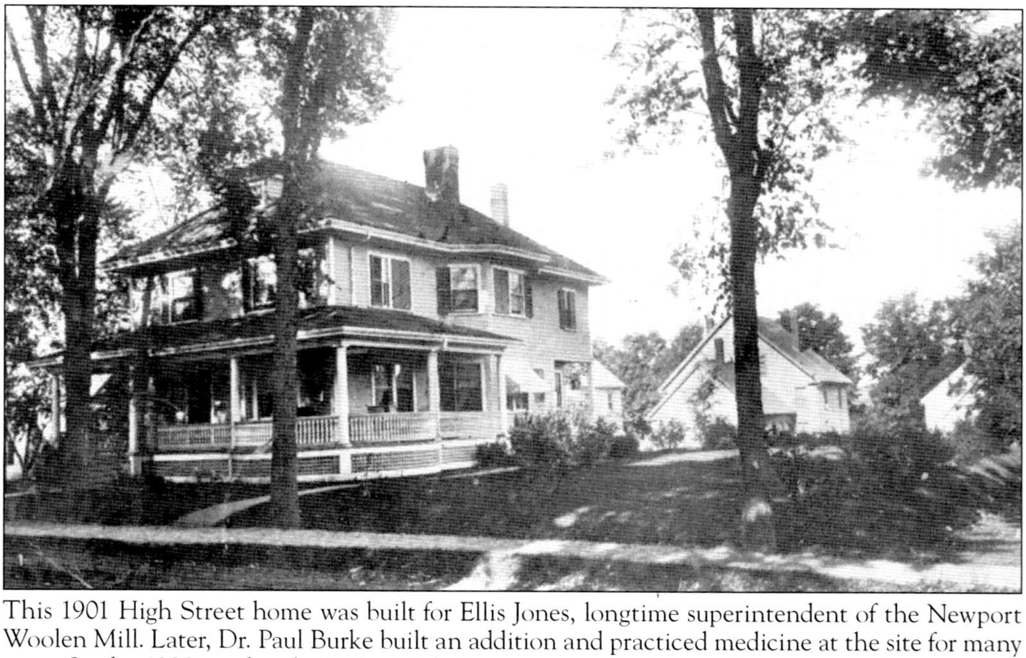

This 1901 High Street home was built for Ellis Jones, longtime superintendent of the Newport Woolen Mill. Later, Dr. Paul Burke built an addition and practiced medicine at the site for many years. In the 1800s and early 1900s, High Street was a popular site for prosperous businessmen, and many of their residences are still private homes.

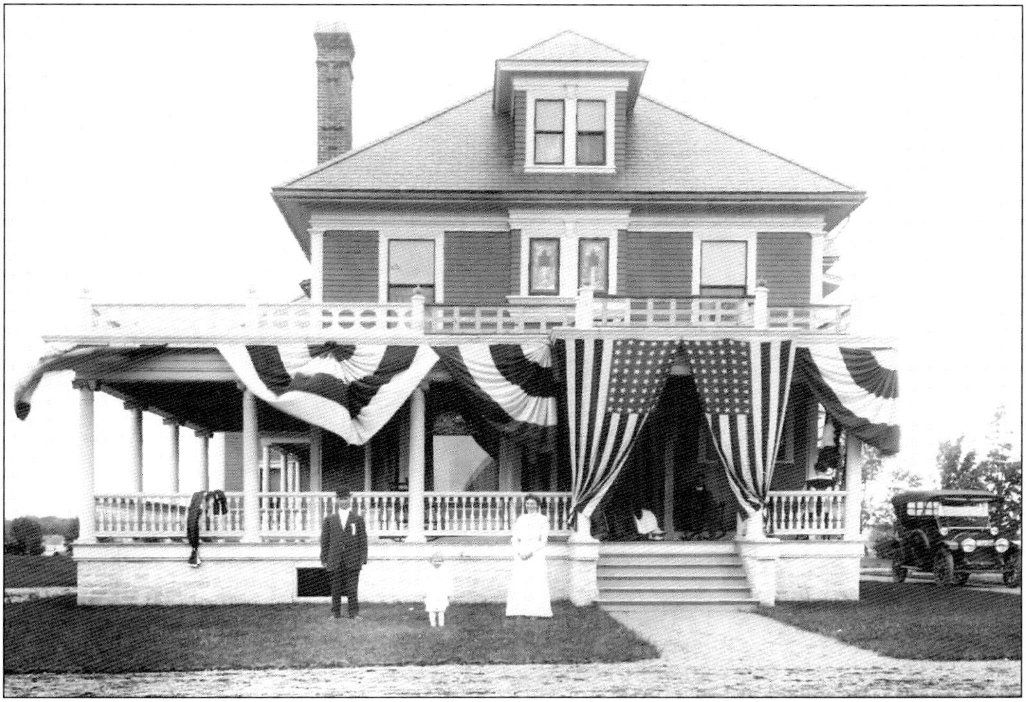

Located on Main Street, this home was built before 1910. Shown here decked out for the 1914 centennial celebration, the home belonged to local businessman John O. Gilman, who also owned Kamp Kill Kare on the lake. For a time in the 1990s, the home was used as a bed and breakfast, but it is once again a private residence in the Gilman family. Photographed in front of the house are, from left to right, John O. Gilman, John T. Gilman, and Rosie Gilman. (Courtesy of the John Dyer family.)

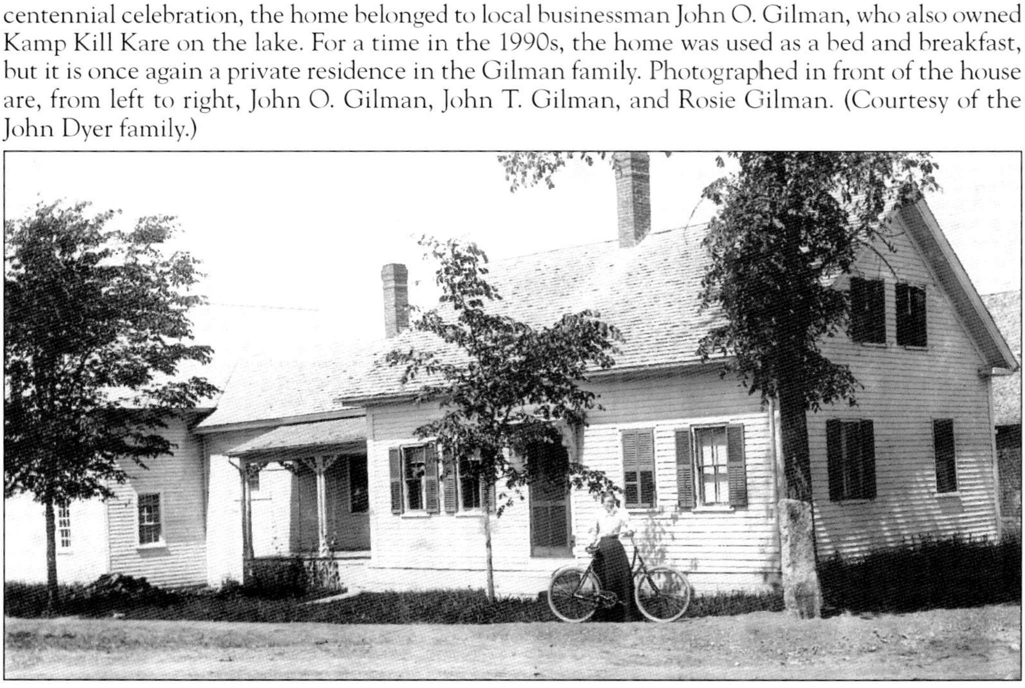

The house at the corner of High and North Streets is now adjacent to the Vic Firth Company, rather than the Cooper Brothers mill, and it looks much the same today. (Courtesy of the Hall family.)

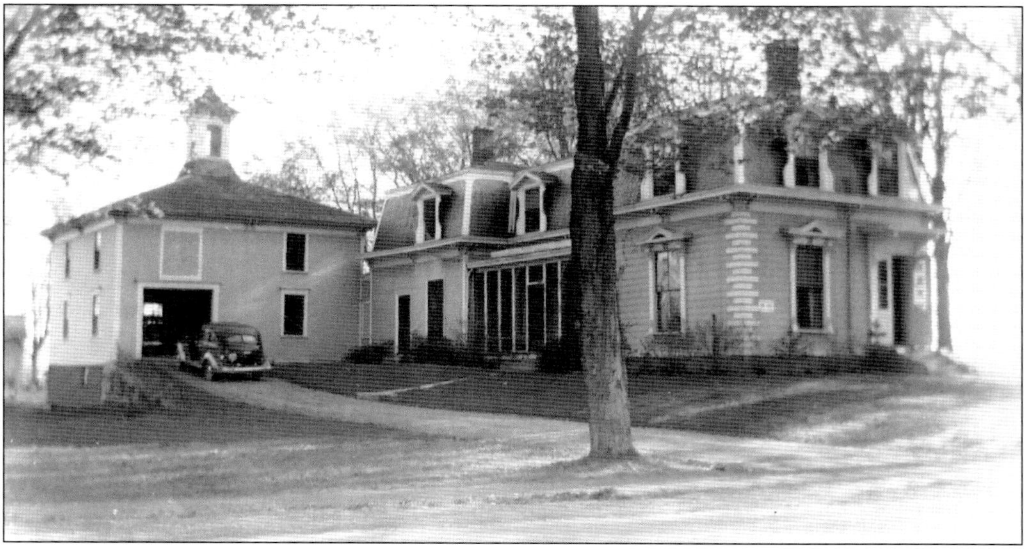

The "old Murch house" on Main Street is better known today as a funeral home. While no longer a residence, the owners have carefully maintained the gracious appeal of the original home.

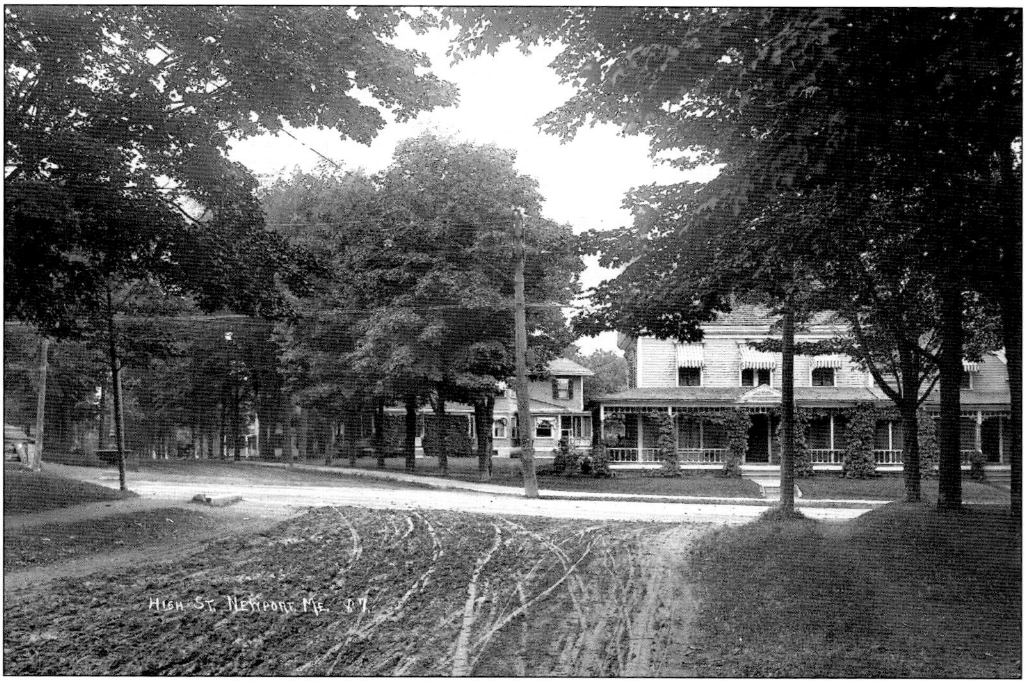

Photographed in the 1920s, the Norris Friend home at the corner of High and Main Streets was torn down and has been the site of many businesses, initially a Bud's Shop 'n Save. At present, a health food store and the offices of the newspaper *Rolling Thunder Express* occupy the site. Behind the Friend home was the residence of Ellis Jones. (Courtesy of the PMM.)

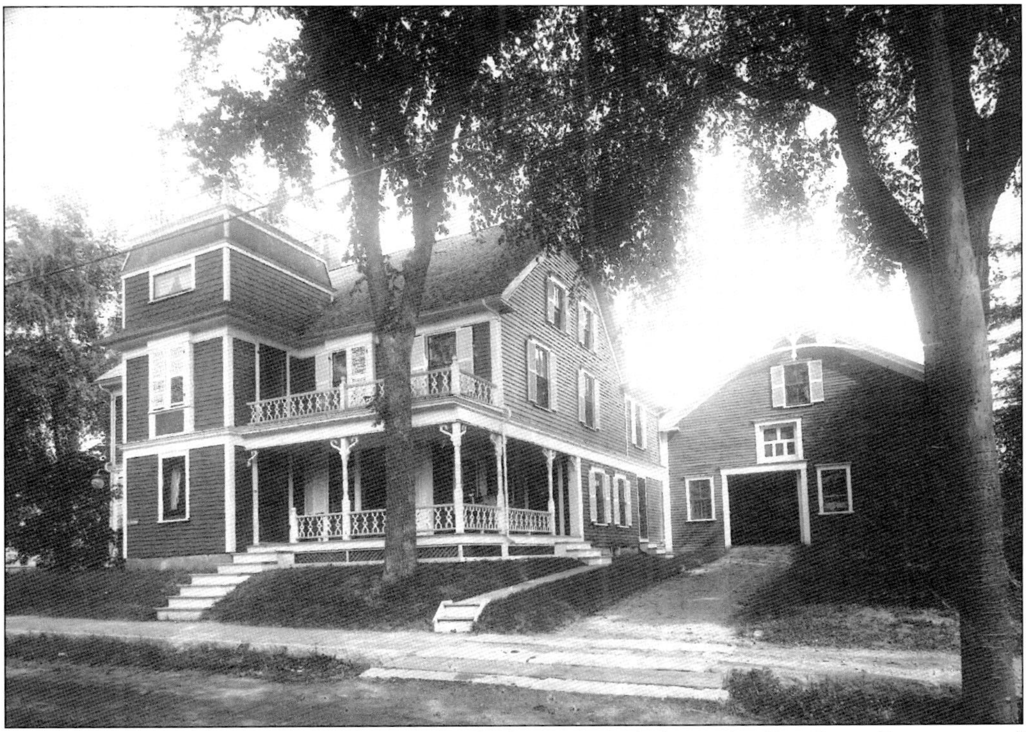

This stately home on the corner of Main and Shaw Streets belonged to Dr. Oscar Emerson, and it is where he lived and operated his practice. It was torn down in 1957, along with the stone friendship wall constructed as a gift by Emerson's friends. Pray's garage is on the site now.

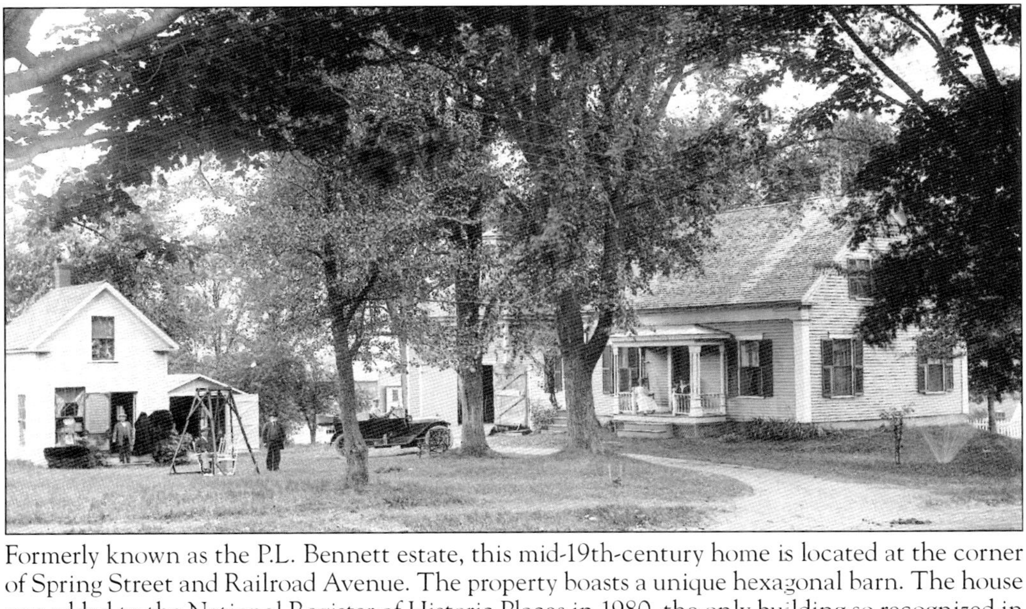

Formerly known as the P.L. Bennett estate, this mid-19th-century home is located at the corner of Spring Street and Railroad Avenue. The property boasts a unique hexagonal barn. The house was added to the National Register of Historic Places in 1980, the only building so recognized in Newport. Pictured from left to right are P.L. Bennett, Mr. Pierce, Mr. Hardy, Bert Brown, Maria Bennett, and her sister Delia Hardy.

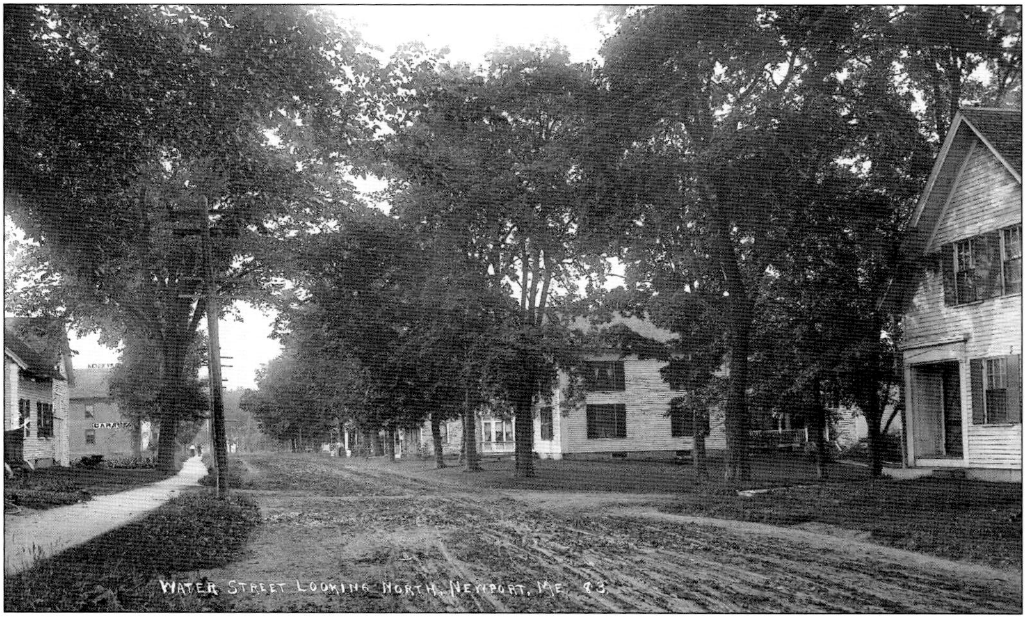

If one stood at the same position today and looked up Water Street toward the lake, several houses pictured here would be missing. It is a quiet, residential side street today, whereas 100 years ago it was a busy thoroughfare leading from the train station and downtown area to the lake.

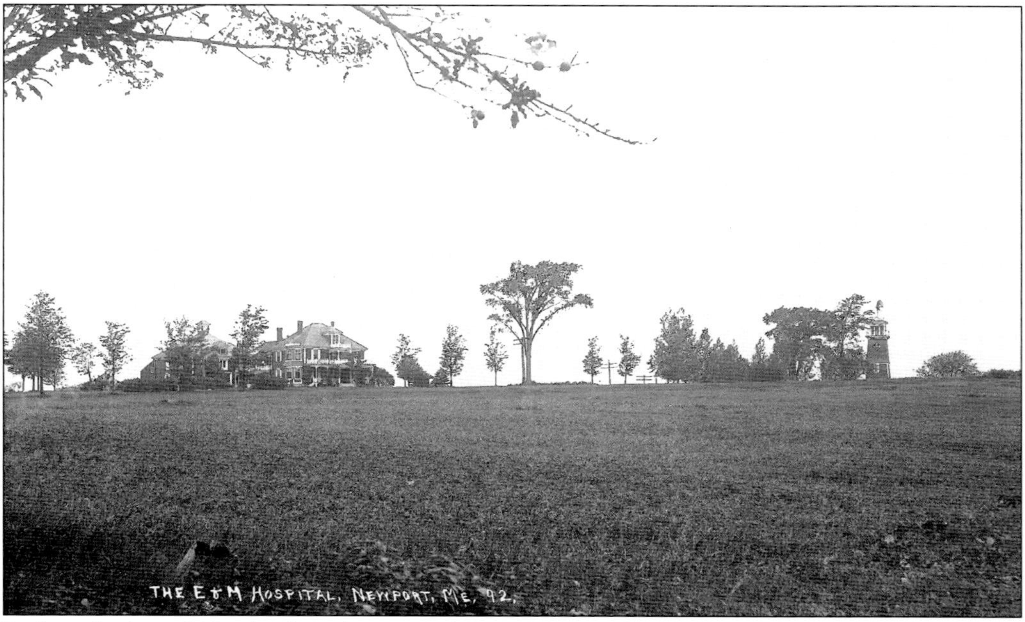

Built in the late 1800s, this large home on the Corinna Road (now Golf Course Road) was built for seasonal resident Dr. Trueworthy. From 1915 to 1924, physicians Oscar Emerson and J.J. McVetty operated a seasonal hospital there. Shown at right is a lookout tower formerly equipped with a windmill for powering a water pump. The home was leveled by fire in the 1920s. The Newport Golf Course was established on the property and opened in 1951. A contemporary private residence was built where the old tower stood, and its design references the tower. (Courtesy of the PMM.)

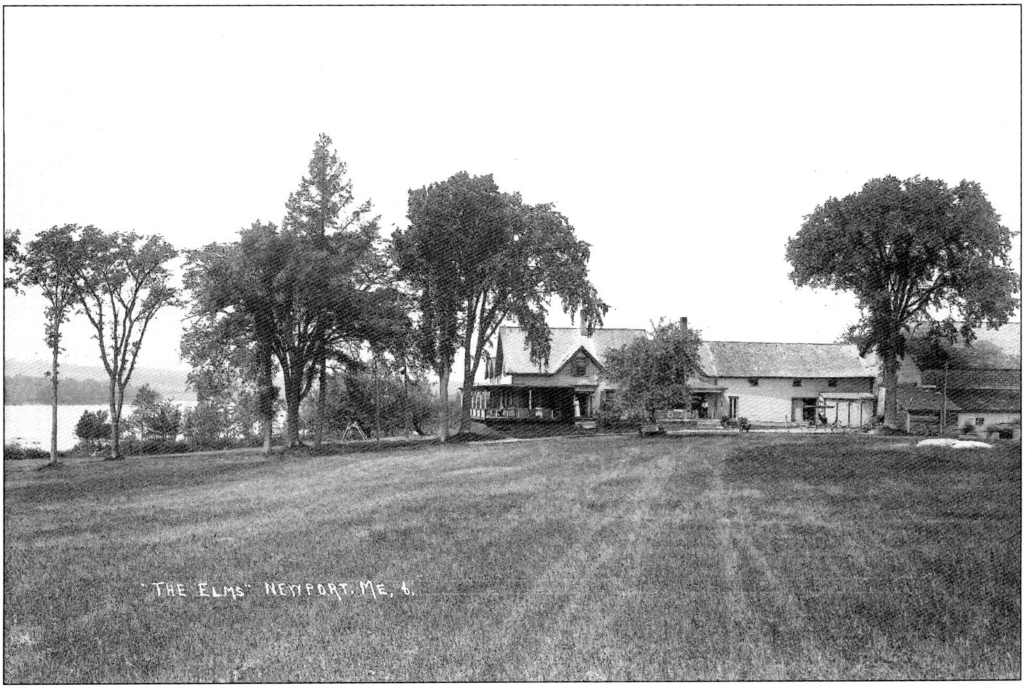

Originally a large farm belonging to Aretas Rowe (descendant of some of Newport's earliest settlers), this outer Grove Street home became a popular inn in the early 20th century. At that time, Newport was rich with elm trees, which contributed greatly to the beauty of the village. (Courtesy of the PMM.)

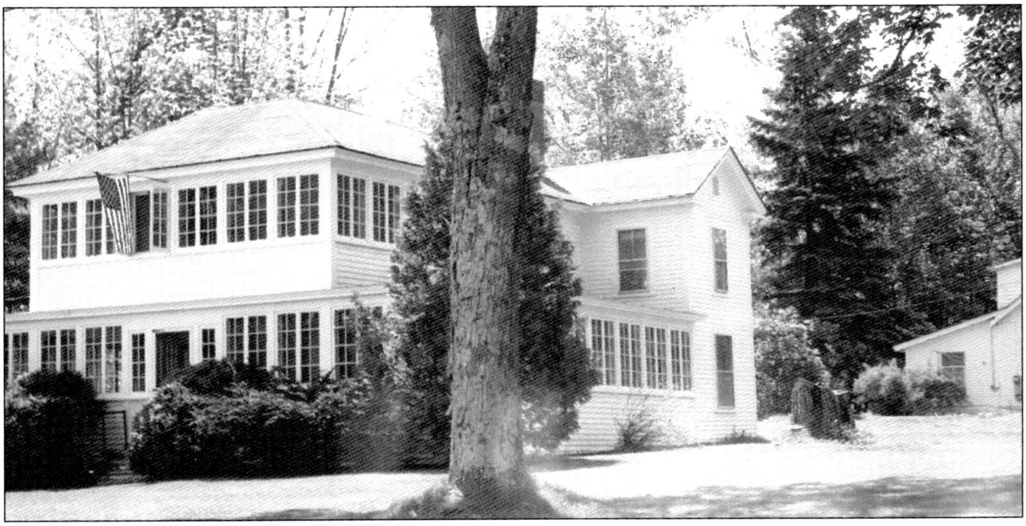

The Kingsburys' home on outer Grove Street housed the Women's Emergency Farm Service summer volunteers who came to Newport in 1943 and 1944. Teenaged girls from all over the country came to do farm labor during World War II. The WEFS girls worked for the Portland Packing Company doing chores, such as weeding fields. They worked up to 10 hours per day, 6 days per week. Later, the home became known as "The Evergreens."

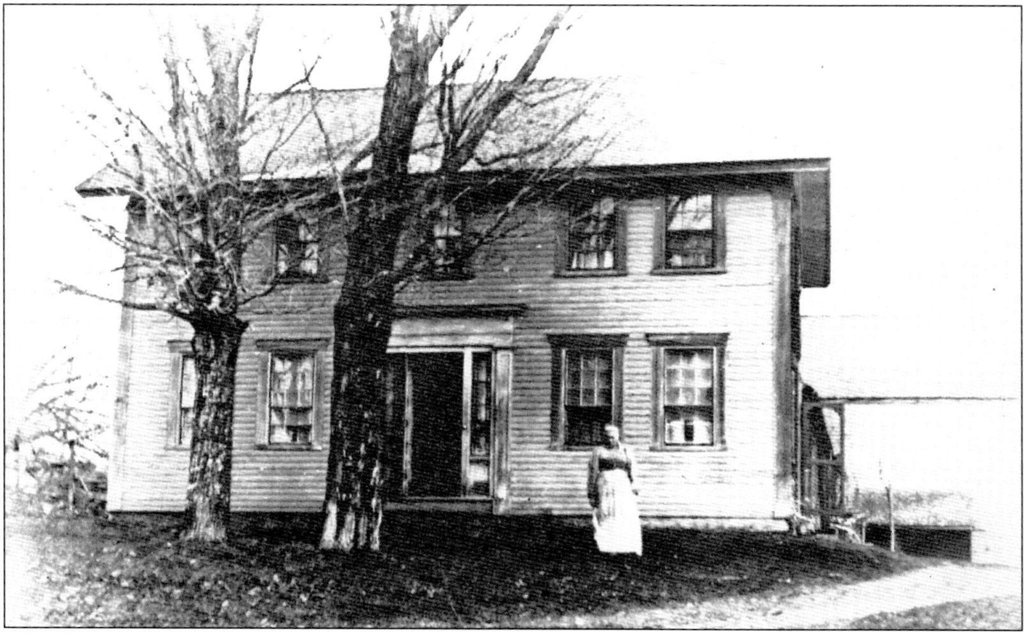

This home, originally the Cochran place, is located halfway up the steep hill on Durham Bridge Road in North Newport. A potato-storage barn set into the hillside remains today, and the same trees appear to be thriving in the front yard.

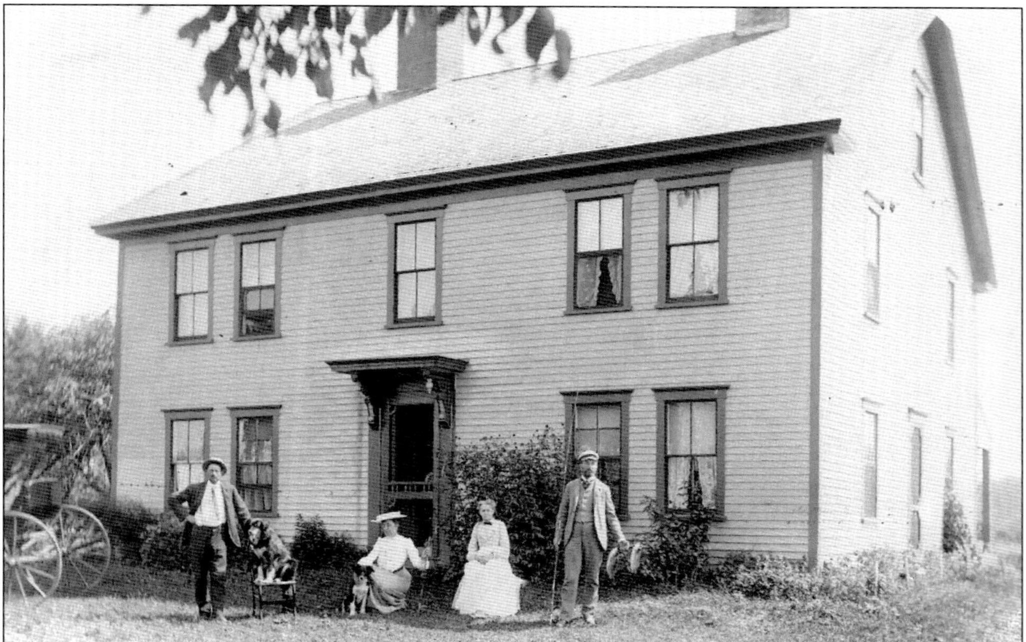

Built in 1807 or 1808 by Nathaniel Burrill, this was one of the oldest frame houses in Newport. It was located in North Newport, near the lake, off the Durham Bridge Road, and it belonged to Hubert E. Turner when this photograph was taken. "Hube" Turner is believed to be the man on the right, displaying a fishing pole and the catch of the day.

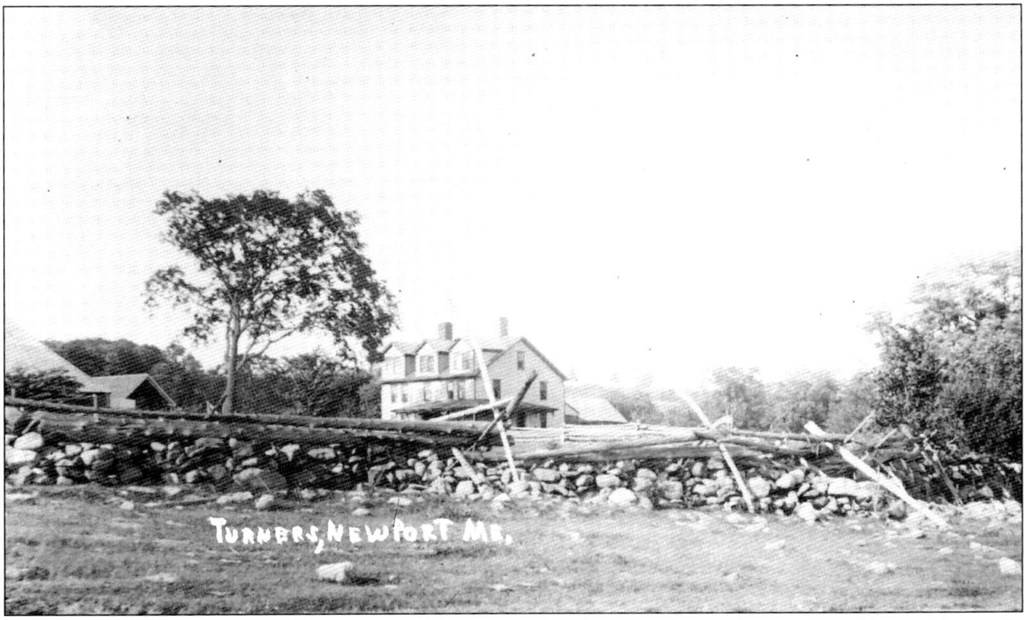

The Turner home was remodeled and expanded several times. (New dormer windows and a wide covered porch can be seen in this picture.) By the early 1900s, the Turner farm was being used as a guesthouse and also had cottages for rent. The evolution of the home reflects the changing economy of the area, from one based on agriculture to one in which tourism played a key role. (Courtesy of Ronald Plummer.)

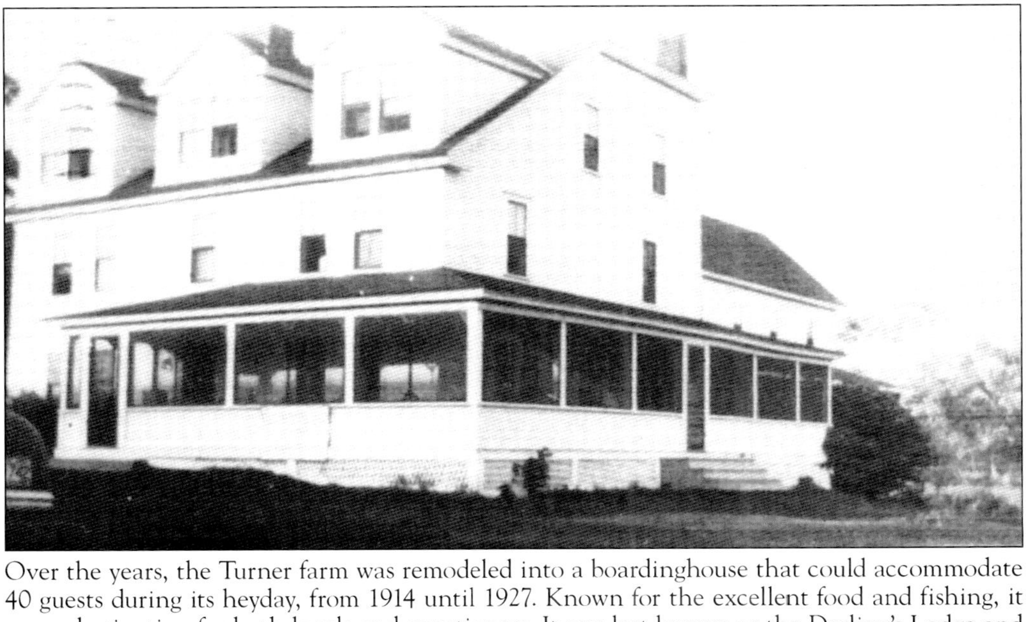

Over the years, the Turner farm was remodeled into a boardinghouse that could accommodate 40 guests during its heyday, from 1914 until 1927. Known for the excellent food and fishing, it was a destination for both locals and vacationers. It was last known as the Darling's Lodge and was torn down in the latter 20th century.

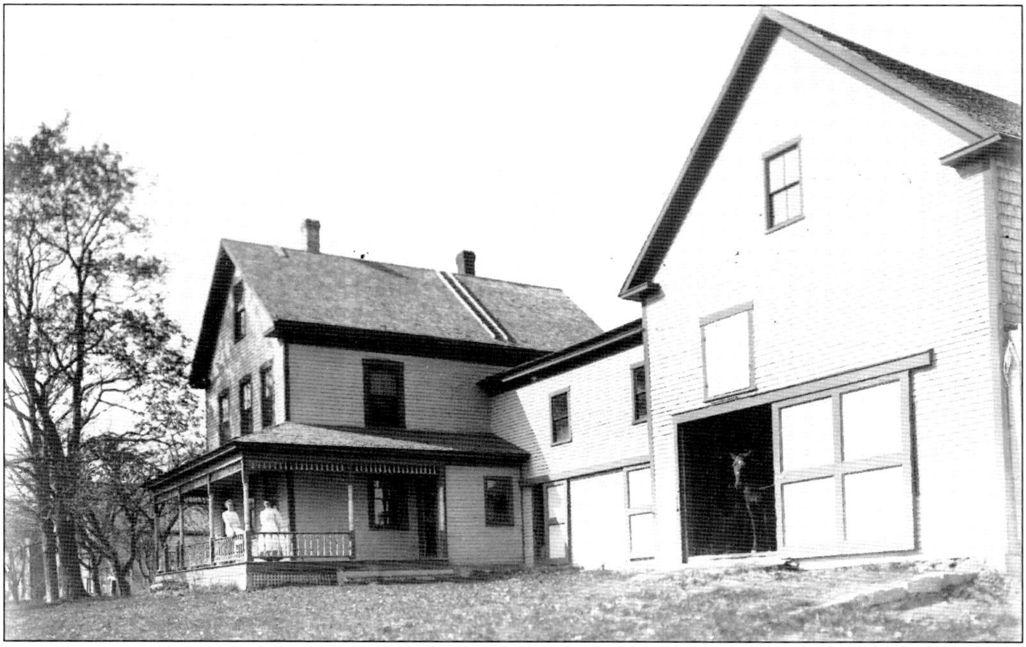

The Bolwell home on Grove Street offered the family a comfortable, farmhouse environment very close to their businesses in town. Grove Street was a popular residential area because of its proximity to town and the lake.

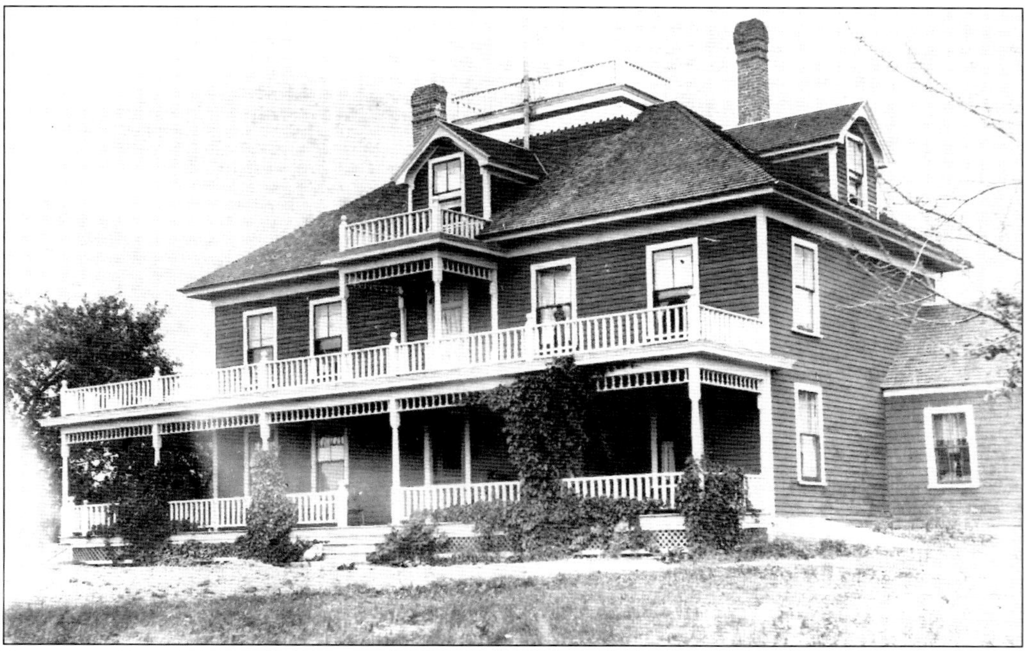

Benjamin Grant's lakeside home is shown about 1910. It was fairly typical of the summer homes built by people "from away," who wanted to enjoy "the cool, comfortable shade and restful scenery of country life, so free, so rich, so full of promise of returning health," per Newport's 1908 Board of Trade publication. The home is now a private residence.

Four

Business and Industry

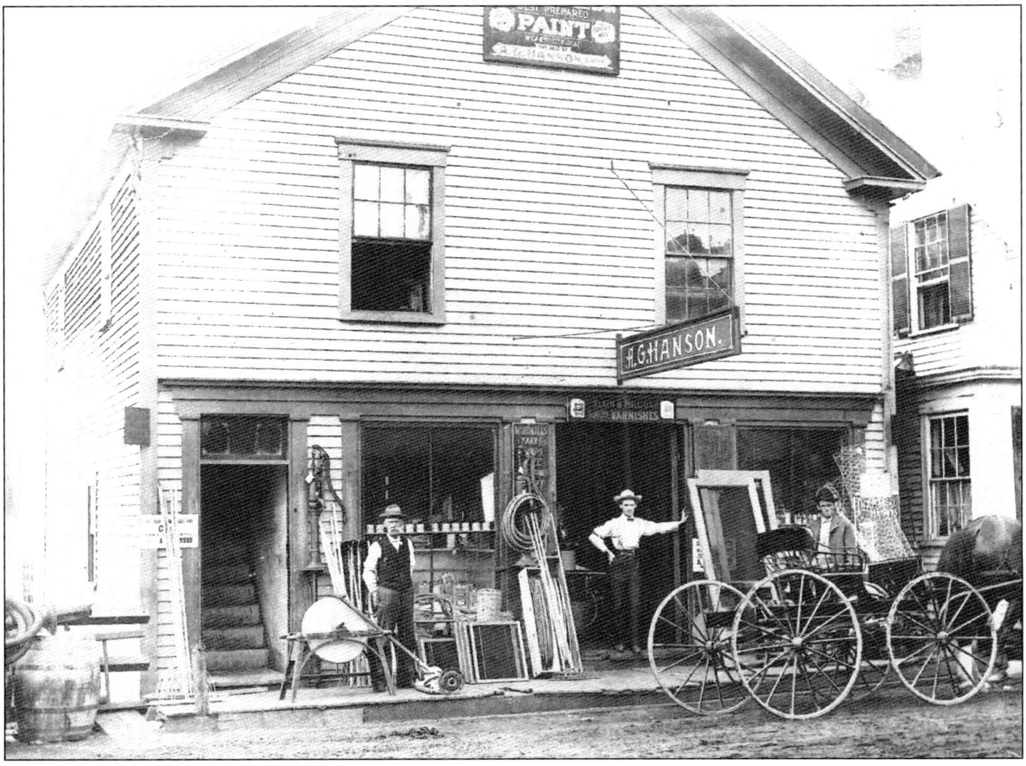

Arthur G. Hanson sold plumbing and hardware supplies, specializing in plumbing and heating systems. Hanson was educated at Maine Central Institute in Pittsfield and then the Bangor Business College. He opened the hardware enterprise in 1900 on Main Street, near the bridge. The building later was the location of Dr. Ralph Dyer's (and still later Dr. John Dyer's) optometry office.

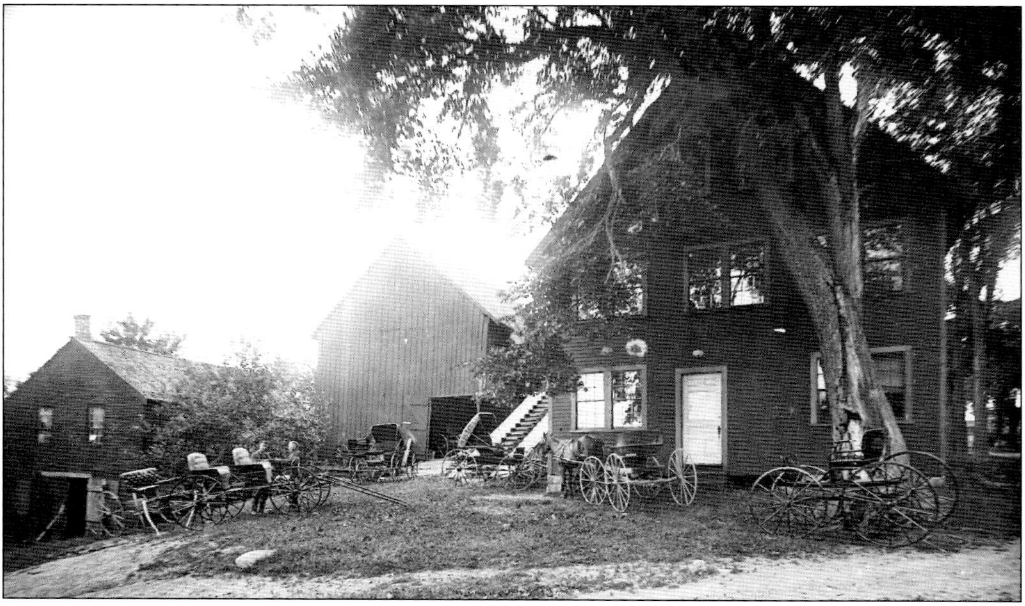

There were a number of carriage shops in Newport over the years. Shown here is the P.L. Bennett Carriage shops (later Clark's Carriage), located on the corner of Elm and Center Streets, near the bridge. Another carriage venture was the shop of G.W. Day on Water Street. That three-story enterprise specialized in painting and varnishing carriages, sleighs, and wagons. In the late 19th century, businesses servicing horses, harnesses, and carriages were common in town.

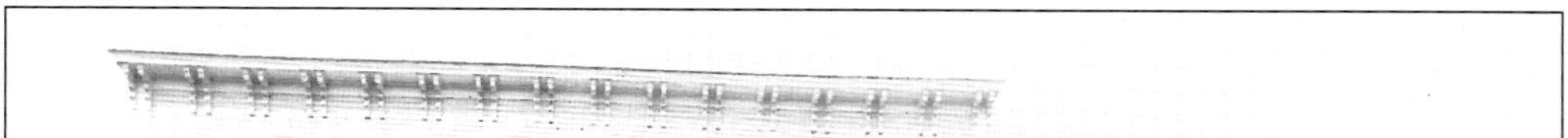

The Croxfords moved to Newport about 1880 and opened a grocery store at the corner of Main and Water Streets. In 1902, they constructed the Croxford building (shown here) on Water Street, where they maintained their large grocery and meat market. In 1912, the building was sold to Hanson and Pingree, and the grocery moved to Main Street. In its heyday, the shop employed three clerks and had a busy delivery service.

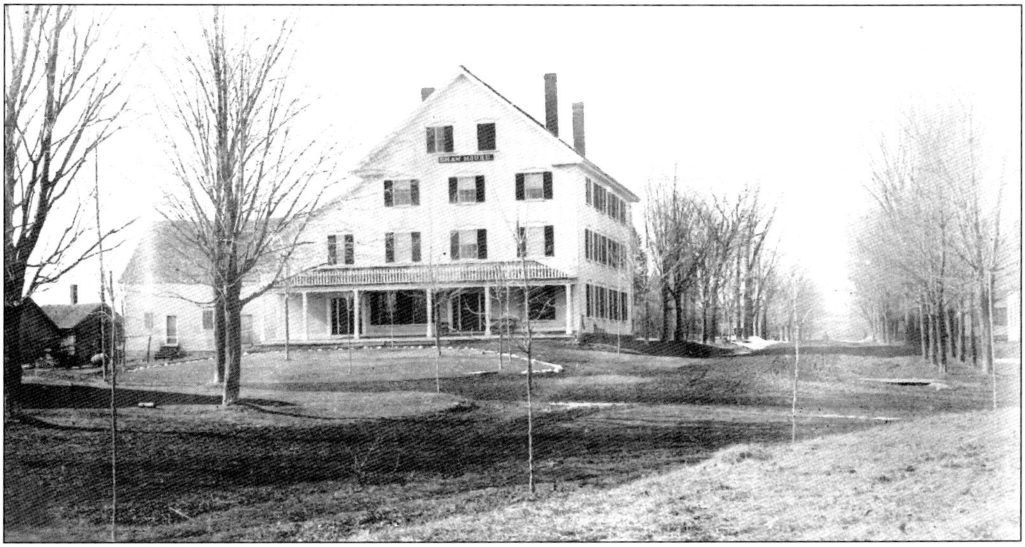

Benjamin Shaw opened the Shaw House on the corner of High and Main Streets in 1861. For a time, it was owned by Charles E. Jones and was called the Jones Inn, ostensibly the location for the 1960 novel *The Inn at the Crossroads* by George Barrett. Residents at the time claimed to recognize many of their fellow citizens in the prurient novel set in the fictional town of Mados. It is now called the Newport Inn and contains apartments for seniors.

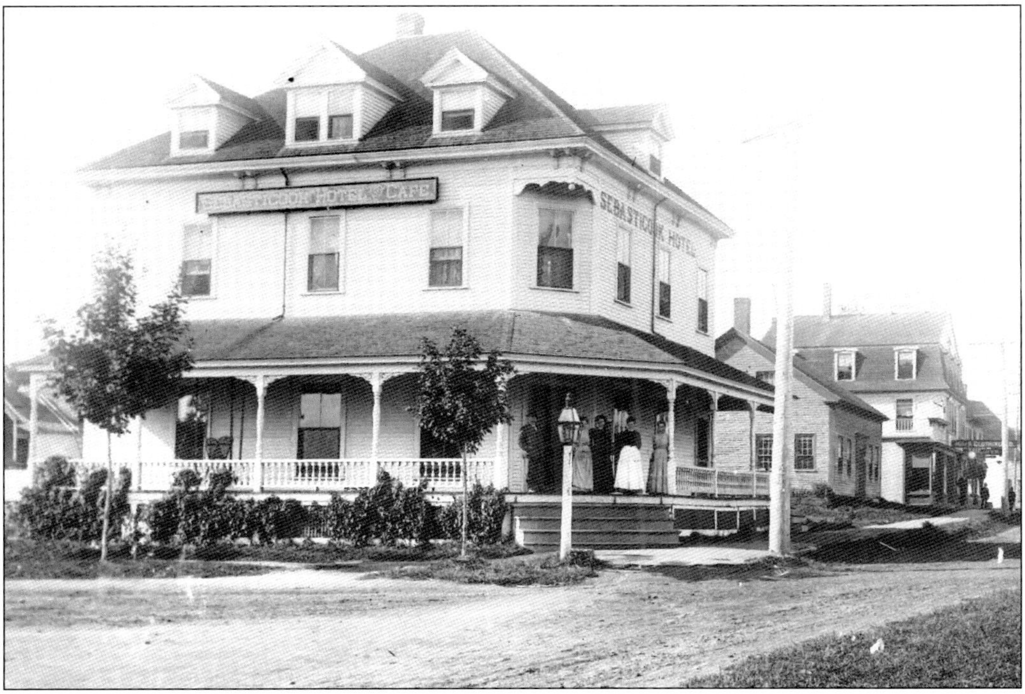

Located near the depot, the Sebasticook Hotel advertised "American and European plans" to travelers. The hotel was upscale enough to offer hot and cold running water in the bathrooms, and a full-service dining room. Located near the both busy Route 2 and the train station, it was a perfect way station for vacationers. The proprietors also sold cigarettes, soda, and souvenirs.

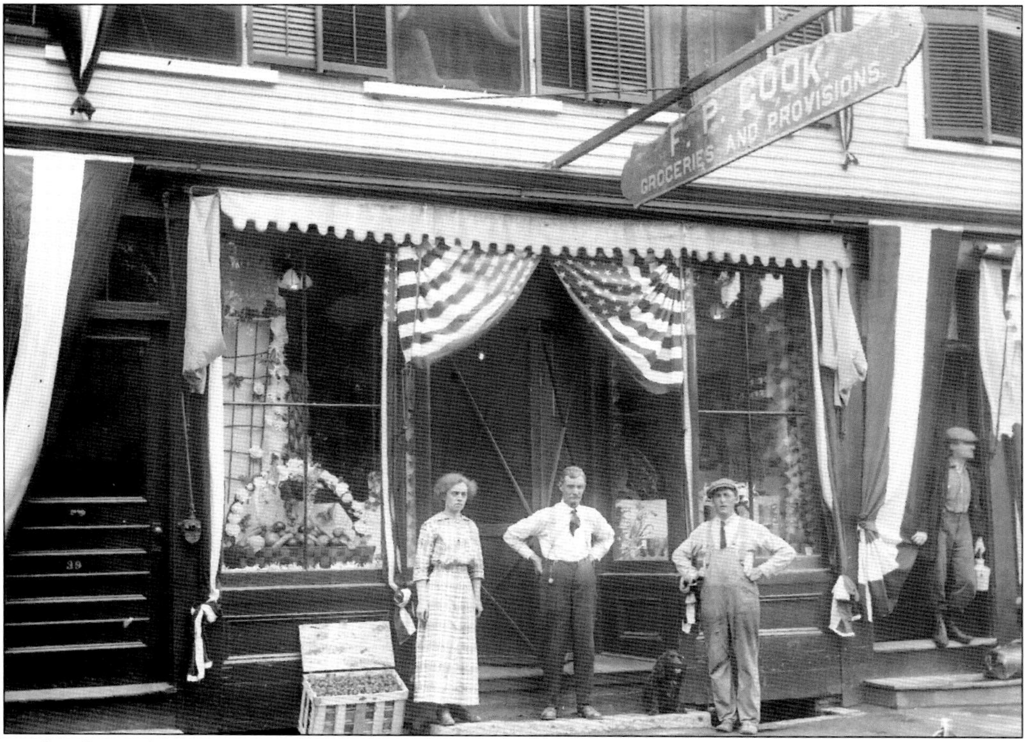

In the days when people traveled primarily by horse, shopping locally was a matter of necessity. Newport boasted all sorts of shops, including multiple groceries. F.P. Cook's was a grocery store on Main Street. This c. 1914 photograph shows, from left to right, Grace Bolwell, proprietor Frank P. Cook, Wallace Stuart, and Sumner Tasker.

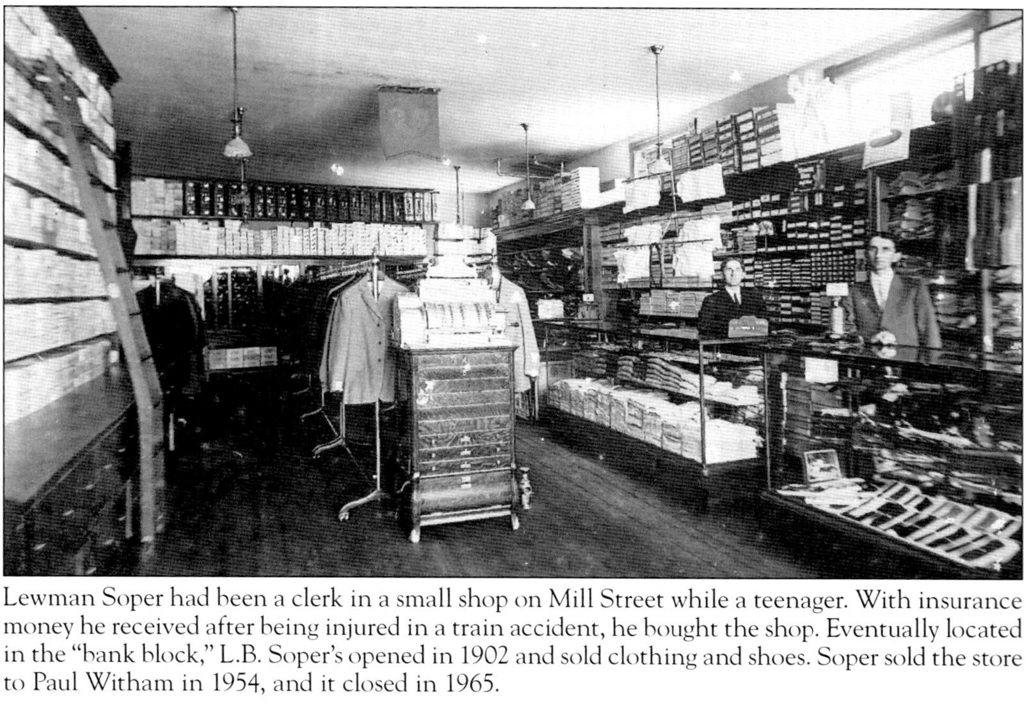

Lewman Soper had been a clerk in a small shop on Mill Street while a teenager. With insurance money he received after being injured in a train accident, he bought the shop. Eventually located in the "bank block," L.B. Soper's opened in 1902 and sold clothing and shoes. Soper sold the store to Paul Witham in 1954, and it closed in 1965.

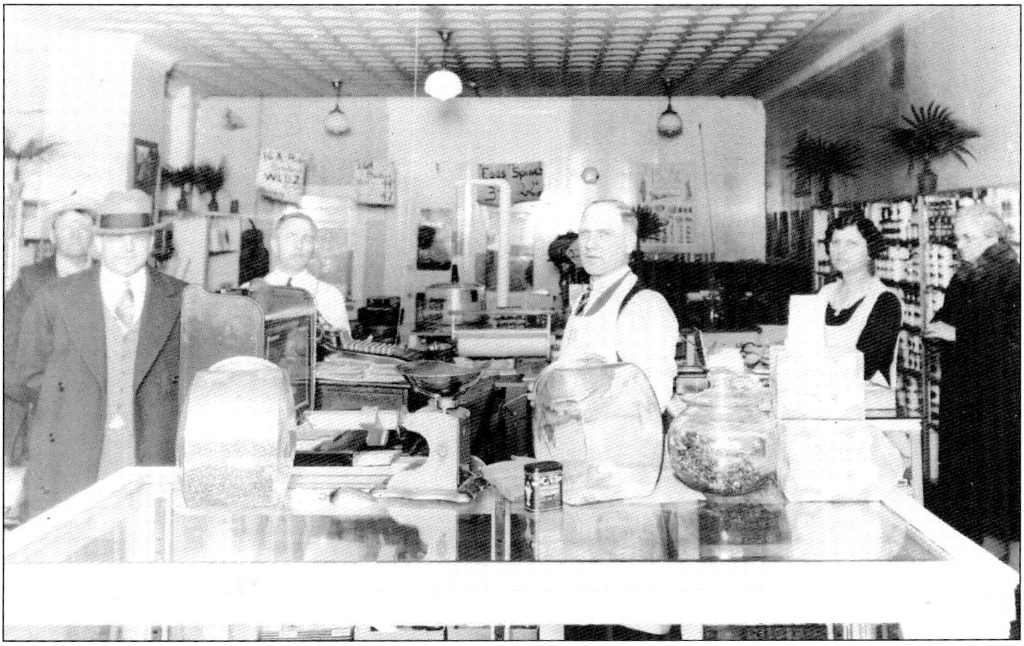

Frost's IGA was located on Main Street in the Judkins and Gilman block, roughly where the Newport Cultural Center now stands. During the 1940s, the store was operated by Rex Frost (center) and his wife, Rena (second from right). The clerk at left was Rex Bartlett. It was purchased in 1953 by "Bud" Homstead.

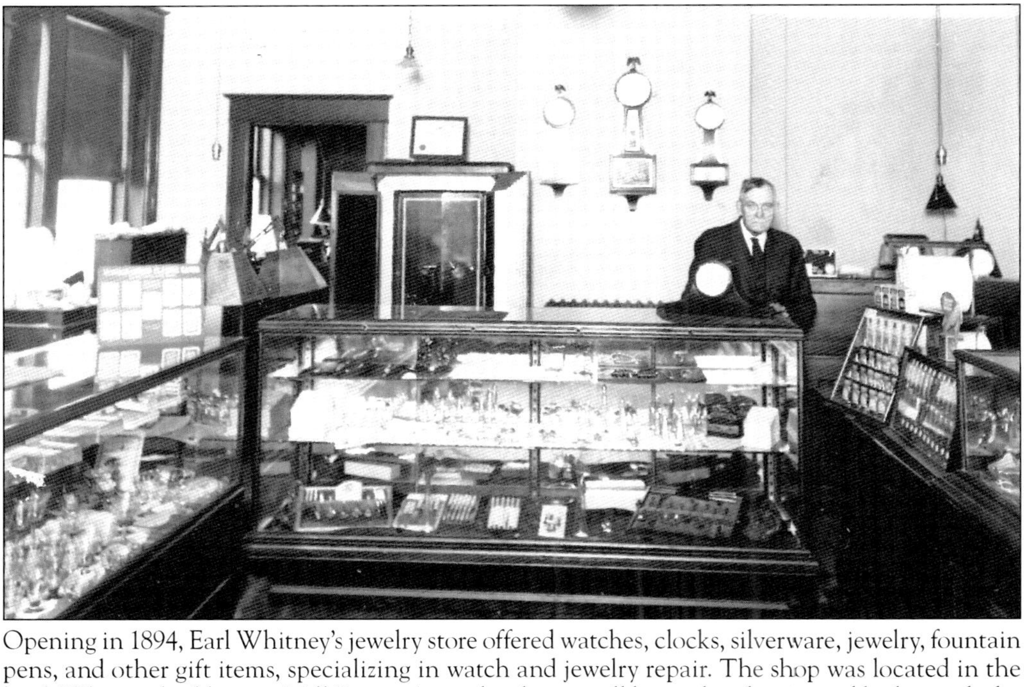

Opening in 1894, Earl Whitney's jewelry store offered watches, clocks, silverware, jewelry, fountain pens, and other gift items, specializing in watch and jewelry repair. The shop was located in the brick Whitney building on Mill Street. A jewelry shop is still located at the site and looks much the same as this photograph. Whitney was known for his generosity and his fondness for children.

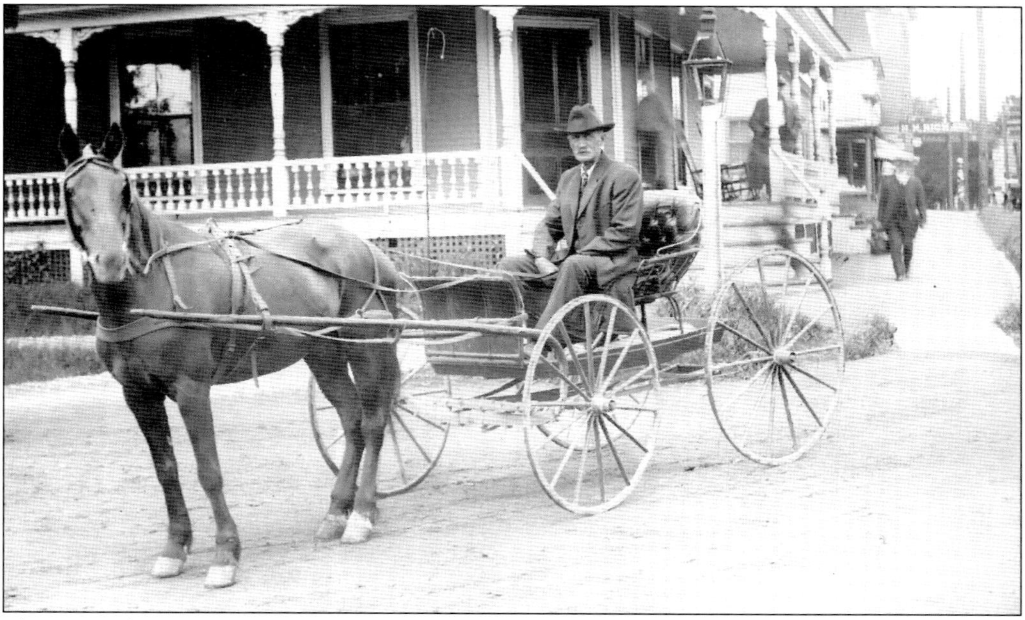

This 1913 photograph shows a horse and buggy in front of the Sebasticook Hotel on Mill Street. The harnesses may have been made by Fred Warren, who ran a harness business in Newport from 1908 until 1927. In the early days, he had business customers that kept up to 300 horses, and each year Warren created 1,500 sets of heavy harnesses as well as light harnesses for other local customers. The evolution of the automobile spelled the end of his business.

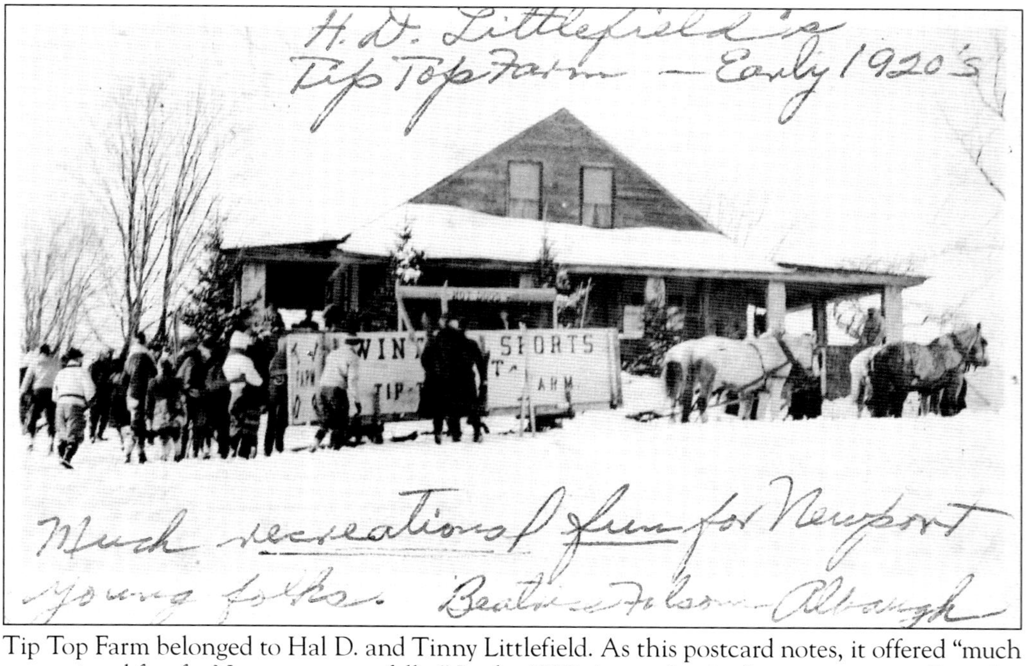

Tip Top Farm belonged to Hal D. and Tinny Littlefield. As this postcard notes, it offered "much recreational fun for Newport young folks." In the 1920s it was the site for winter sports, Saturday night dancing, a tea house, and a site for hosting birthday parties.

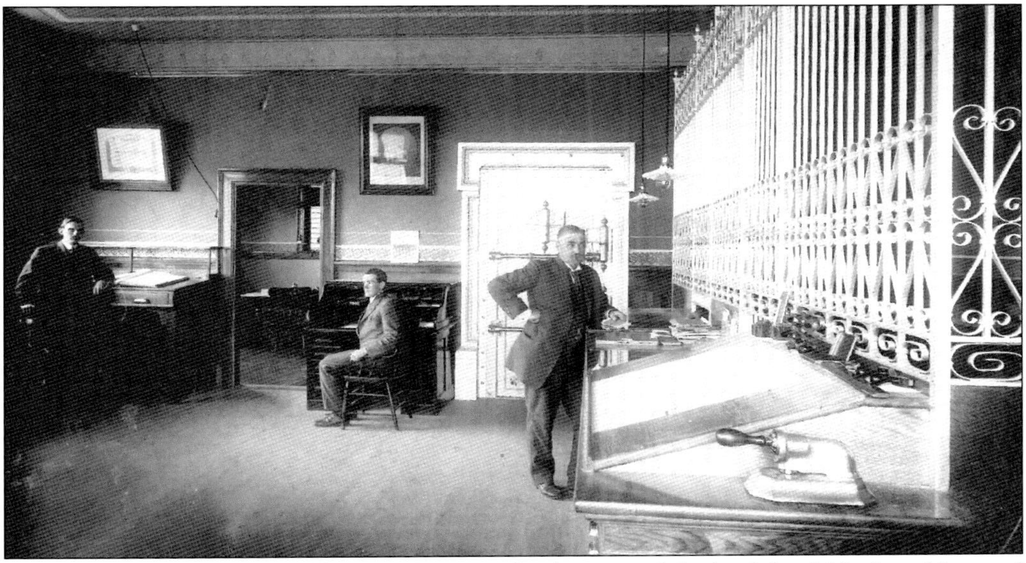

Founded in 1893, the Waterville Trust Company bank occupied the brick bank block and featured a state-of-the-art vault installed by the Remington Sherman Company. C.H. Morrill (previously assistant postmaster) was the cashier for many years. O.H. Judkins and James M. Sanborn were directors, and Rosie (Soper) Gilman was the bank assistant.

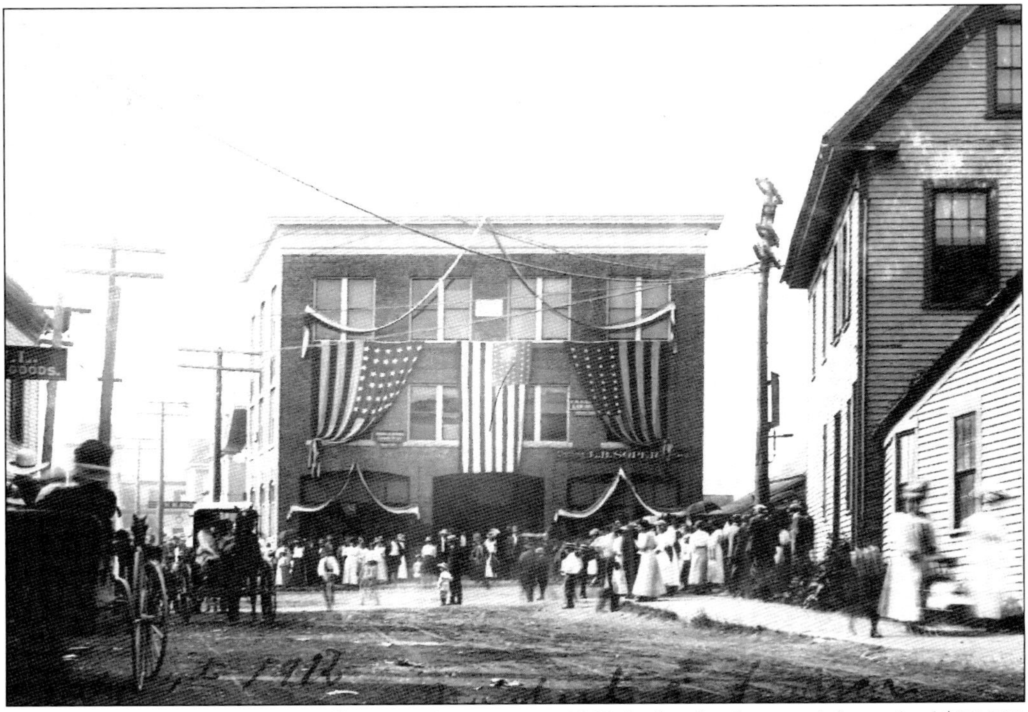

Formerly known as the Waterville Trust Company, in 1927 the bank advertised that it had $25,000 in capital and $60,000 in surplus. The lower level of the bank building housed L.B. Soper's clothing and shoe store. Offices were located on the second floor, and the Knights of Pythias Hall occupied the third. Later, district courthouse offices were located on the upper floors.

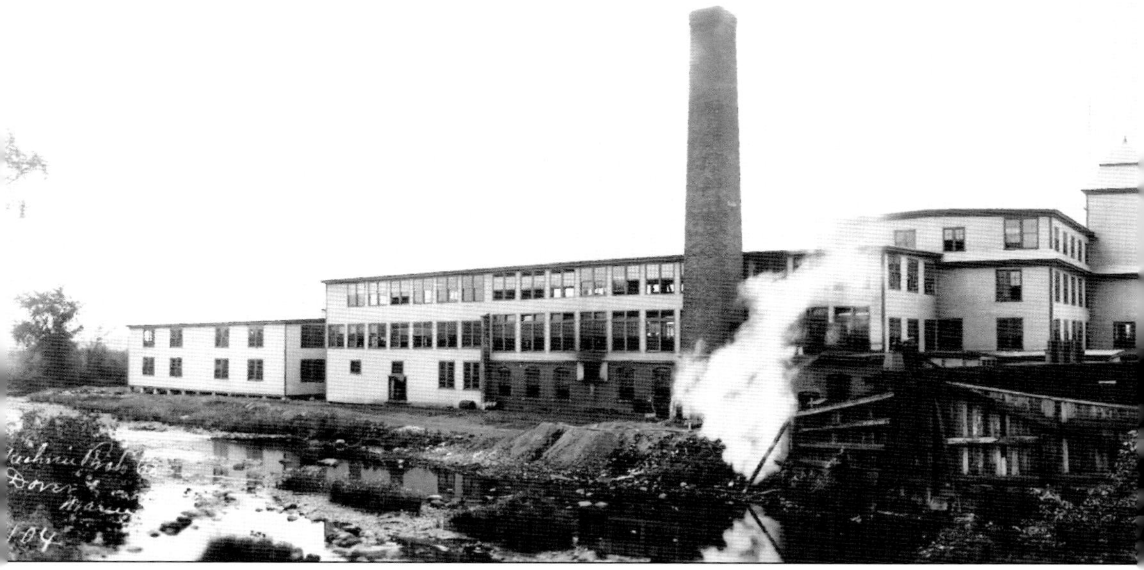

In 1891, Newport businessmen pooled their resources to form the Newport Manufacturing Company. The corporation purchased the lower (Main Street) dam (with water rights to the river), the flume, and land on either side of the river, including a sawmill and the former gristmill location on the west side. Ground was broken for the locally owned mill at a blow-out Fourth of July celebration that year. Posters advertising the event declared, "The Prince is Come, and Miss Newport, the SLEEPING BEAUTY, is to be Awakened by the Kiss of Business: In honor of which event the citizens will hold a GRAND JOLLIFICATION." To celebrate completion of construction, a concert ball was held on Thursday evening, December 24, 1891, with special trains bringing guests from afar. The ball featured 18 dance sets and an intermission. Though the mill changed hands, it continued to prosper and was enlarged several times. In 1908, the mill was called "the source of livelihood for the majority of the townspeople," with 175 directly employed that time. It specialized in woolens for menswear.

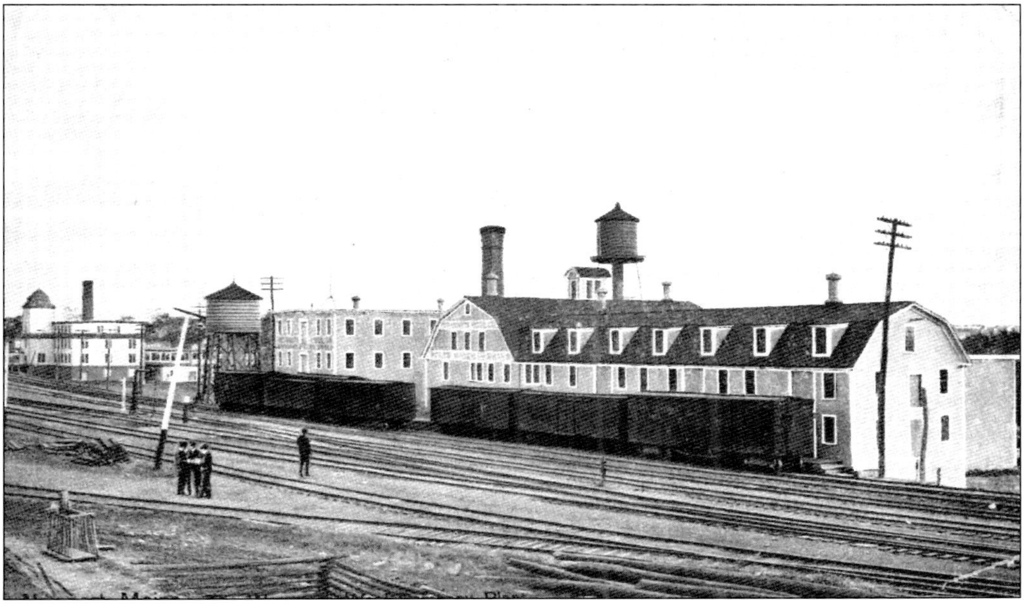

Founded in 1902, the Weymouth Wool Company produced pulled wool products. In November 1911, the company's office was burglarized. After a shoot-out, Officer Hefferen captured one burglar and pursued two others to Pittsfield via train. Officials sounded Newport's fire whistle to raise the alarm the night of the burglaries, which caused "a big portion of the village to turn out and excitement ran pretty high for some time."

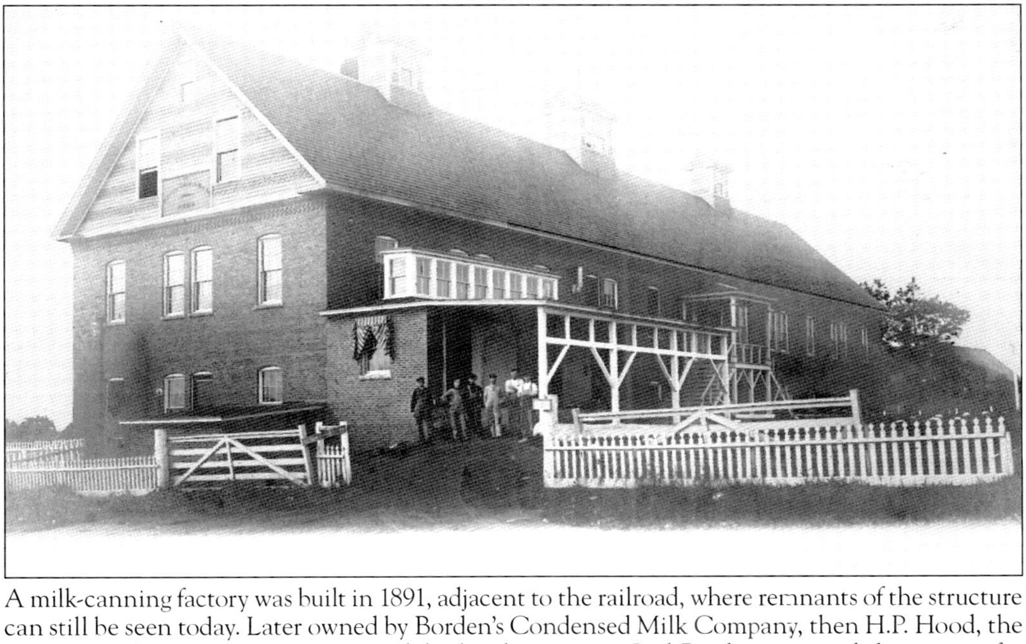

A milk-canning factory was built in 1891, adjacent to the railroad, where remnants of the structure can still be seen today. Later owned by Borden's Condensed Milk Company, then H.P. Hood, the factory was long an important part of the local economy. Gail Borden patented the process for canning evaporated milk, which was especially important in the days before refrigeration.

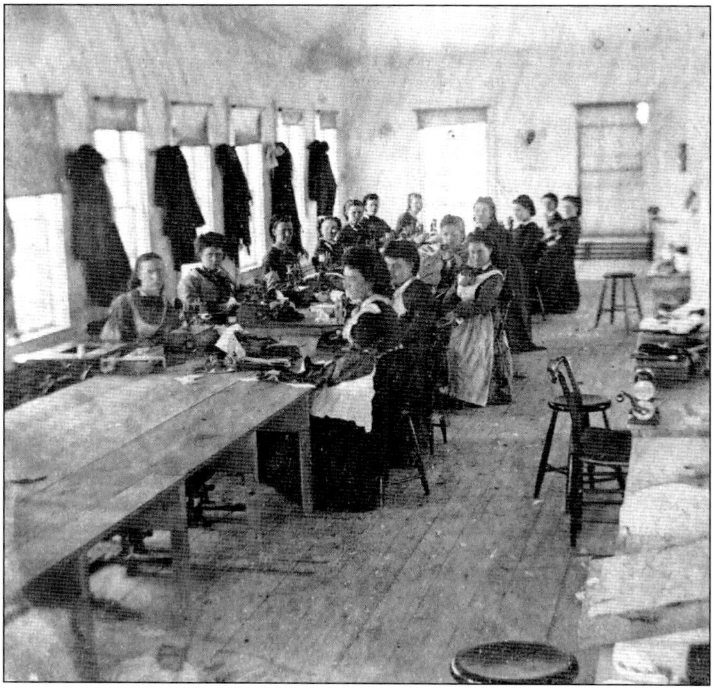

The Newport Shoe factory was a small concern located on Railroad Avenue in the late 1800s. Women working in the stitching room are shown here. In 1905, the Kingsbury Manufacturing Company incorporated. The company tanned leather and produced moccasins that were sold throughout the United States and Canada. Within a few years, the Kingsbury plant was a 3,500-square-foot enterprise.

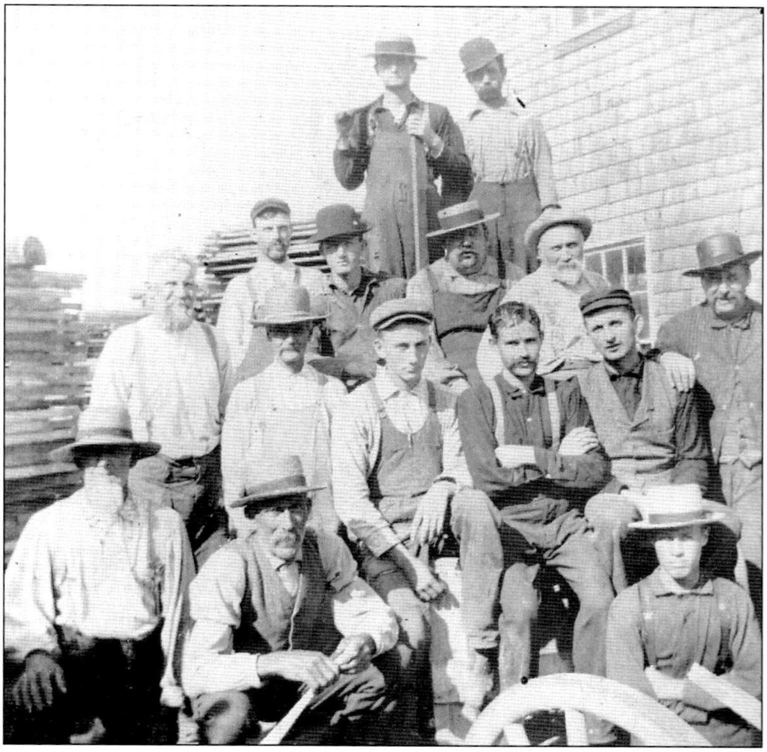

In 1892, Freeman and Alexander Cooper moved to Newport, establishing the Cooper Brothers veneer mill on the lower cove of Sebasticook Lake and later building nice homes up the street. In the early 1900s, the mill used 225 train cars of logs per year. Specializing in veneer for carriages and sleighs, mill waste products were used by the Newport Box and Novelty Company next door. This late-19th-century photograph shows the Cooper mill crew.

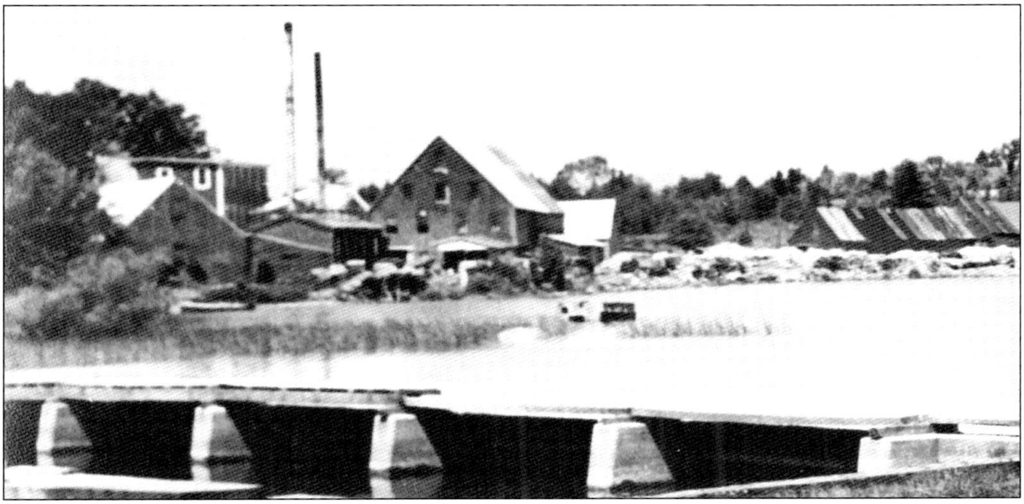

In 1906, the Cooper brothers joined P.L. Oakes in establishing the Newport Box and Novelty Company, employing 15 to 20 people. The building, which still stands as part of the Vic Firth Company, featured state-of-the-art machinery, an elevator, and fire-proofing technology. In 1913, the mill and box company merged to form the Cooper Brothers Company.

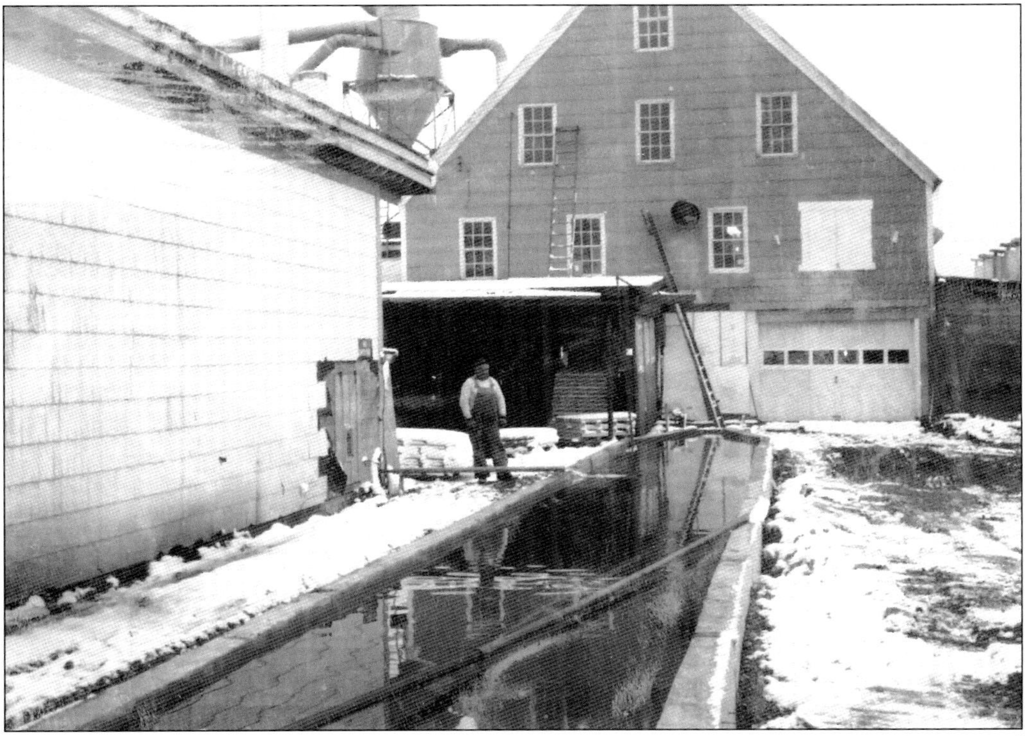

The Banton brothers took over the former Newport Box and Novelty Mill in 1926 and continued to make wood novelty items, many of which were featured in a segment of the 1936 silent film *The Movie Queen*, an advertising film set in Newport. This 1942 photograph shows the pool in which logs were cleaned before they were run through the mill. John Blynn stands at the rear of the pool.

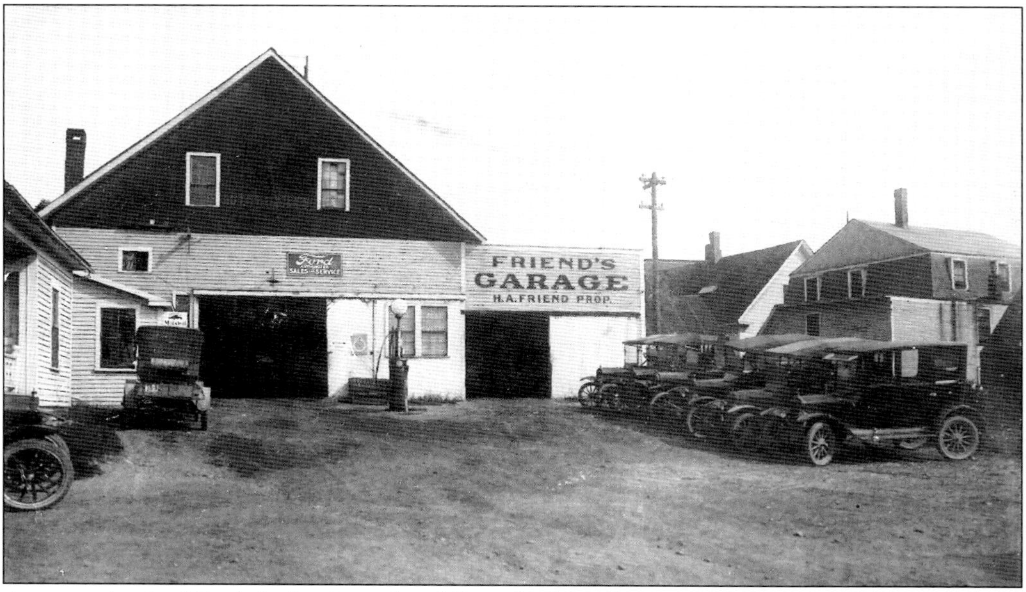

As an authorized Ford dealer, Friend and Friend sold and maintained automobiles, trucks, and tractors. The company was founded by Harry Friend and his son Norris when the latter returned from service in World War I. Their first location was on Railroad Avenue, shown here. Even in the cramped yard, there was room for a gas pump by the garage.

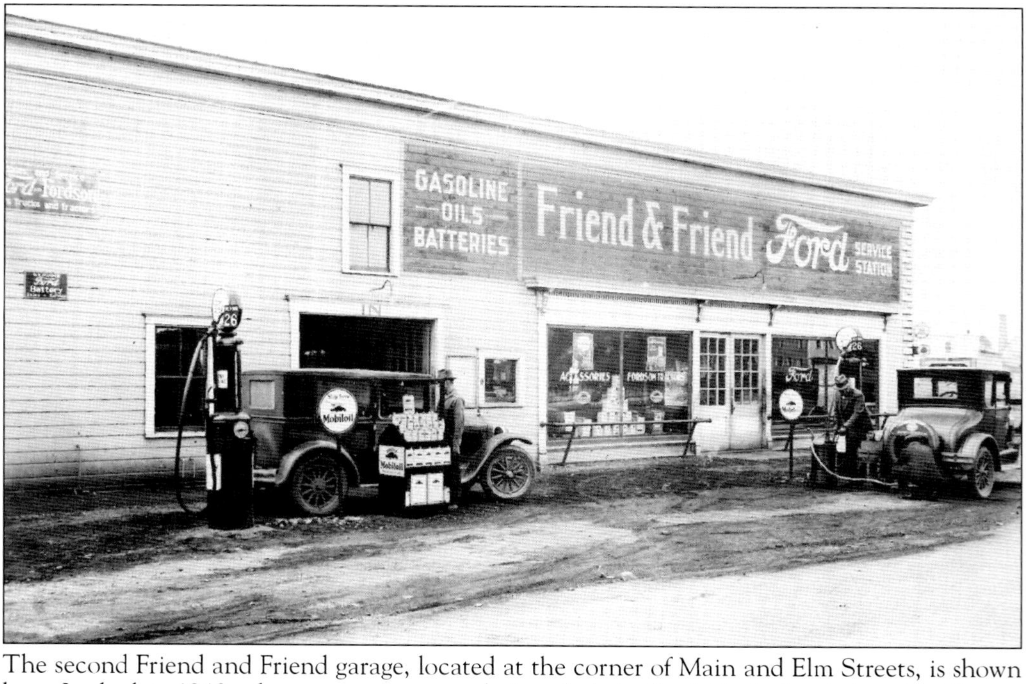

The second Friend and Friend garage, located at the corner of Main and Elm Streets, is shown here. In the late 1940s, the company custom-designed a hybrid vehicle for local physician George Higgins. The crew fit a 1938 Chevrolet body over a surplus Army Command and Rescue chassis to create an early sport utility vehicle that enabled the good doctor to make rural house calls in the winter.

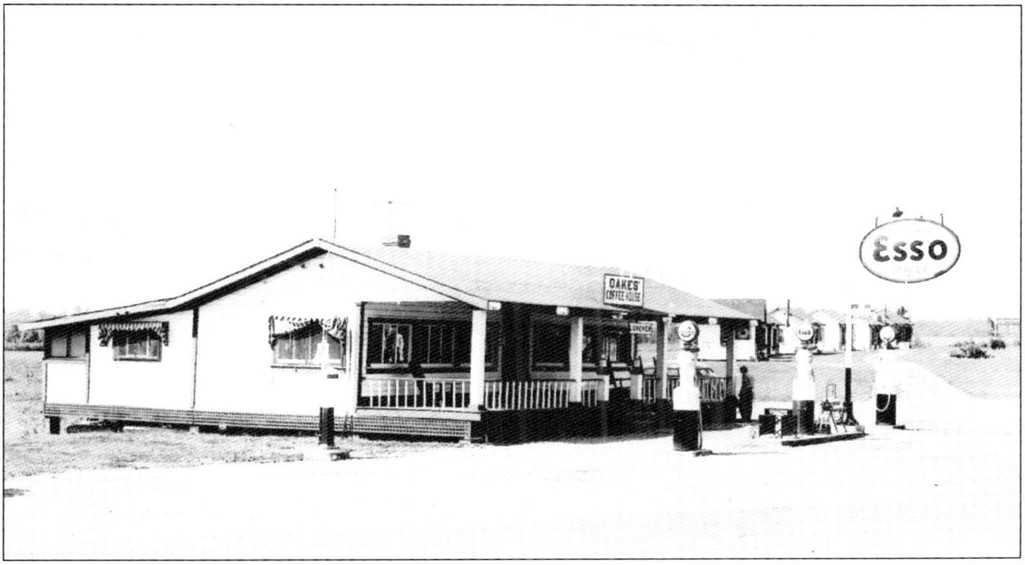

P.L. Oakes Coffee House and cabins were located on Route 100 at the Triangle. There was a row of cabins available for travelers (plus a "dog house" cabin for the girls who worked there to stay in), gas pumps, and a coffee shop.

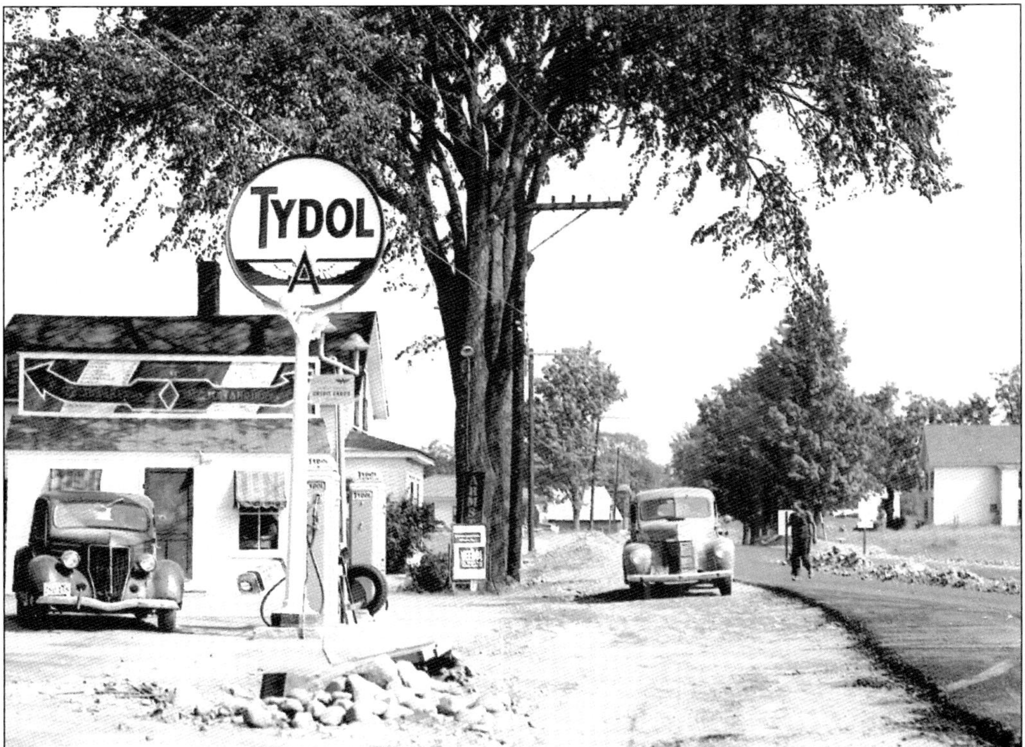

During the 1950s, this Tydol service station on Main Street was owned by Merton Davis and his wife, but it burned down on Christmas Day in 1967. For many years thereafter, an A-frame building housing the Pine Cone Realty office was on the site.

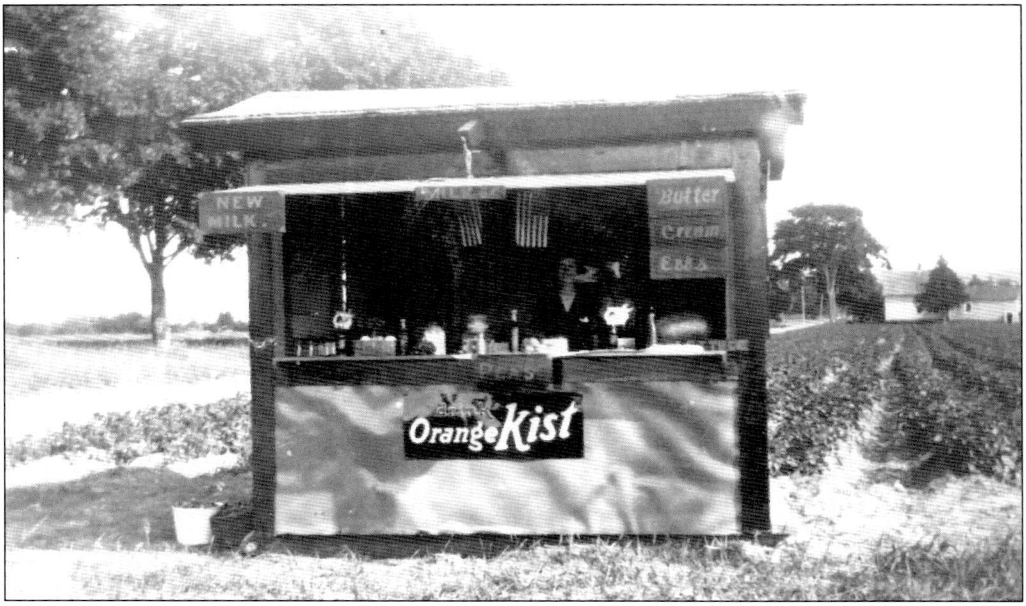

Helen Tardy operated a stand at Tardy's Corner, the corner of Route 7 (the Corinna Road) and Camp Benson Road. In this photograph, Lena Prescott works the stand, which was eventually expanded into a shop and a little restaurant. The Orange Kist soft drink advertised here might have been bottled at the Newport Bottling Works on North Street. (Courtesy of Maude Smith.)

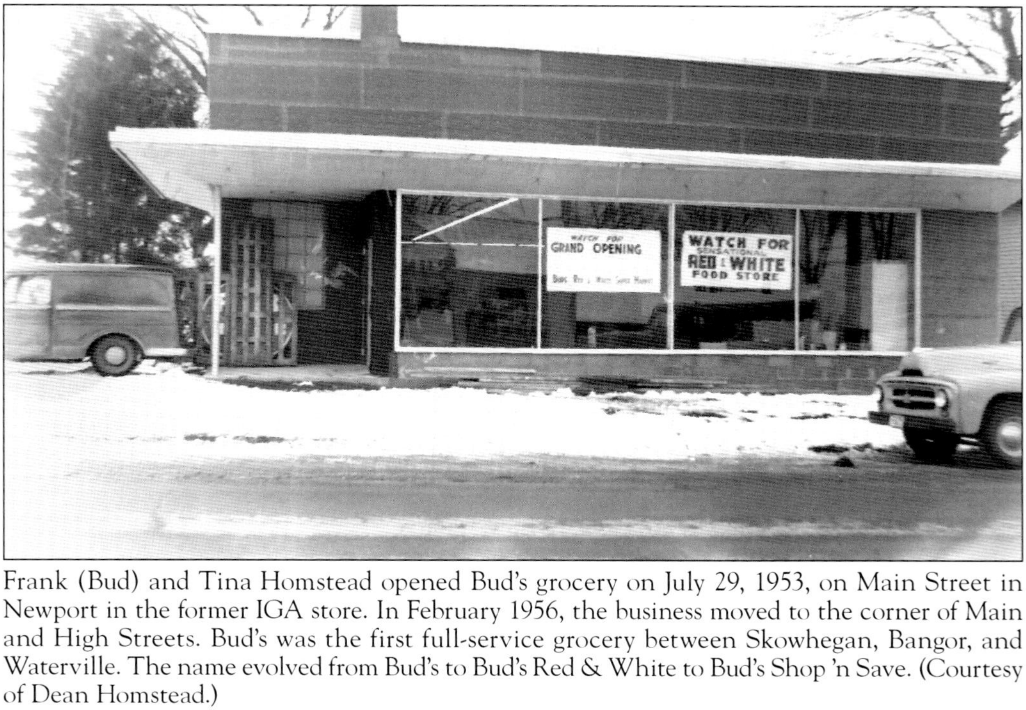

Frank (Bud) and Tina Homstead opened Bud's grocery on July 29, 1953, on Main Street in Newport in the former IGA store. In February 1956, the business moved to the corner of Main and High Streets. Bud's was the first full-service grocery between Skowhegan, Bangor, and Waterville. The name evolved from Bud's to Bud's Red & White to Bud's Shop 'n Save. (Courtesy of Dean Homstead.)

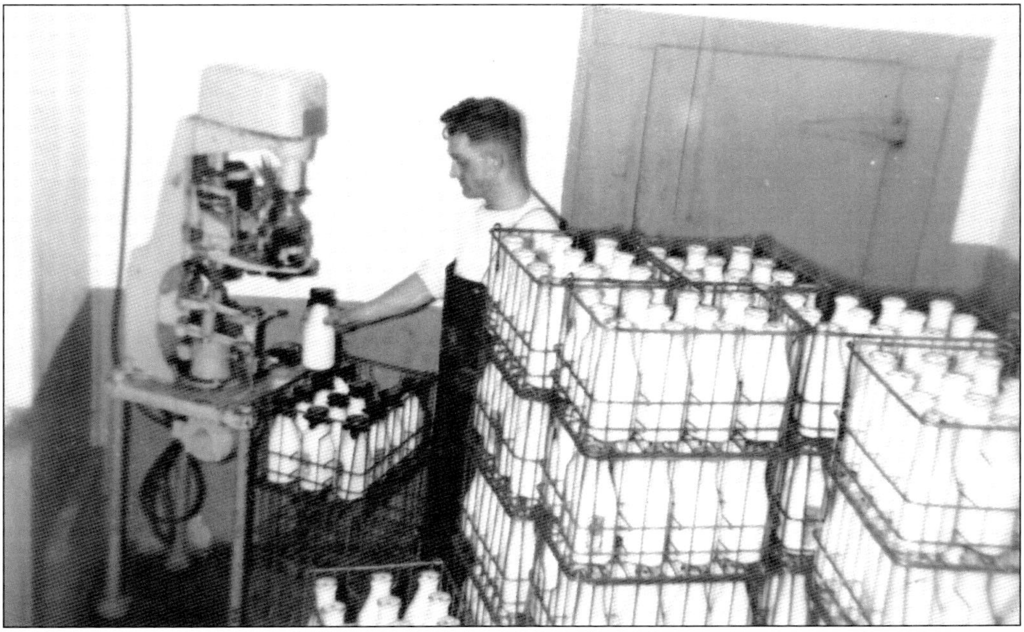

Located on the Corinna Road opposite Sebasticook Lake, Lakeview Dairy was a fixture in town for many years. The Sebasticook Valley has a rich agricultural heritage, with dairy farms and processing plants playing an important role in the local economy. Shown here around 1950, Errald Turner seals milk bottles. (Courtesy of Errald Turner.)

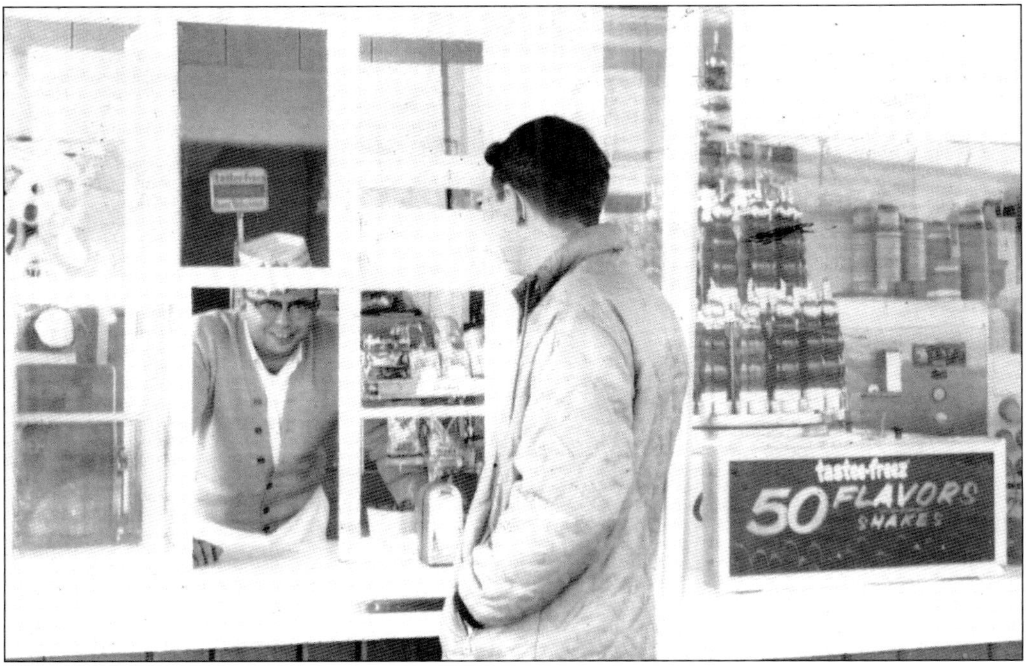

Long a destination at the Triangle (the junction of Routes 2 and 100) in Newport, the ice-cream stand there still opens seasonally. Here, customer Sid Smith talks to Howard Shapiro, who owned a Tastee-Freeze in the 1950s. (Courtesy of Maude Smith.)

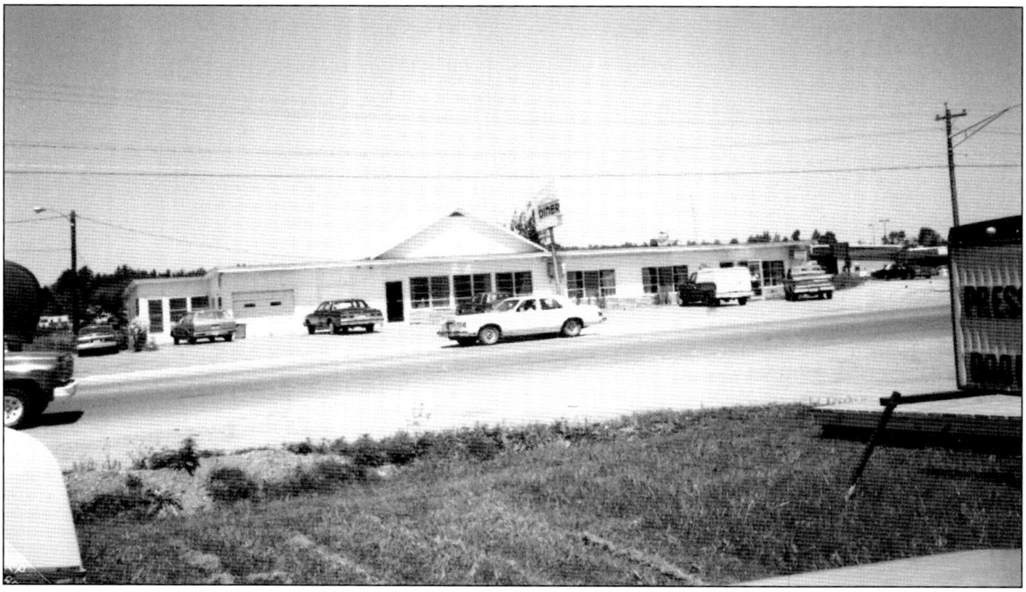

Located on Route 100 just outside town, Shorette's Diner benefited from Newport's location at the junction of major thoroughfares. Across the road was a large parking lot suitable for large trucks. Shorette's stood where the Irving truck stop is now located. Newport's first fast-food restaurant, a McDonalds, opened in 1985 opposite the diner/truck stop location. (Courtesy of Dale Carsley.)

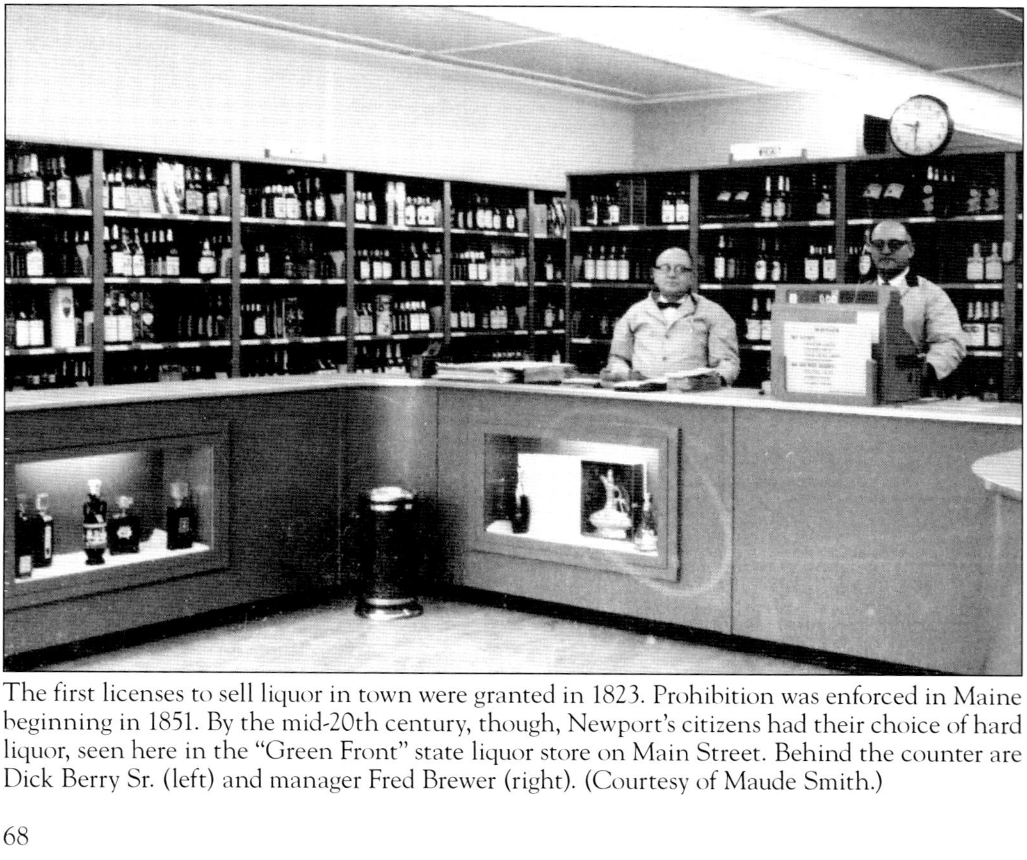

The first licenses to sell liquor in town were granted in 1823. Prohibition was enforced in Maine beginning in 1851. By the mid-20th century, though, Newport's citizens had their choice of hard liquor, seen here in the "Green Front" state liquor store on Main Street. Behind the counter are Dick Berry Sr. (left) and manager Fred Brewer (right). (Courtesy of Maude Smith.)

Five

CHURCHES AND SCHOOLS

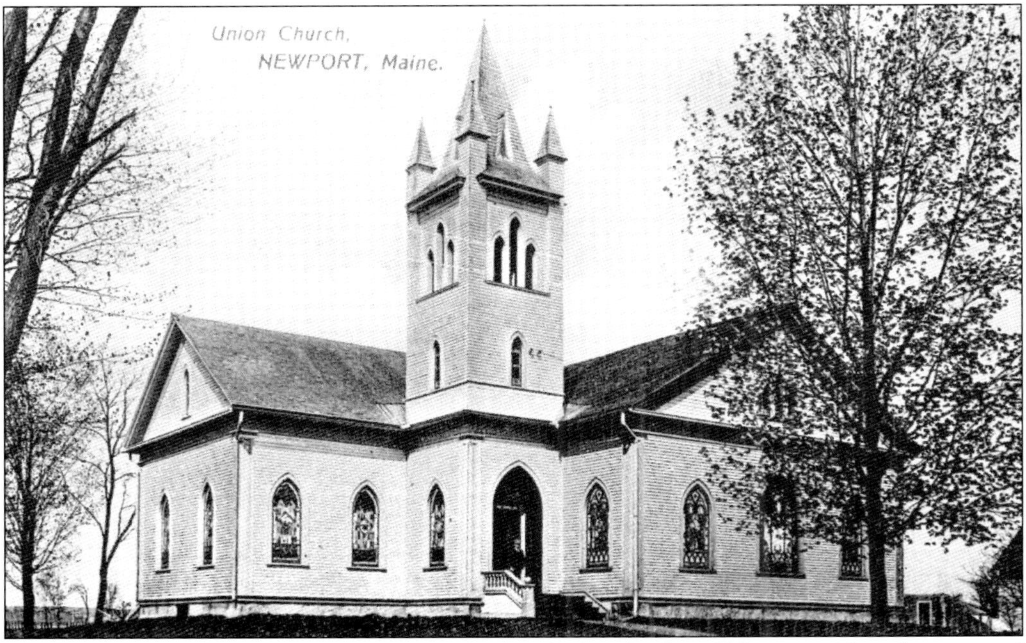

The origins of High Street Congregational Church date back to February 1831, when several Newport families formed a congregation. The church itself was built in 1837 through the combined efforts of Methodists, Free Will Baptists, Congregationalists, and the Universalists.

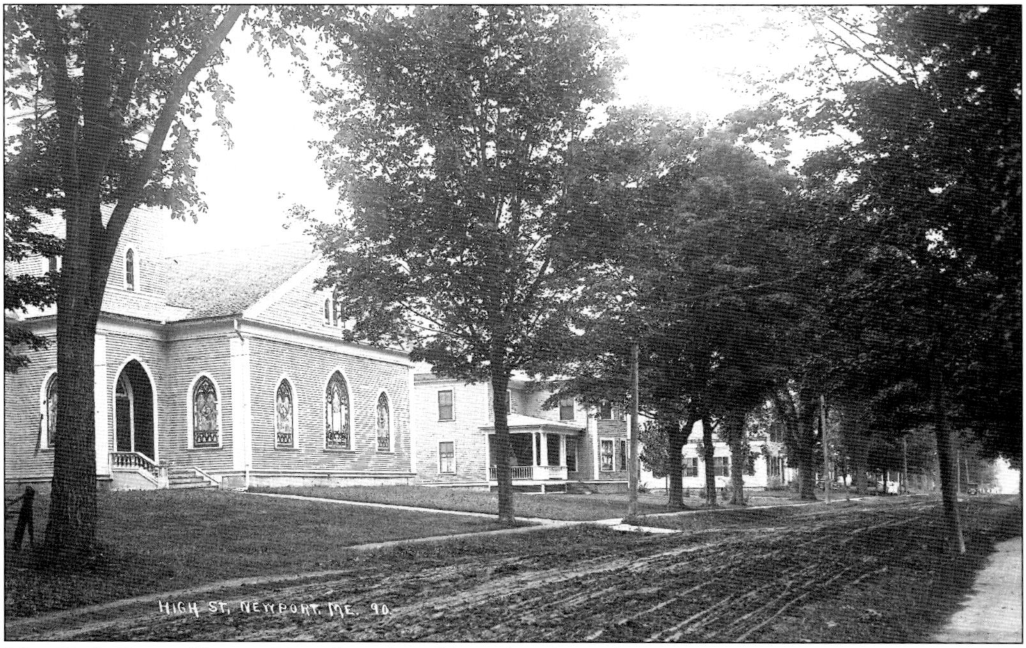

The High Street Union Church is the oldest church in the town. It was extensively remodeled in 1902 and again in 1948. In the 1940s, a parsonage was built adjacent to the church. Although most of the mighty trees on High Street are gone, many of the fine old homes still exist. (Courtesy of PMM.)

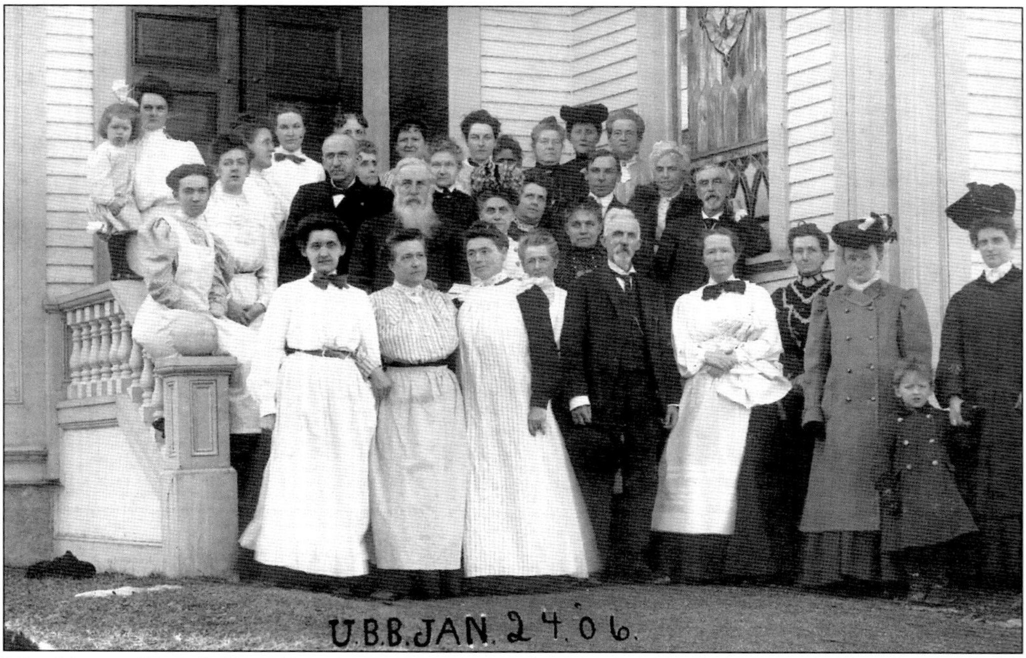

The Union Church Busy Bee Society poses on the steps of the High Street Union Church in this January 1906 photograph. The Busy Bees raised money to support and improve the church and community and held social events as well.

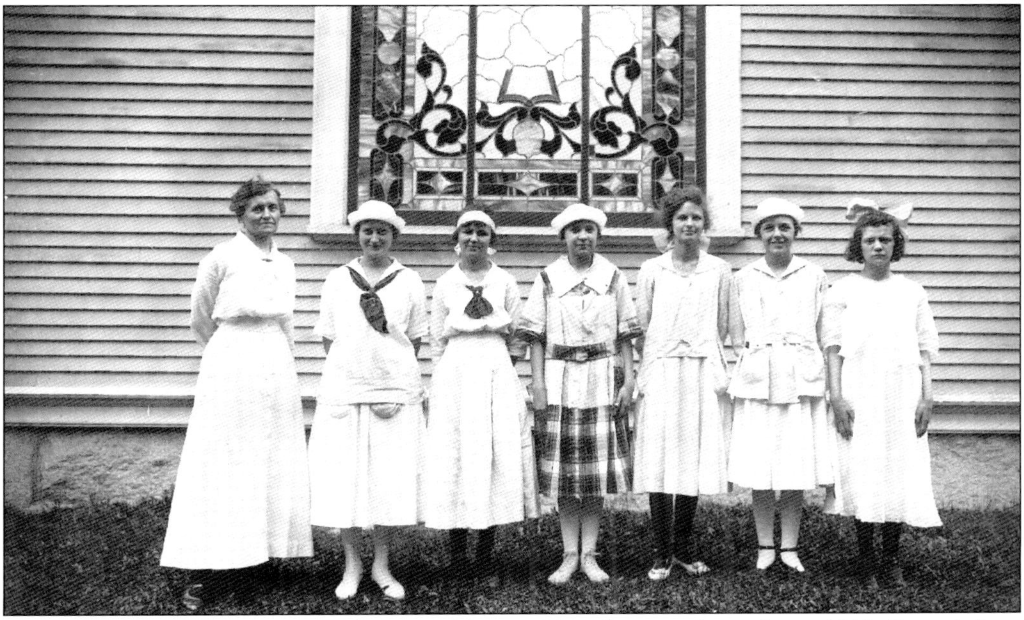

The Sunday school class at High Street Union Church poses here about 1918. From left to right are teacher Clara (Bickford) Chase, Thelma (Littlefield) Knight, Mary (Bowen) Carlsley, Madeline (Miles) Hall, Kathleen (Bickford) Folsom, Grace (Miller) Wightman, and Dorothy (Burrill) McKenzie.

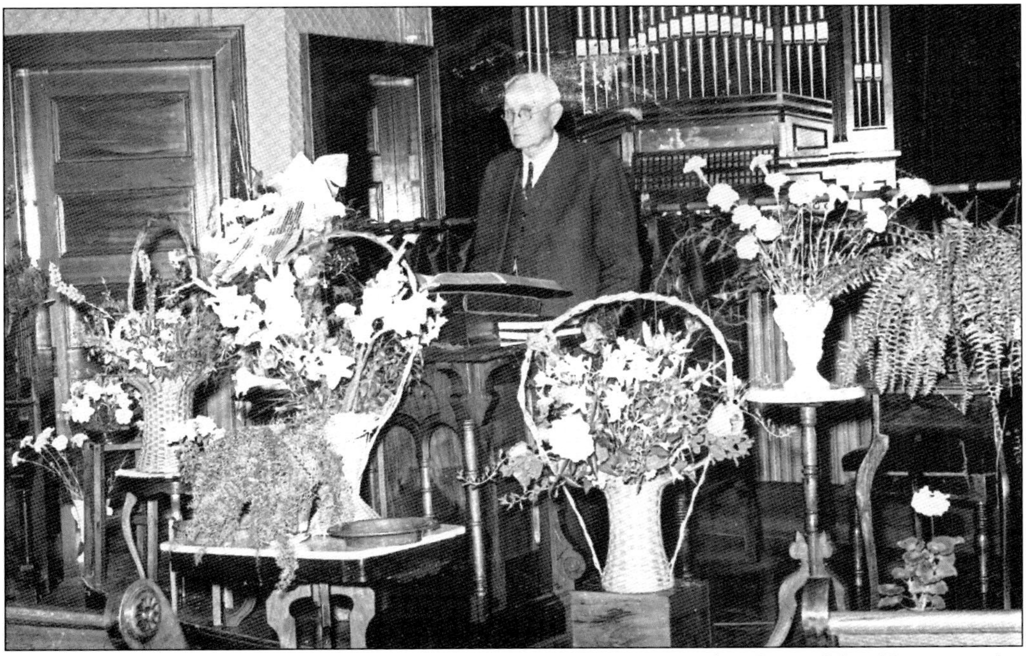

This interior view of High Street Union Church shows Rev. John Reynolds officiating the church's 1937 rededication ceremony. Reynolds had retired after 25 years in the High Street pulpit. The church building was 100 years old that year and had been remodeled in advance of the August ceremony.

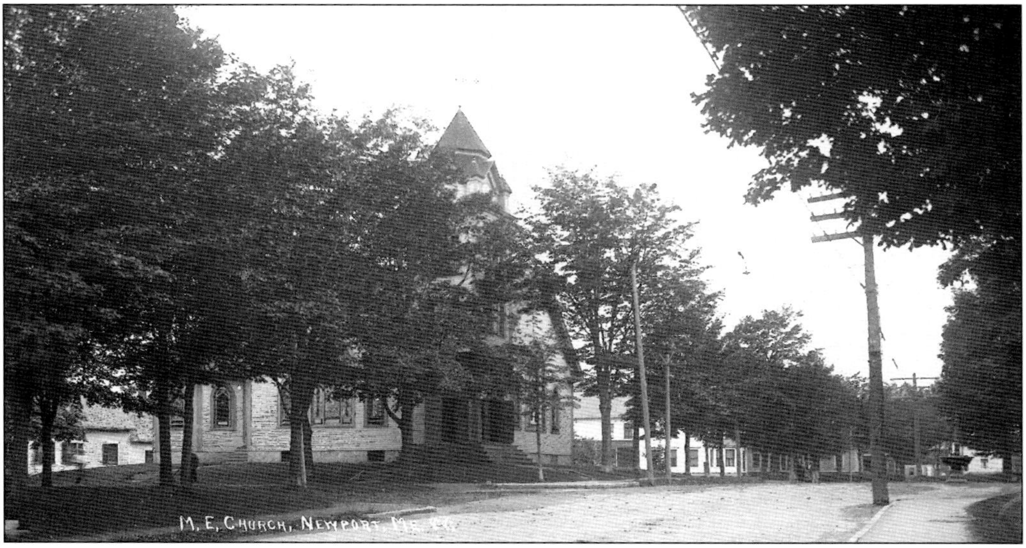

Initially, Newport Methodists shared an edifice with other denominations until the 1850s, when they built a church on Shaw Street. In 1902, the People's Methodist Episcopal Church was built on the corner of Main and Spring Streets for about $10,000. At the time, the parsonage was located on High Street. In 1948, a new parsonage was built adjacent to the church, featuring a state-of-the-art heating system and an underground passage to the church.

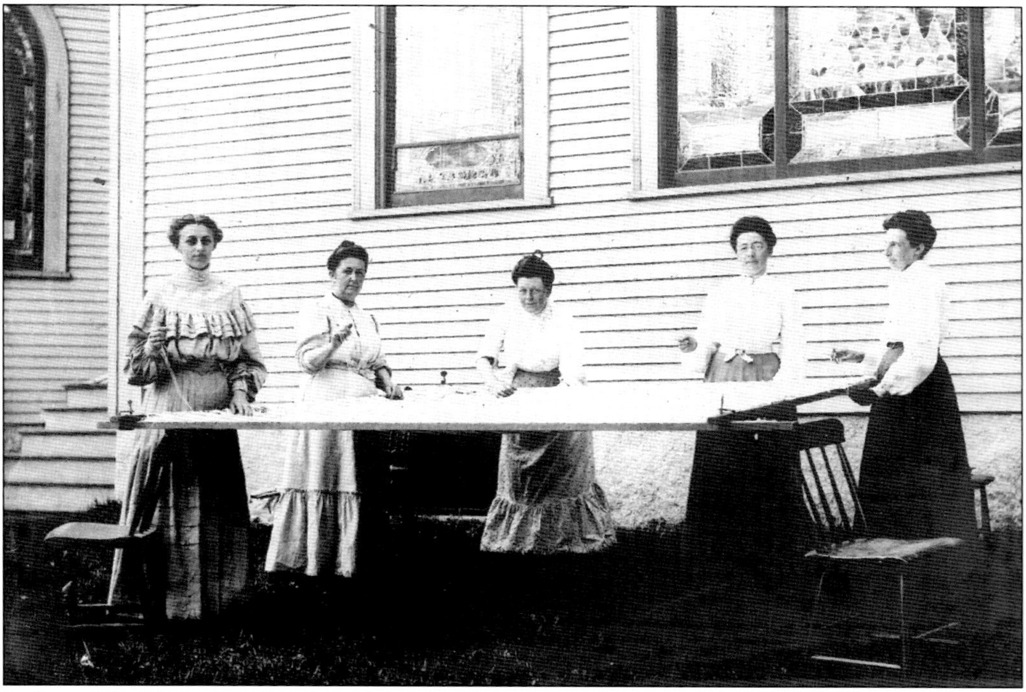

Ladies of the Methodist church work on a sewing project (perhaps a quilt for one of their fundraising fairs). Pictured are ? Stuart, Eva Merrill, Mrs. Hollowell, Mrs. Dow, and Nina Judkins. The Ladies Aid Society of the Methodist Episcopal Church was a busy group, and they raised almost $600 in 1904 alone.

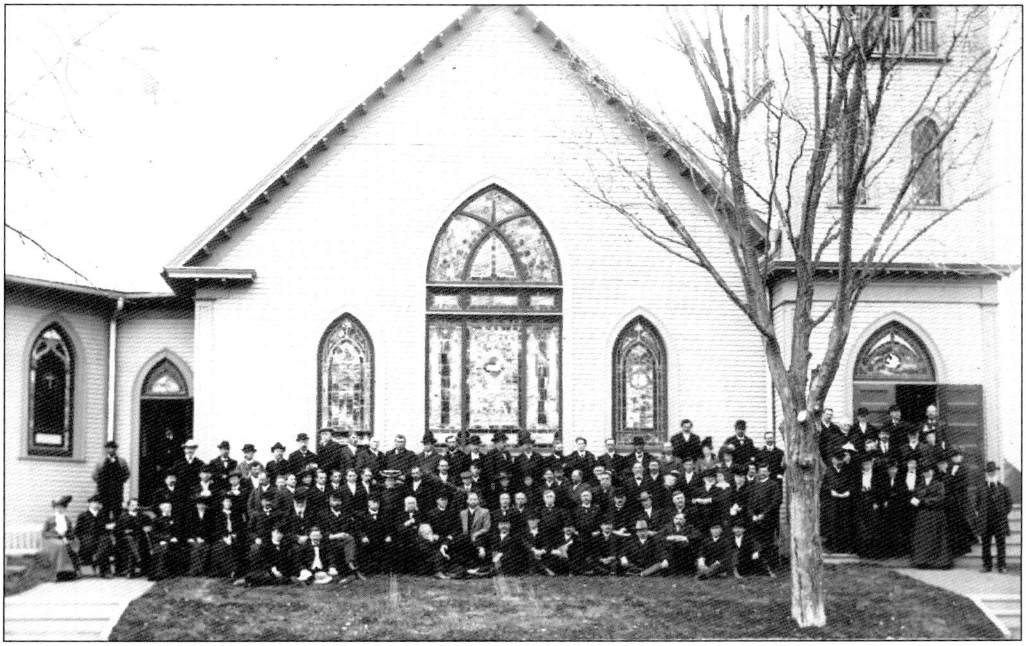

This formal portrait of the Methodist congregation may have been taken when the new church on the corner of Main and Spring Streets was dedicated in 1902. The original Methodist Church on Shaw Street was sold to the Knights of Pythias, but the night the sale was finalized, the building was destroyed in a fire that spread from a railroad freight house. (Courtesy of the John Dyer family.)

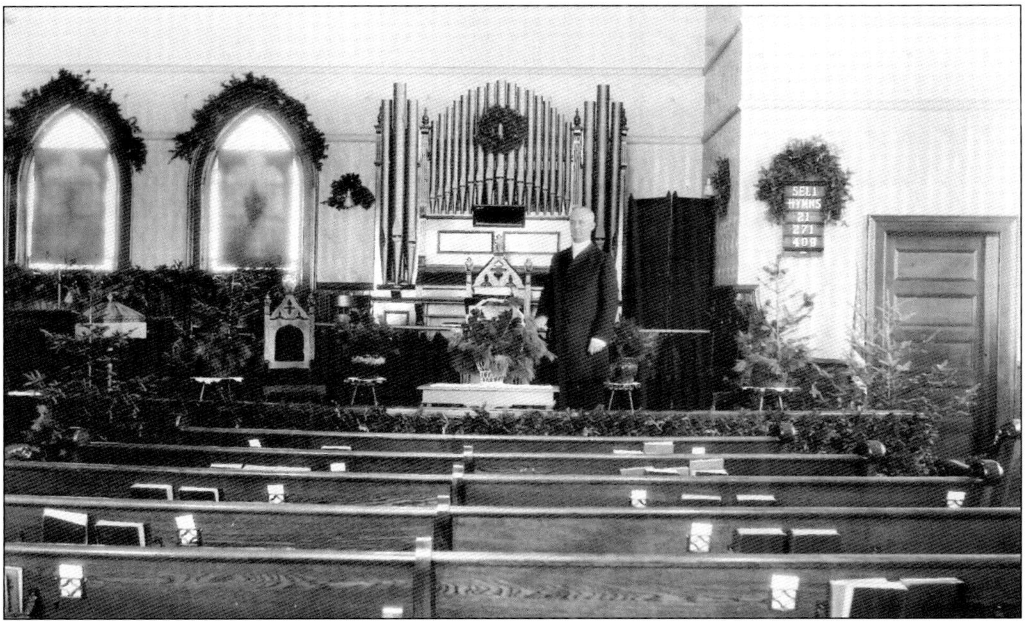

The structure on Main Street, built in 1901, was the third church to be used by the Methodists in Newport. The first minister to settle in the town was a Methodist, Rev. John Whitney, in 1825. This image shows the interior of the church about 1925. (Courtesy of the John Dyer family.)

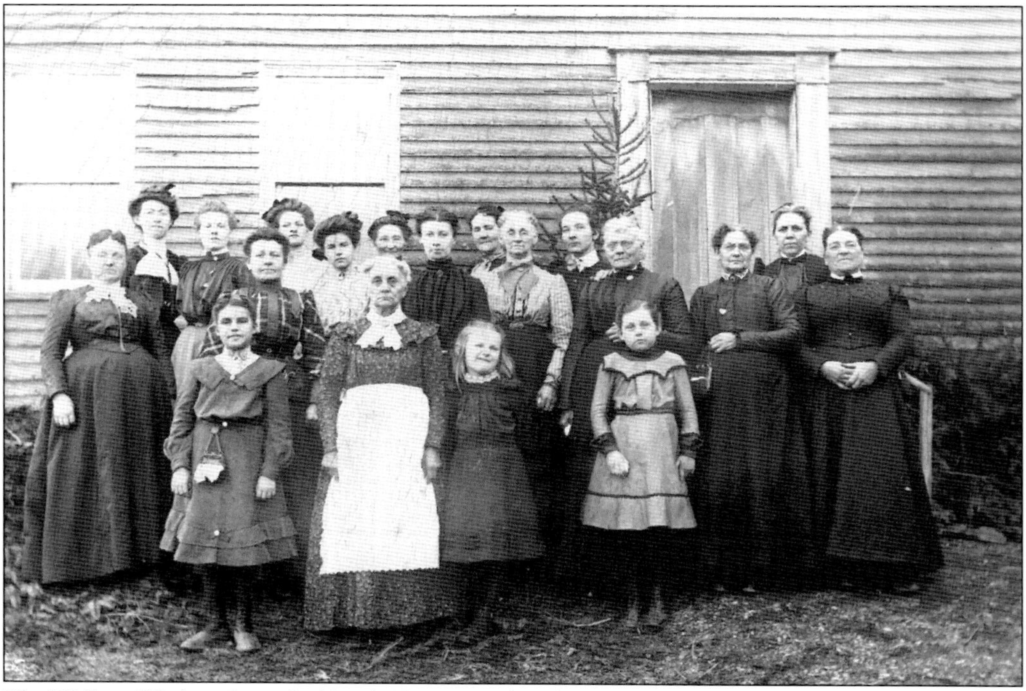

The Willing Workers from the North Newport Church are pictured in 1903. The group participated in community projects, assisted people in need, and supported the Sunday school. The energetic group contributed to the upkeep of the church and paid for a new tin ceiling that was installed in the church before the 50th anniversary celebration in 1907. (Courtesy of Dody Duplisea.)

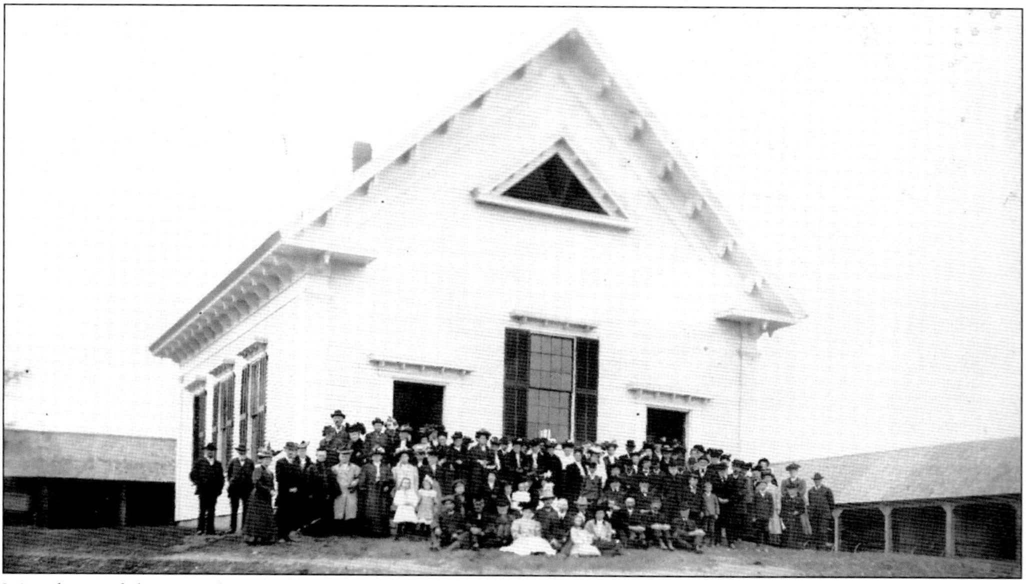

Members of the North Newport Christian Church, built in 1857, held a 50th anniversary celebration in October 1907, shown here. Note the horse sheds on the north and east sides of the church. Congregants could purchase designated stalls to shelter their horses on Sundays. (Courtesy of Dody Duplisea.)

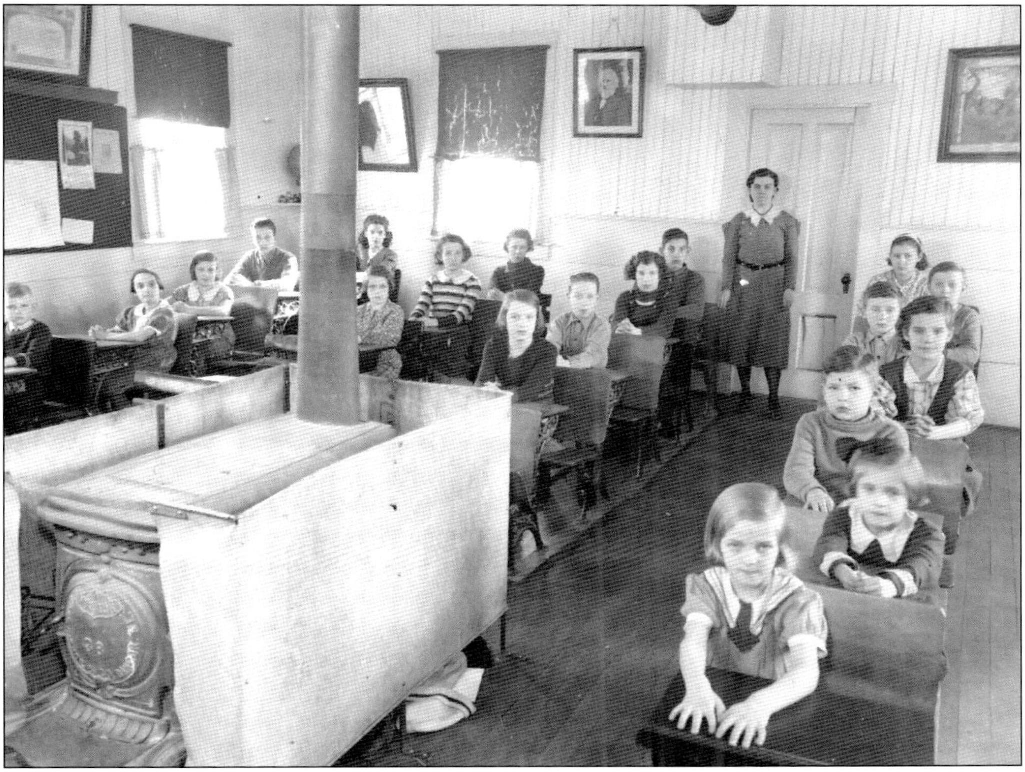

All students in the eastern part of North Newport went to the Hubbard School. Pictured in 1938 are, from front to back, (far left row) Basil Sterns, Rita Lancaster, Arlene Gray, Leon Gray, and Doris Russell; (second row) Winona Gray, Evangeline Gray, and Barbara Townsend; (third row) Beatrice Russell, Robert Gray, Elizabeth Jackson, and Silas Jackson; (fourth row) Gloria Gray, Helen Gray, Elmer Jackson, Bertha Russull, Howard Gray, Fred Townsend, and Barbara Gray. Standing is teacher Geraldine Smith. (Courtesy of Dody Duplisea.)

Students from the west side of North Newport attended the Coburn Corner School. Rural schools were vital in an era when even local travel could be difficult. In 1876, the superintendent of schools implored, "Parents; visit the school more, proffer aid and sympathy to the teacher; interest yourselves in the studies of your children; see that their books are of the right kind . . . acquit yourselves of all the duties of parents."

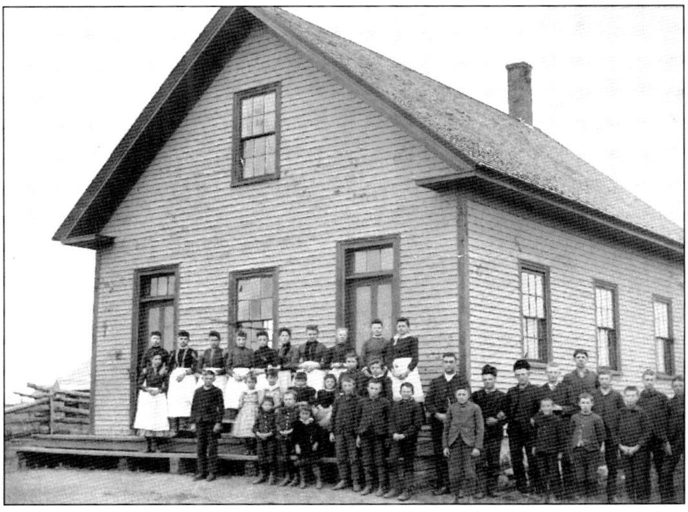

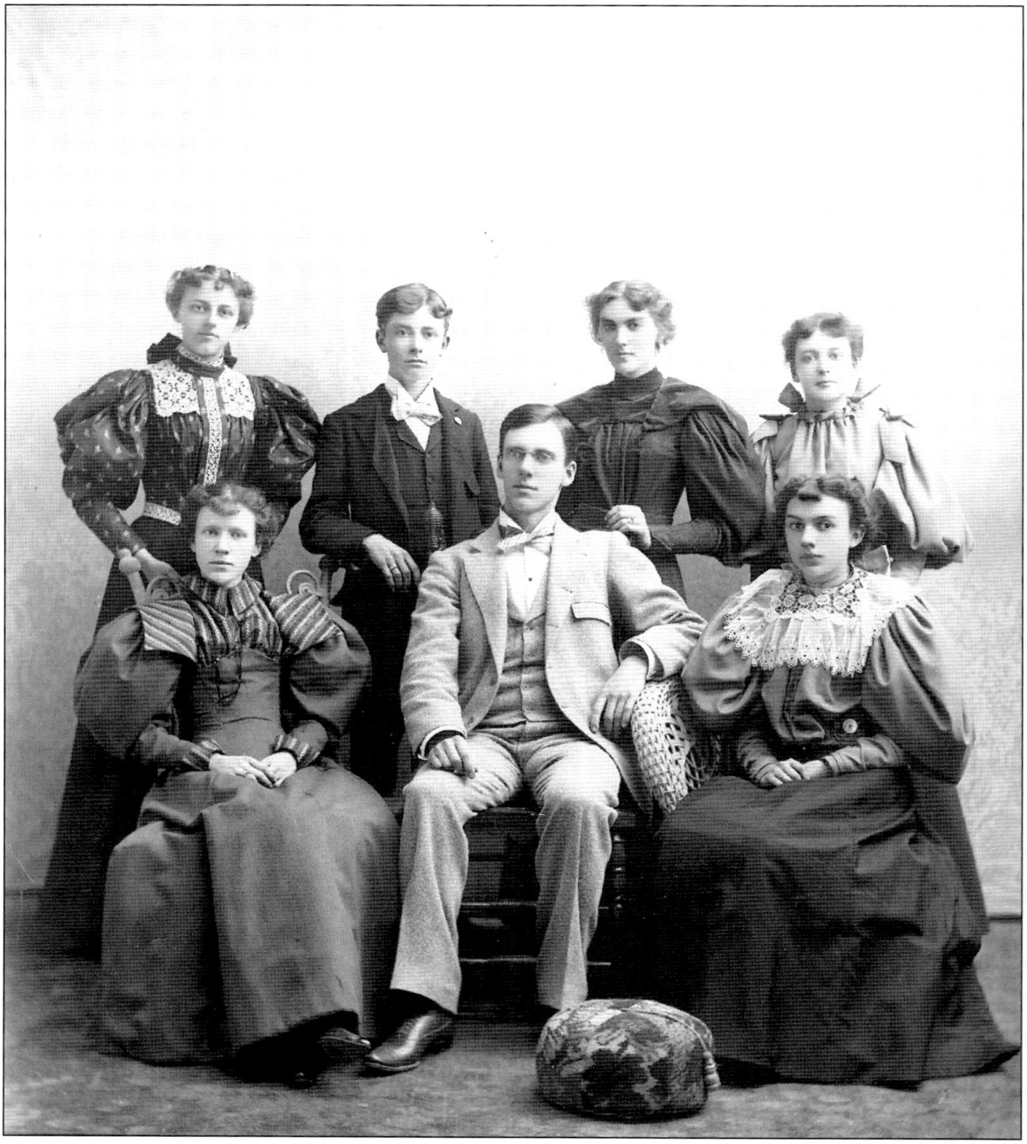

While attending grade school was encouraged, few made it through high school. In 1896, the school superintendent, Homer Benson, bemoaned low teacher salaries, the short school year, and the poor condition of the schools. Whether or not the town should fund a high school was hotly debated. By 1899, the town provided $290 toward the high school and the state funded a similar amount. As for Newport's students, Benson noted problems with truancy and tardiness. These scholars, the Newport High School class of 1896, must have been the more studious among their peers. In this class are Nina Judkins, Rose May Soper (who married John O. Gilman), Mildred Goding, John Hallowell, Mary Hallowell (who married Ralph Dyer), and Glennis Fletcher. Note the elaborate dresses worn by the women, featuring leg-of-mutton sleeves.

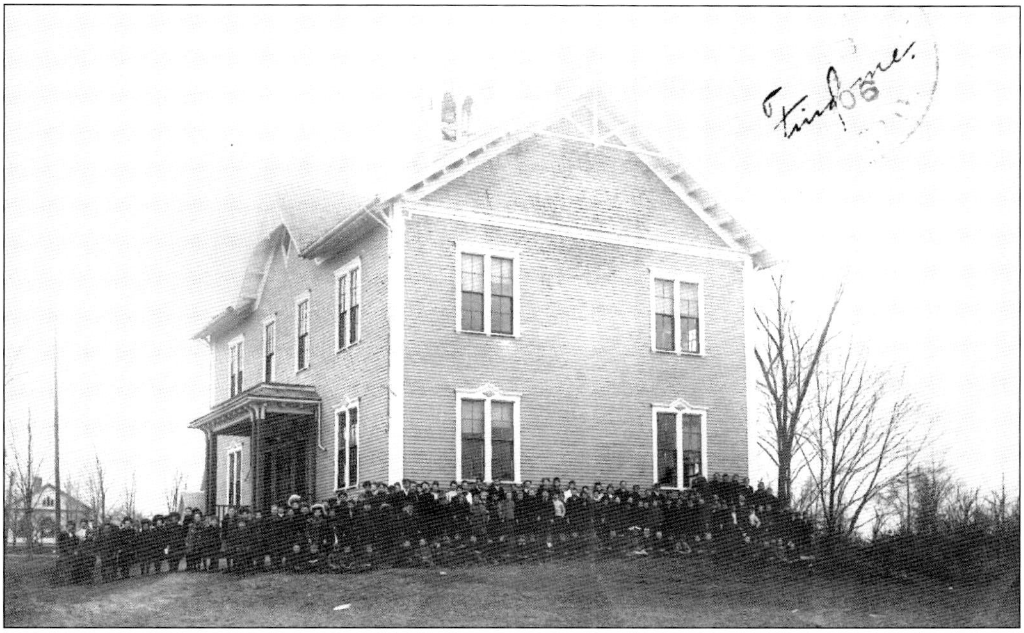

The grammar school, photographed here about 1900, was built on Shaw Street in 1874. This image was taken before the structure's first major remodel. Alice Harriman is one of the school's most prominent alumnae. She was born in Newport in 1861 and graduated from Newport High School. She moved to Montana and later to California, where she become a celebrated journalist, Native American advocate, author, and publisher. She was also an intrepid traveler, career woman, and scholar. The High Street Union Church is visible at left.

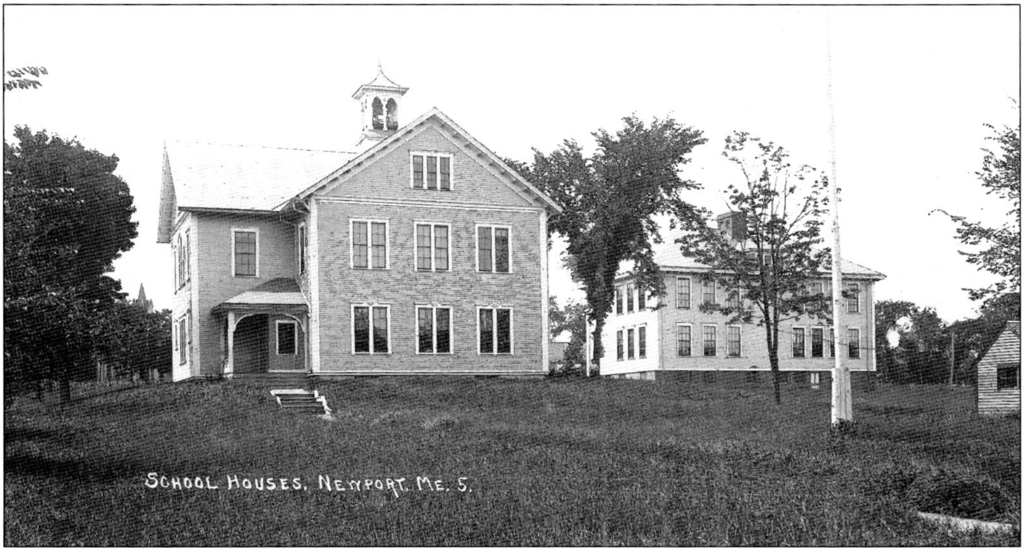

Shown in this later view from Water Street, the District No. 2 (grammar school) schoolhouse was built in 1874 to accommodate all grade levels. Located between Water and Shaw Streets, the school was convenient for town residents. It was remodeled in 1910, and the upstairs was set aside for high school classes. Both schools were torn down, and modular housing units were installed on the site in 1973. (Courtesy of the PMM.)

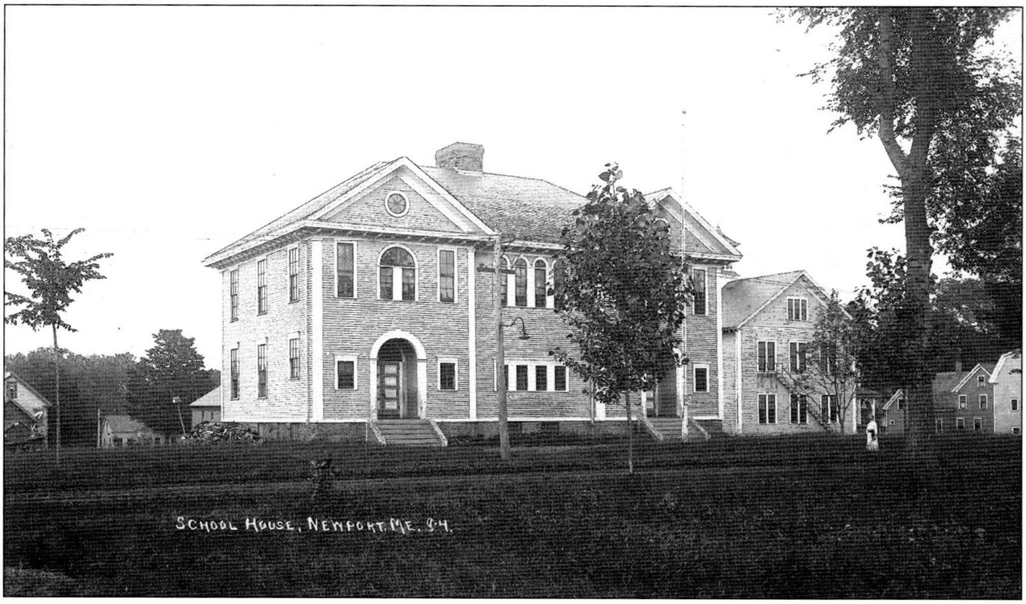

In 1910, a new grade school building was constructed on Shaw Street for $15,000. A new high school was built on Elm Street (the current elementary school) in 1952, and a gym (with cafeteria) was added in 1965. Both of the Shaw Street schools were torn down around 1970. By the early 1960s, a proposal to form a consolidated school district with area towns was hotly debated. The Nokomis Regional High School opened in 1967. (Courtesy of PMM.)

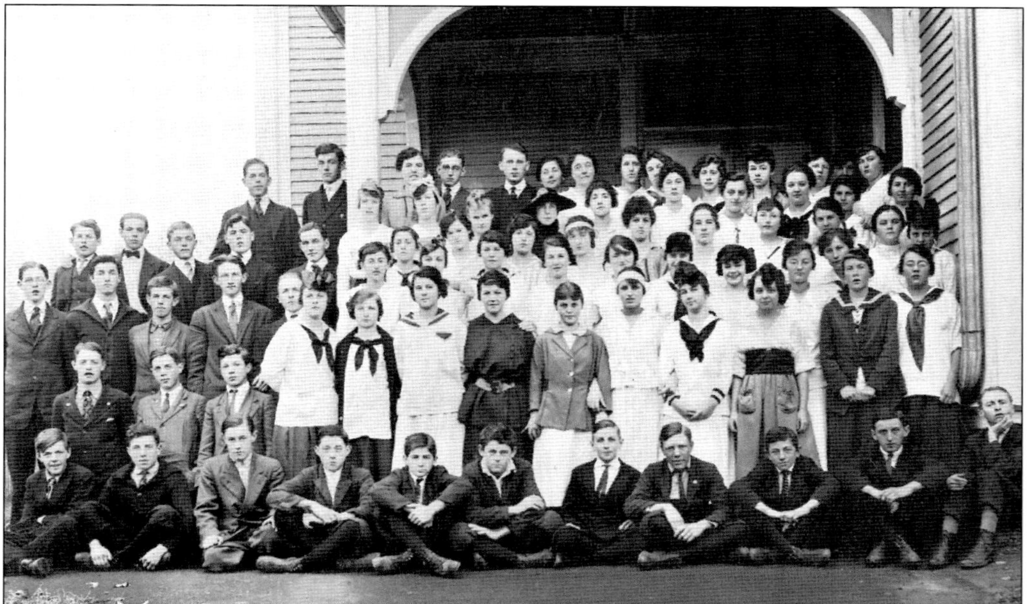

By 1917, many more students were attending the high school. Students here pose on the steps of the old high school building, the boys in jackets and ties, the girls in sailor-style tops. Classes at the high school were smaller, although grade school classes often numbered more than 30 students per class.

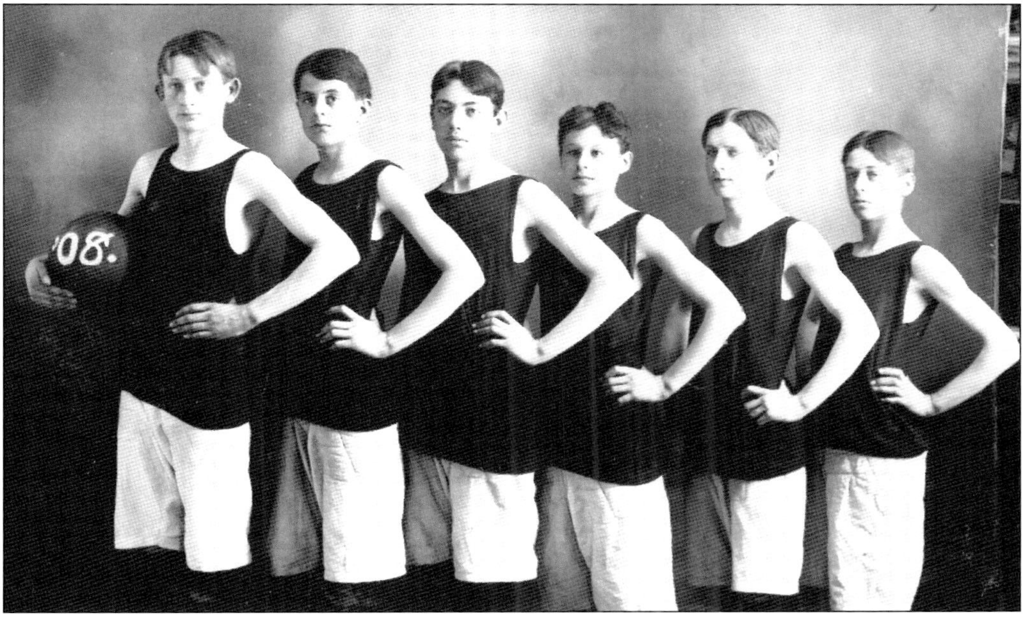

School funding was a contentious issue as far back as the 1890s. Other issues sound familiar today, including the need to balance sports and studies. The 1908 Newport High School basketball team is shown. Pictured here are, from left to right, Sheldon Bracket, Lewis Barrows (future Maine governor), Charlie Matthews, Clyde Reynolds, Hubert Wardwell, and Louis Sanborn.

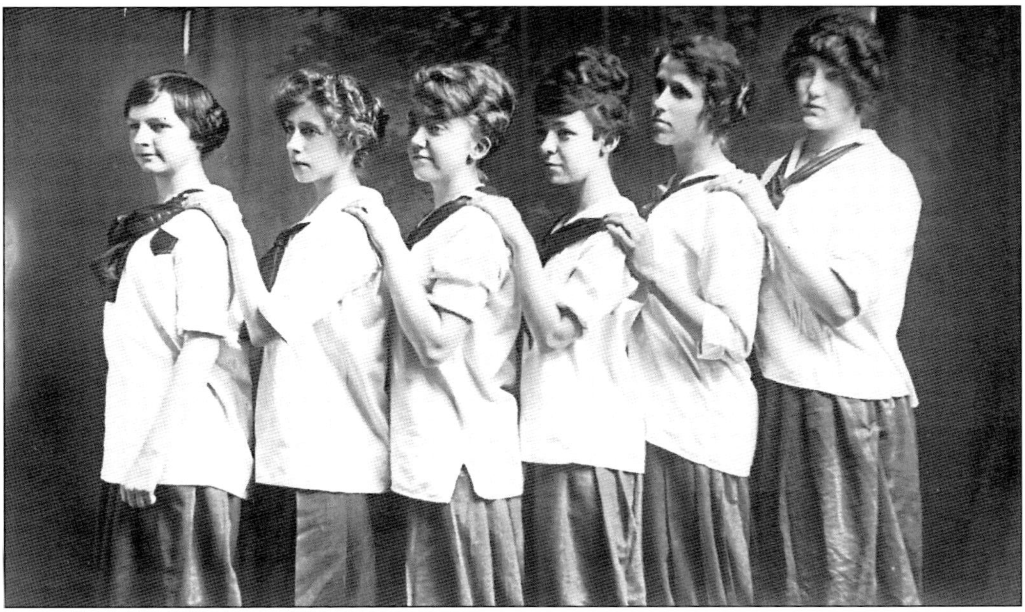

In 1915, tuition to Newport High School was $10 per term. Students could choose between two courses, Latin-Scientific and Commercial. They were also encouraged to take part in athletics. Basketball was the only sport offered to girls. The 1914 team shown here is, from left to right, Eleanor Hatch, Dolly Croxford, Gladys Beau, Bernice Ponton, Ethel Brawn, and Velma Ellis.

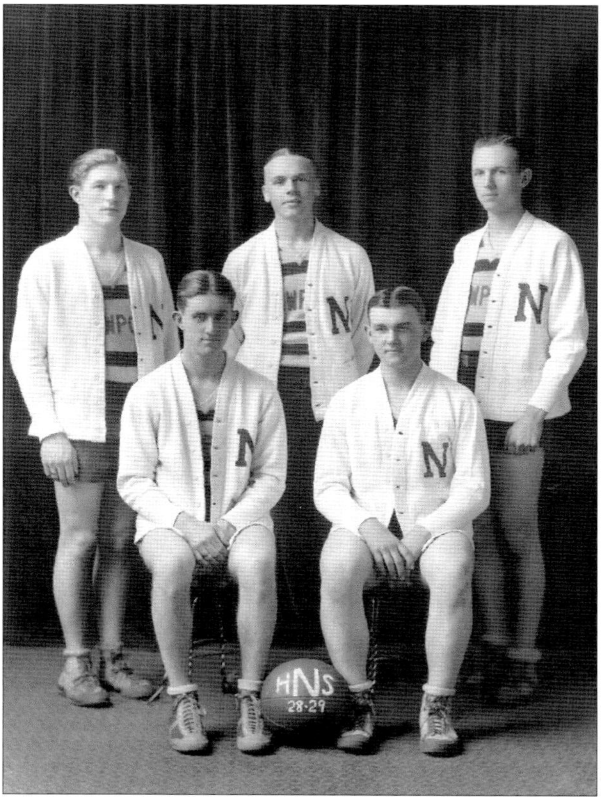

Featured in this photograph is the starting lineup for the 1928–1929 Newport High School basketball team. The team celebrated 10 wins versus 6 losses that year. Pictured are, from left to right, (seated) Jasper Colby and Jack Evans; (standing) Harold Fraser, Malcolm Murray, and John T. Gilman. (Courtesy of Goody Gilman.)

The Newport High School Winter Carnival was held January 31, 1948. Skiing competitions were held on Tip Top in the morning, and skiing and snowshoeing events were held in the afternoon. After a dinner at the Grange hall, the carnival king and queen were crowned at a dance at the Armory. Pictured below are, from left to right, (first row) Thelma Patchell, Inez Sewall, Carrie Sewall, M. Rich, and Jean Boylan; (second row) Gary Richardson, James Smith, Richard Williams, Robert Gipson, Lauren Small, and Ivan Fletcher. (Courtesy of Dale Carsley.)

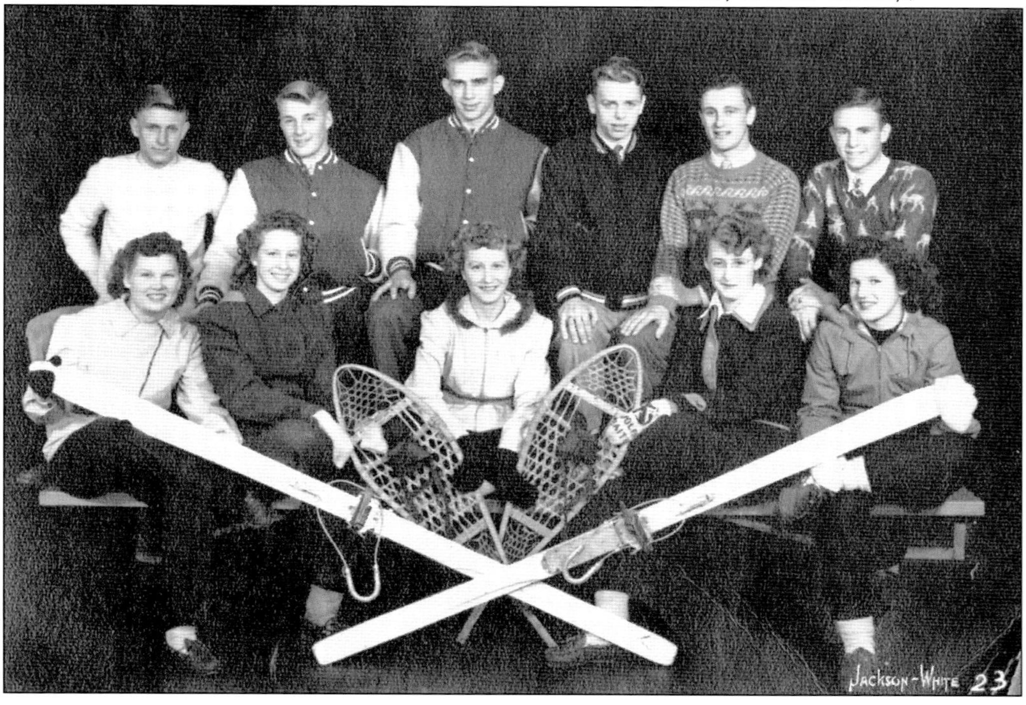

Six

PEOPLE OF NEWPORT

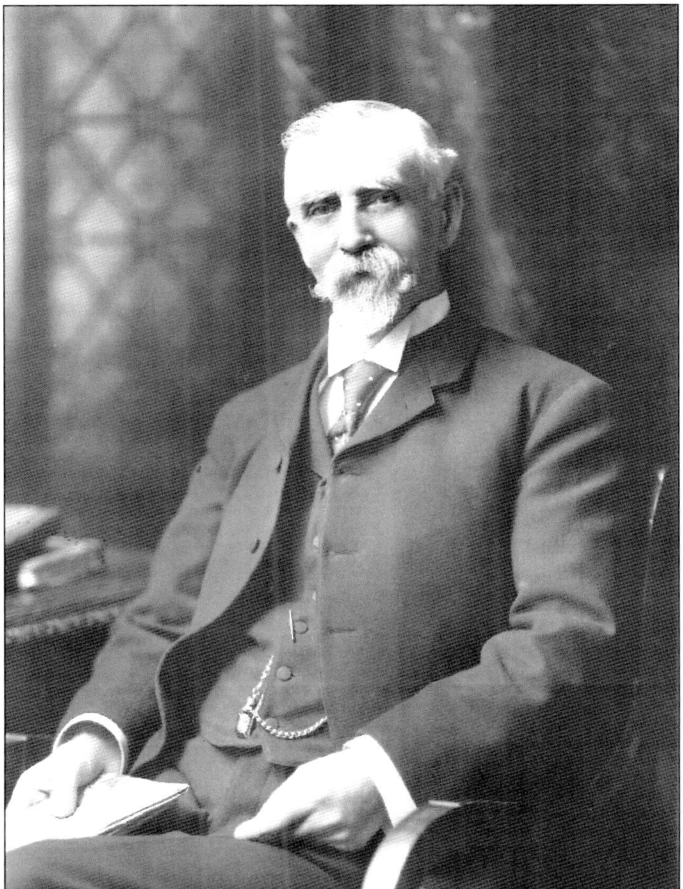

Born in Wales and educated in the United States, Ellis Jones was superintendent of the Newport Woolen Company, beginning in 1896. He was active in town life and built a large home on High Street in 1901. (The house is now adjacent to the retail building on the corner of High and Main Streets.)

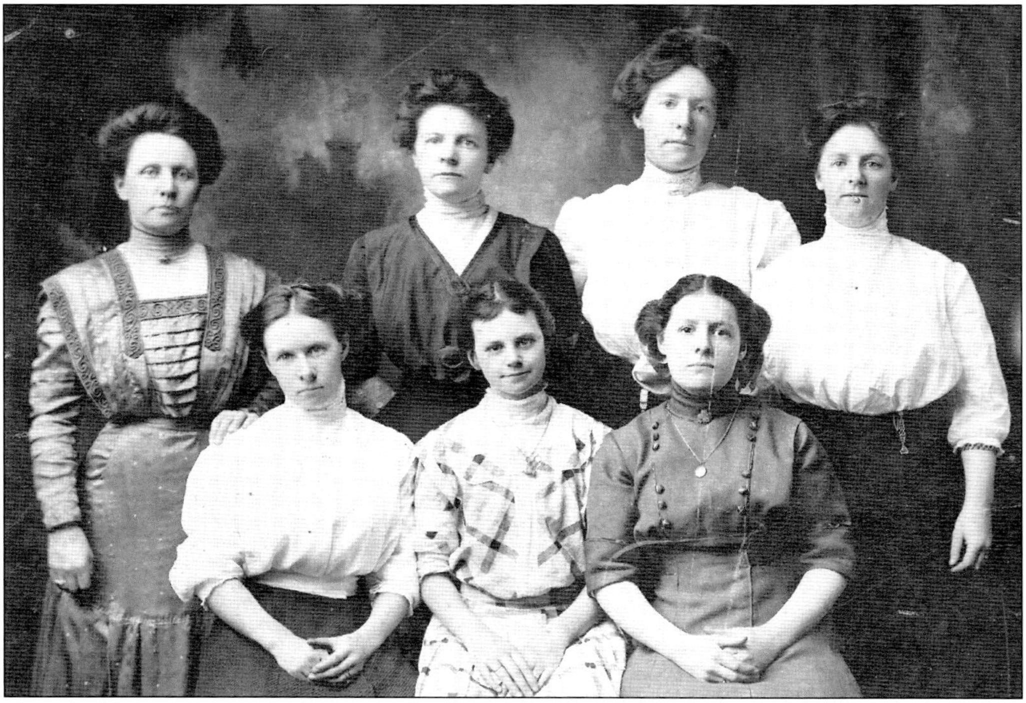

Identified here are Daisy Whitney (second row, second from left) and Ida Reilly (second row, far right). This photograph is believed to be a portrait of some of the town's early schoolteachers. In 1890, there were 11 districts in town. At the end of each term, the students, the school, and the teachers were evaluated by the superintendent and the results were published in the town report. Teachers were usually young women from the area. They earned between $2.50 and $5.50 per week.

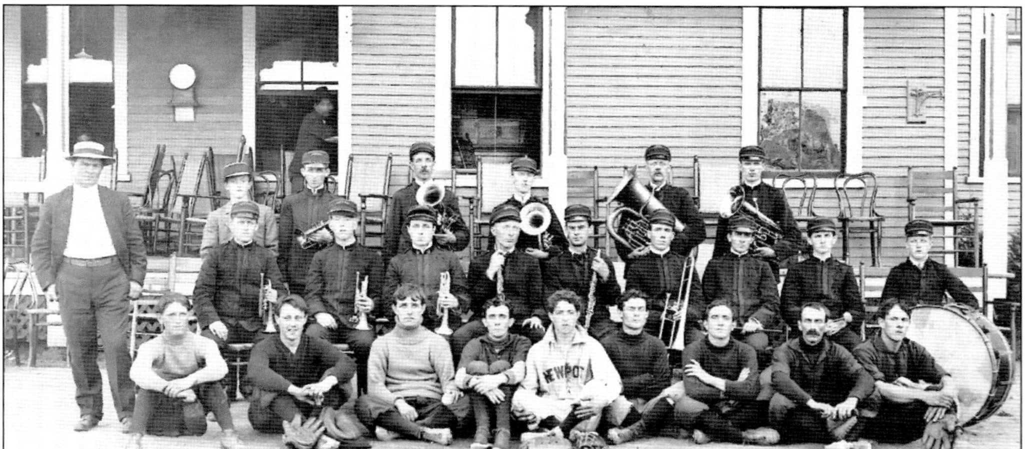

This marching band was led by Ralph Dyer for many years. Regulars included Ben Shaw, Frank Merrill, Herb Jones, Harry Merrill, Harry Stevens, George Newton, Mike Kingsbury, Seth Banton, Roy Moore, Charles Hubbard, and Robe Young. Optometrist Ralph Dyer's name was synonymous with the band. Newport resident Byron Fraser noted in a poem called "Lost in Thirties," "Ralph Dyer is our optometrist. / He sells instruments at his stand. / He can adjust your eyes to 20-20 / Or fix you up to join the band."

The Reverend John Webster became pastor at High Street Union Church in 1889, serving for several decades. He was described as an "earnest, devoted pastor." The 1837 church (now a Congregational church) building is the oldest in Newport.

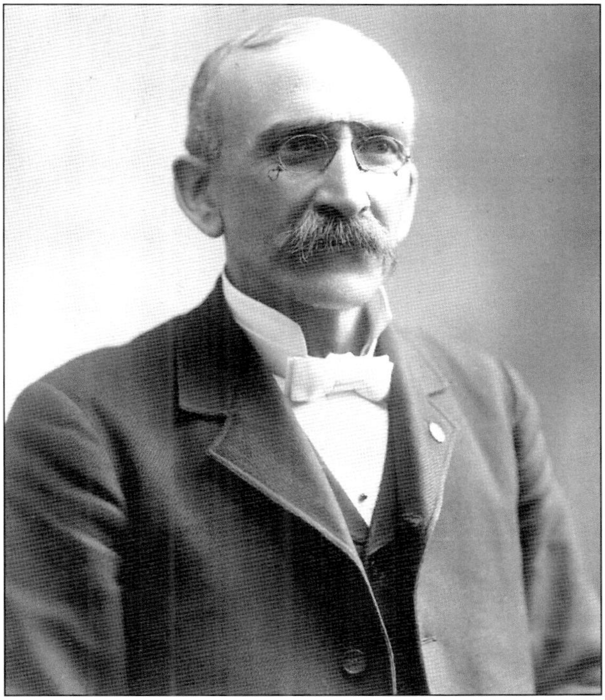

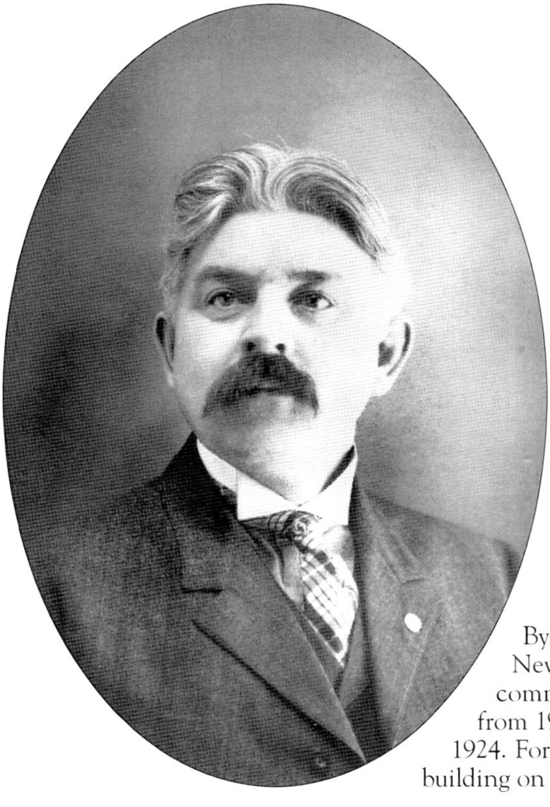

Byron G. Croxford operated a dental practice in Newport for 35 years. He was very active in the community and served as a state representative from 1921 to 1922 and a state senator from 1923 to 1924. For many years, his office was in the Croxford building on Water Street.

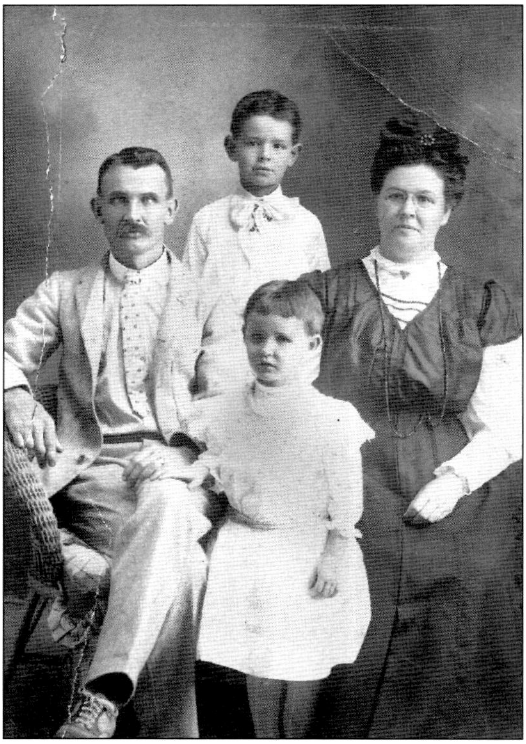

Shown in this c. 1910 image are Otis and Edna Bowen and their children Milton and Mary. In 1934, a scholar interviewed Otis about his experiences cutting ice in his youth, and the interview was recorded on aluminum records. Bowen's stories illustrate the remarkable fortitude necessary to travel and work on the ice and the vital importance of horses in those days as well. Even as a 17-year-old, Otis Bowen was working with teams of up to six horses. (Courtesy of Dale Carsley.)

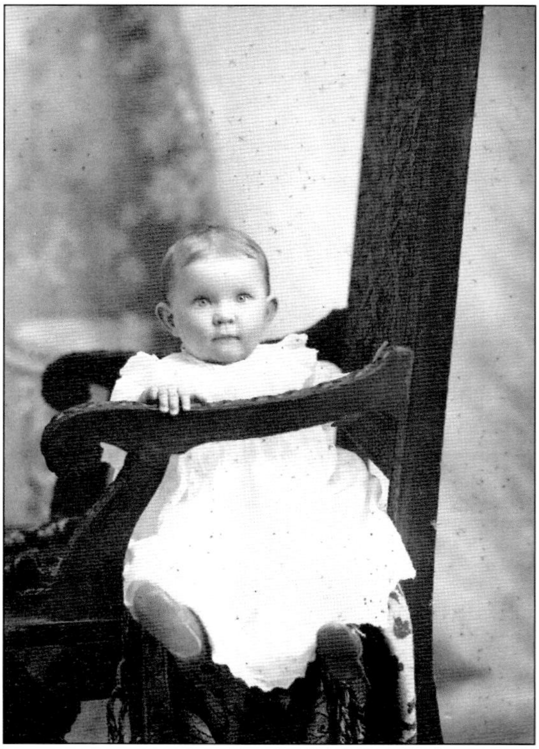

Baby Madeline was the namesake of the steamboat *The Madeline*, owned by her father, Homer Miles. The family lived on Water Street, and when Madeline was a teenager, she operated her own boat-rental business. Madeline (Miles) Hall later taught business courses in Newport schools for 32 years and was a much-loved instructor. She also contributed to the preservation of Newport history over the years as an early and active member of the Newport Historical Society. (Courtesy of the Hall family.)

Dr. Oscar Emerson lived on the corner of Shaw and Main Streets. In a poem, Byron Fraser recalled, "We have two doctors in our town / They both can cure our ills. / Doc Emerson is handy with the knife. / Doc Higgins gives us pills. / No matter what the problem is, / It's the same for man or pup. / Hig is big he'll hold you down, / While Emerson carves you up."

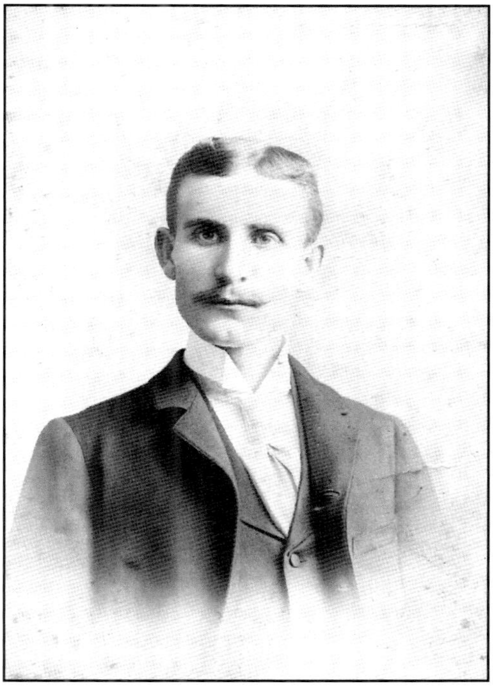

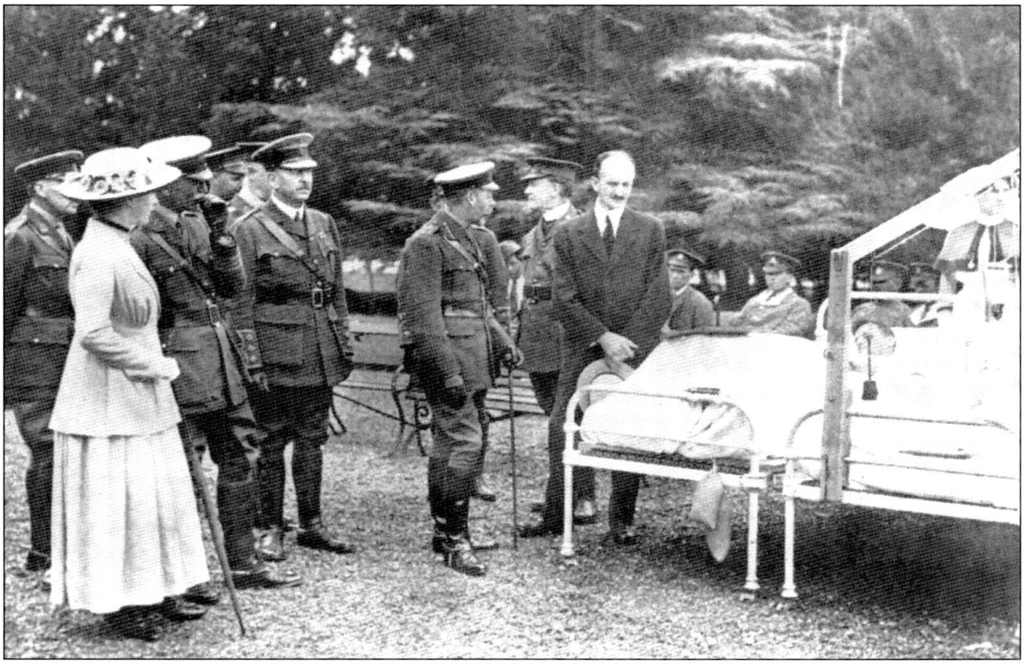

Dr. Jefferson Hawthorne was born in 1873 in Pittston and practiced medicine in Newport for 20 years. He is reported to have served in the British Army from 1916 until 1919 and the Armenian Far East from 1919 to 1921. In this photograph, the doctor is at the bedside. Also pictured are Major Reed, Princess Mary, Colonel Symons, Colonel Loucus, and King George V. The picture was taken at Netley Hospital, near Southampton, England. Hawthorne died in 1936.

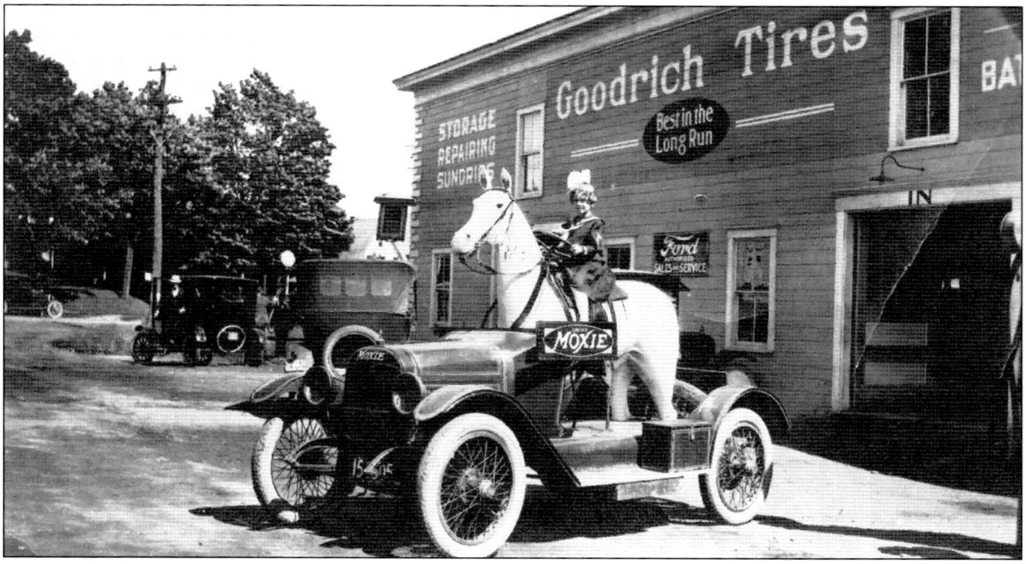

The Friend and Friend garage was located on the corner of Main and Elm Streets, on the east side of the river. Barbara Weymouth is photographed perched atop the "Moxie Horse," a promotional vehicle for the popular Moxie soft drink. Note that Barbara is holding fast to the horse's "steering wheel."

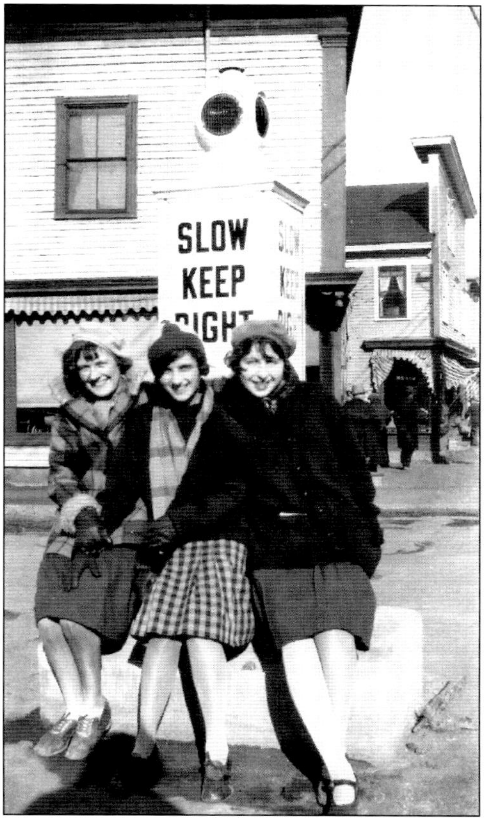

In this 1928 image, three friends pose on the concrete base of the traffic sign at the intersection of Main, Water, and Mill Streets. Pictured are, from left to right, Estelle (Wiseman) Gilman, Bunny (Folsom) Albaugh, and Helen (Gray) Wilcox. A few years after this photograph was taken, Newport's first traffic light was installed over the site.

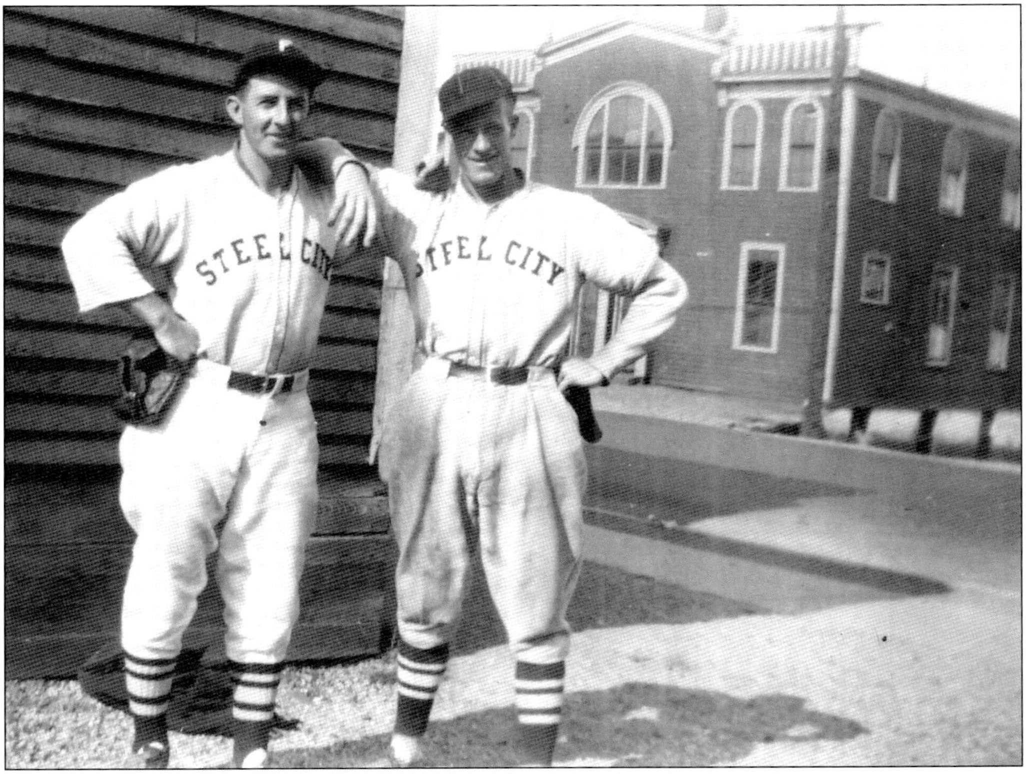

"Bullet Bill" Jarvis was a noted baseball player for 27 years. In a particularly memorable 1936 Maine All-Stars game, he pitched against seven Boston Red Sox batters, striking out five and allowing no hits. Jarvis was invited to try out for the 1936 Olympics and was inducted into the Maine Baseball Hall of Fame. Jarvis (right) poses with Steel City teammate Stan Towle. (Courtesy of David Jarvis.)

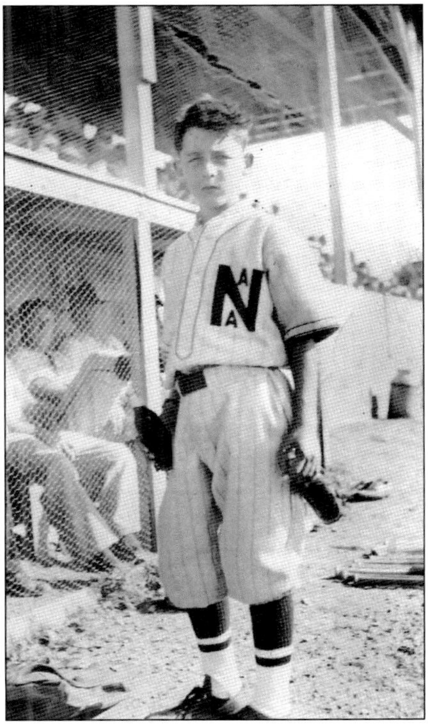

Donn Fendler and his family summered in Maine and made their full-time home in Rye, New York. In the summer of 1939, he took a trip to Mount Katahdin with family. Donn became disoriented in the fog and ultimately spent nine days lost. His story drew nationwide attention, as hundreds of searchers combed the mountain looking for him. Thousands of schoolchildren have read Thomas Egan's book about Donn's ordeal, *Lost on a Mountain in Maine*. In 2011, Donn published a new graphic novel about his story (with Lynn Plourde and Ben Bishop) called *Lost Trail*. Here, Donn is shown in 1940 when he served as bat boy for the Newport A.A.'s baseball team. (Courtesy of Tebob Buckland.)

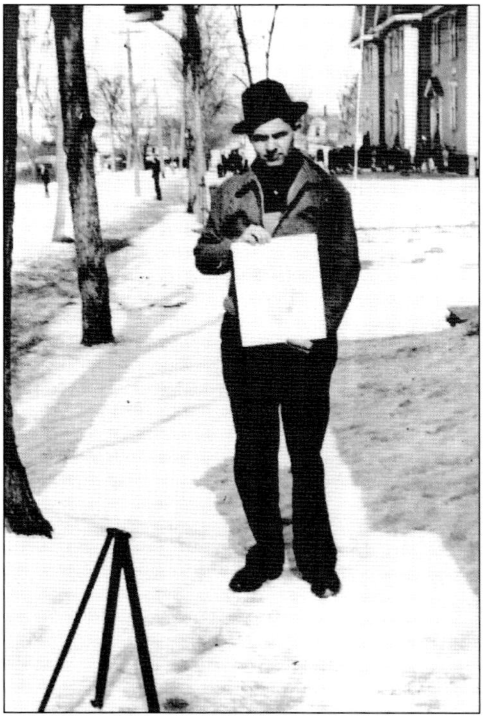

Greydon Piper graduated from Newport High School in 1934, attended art school, and served in the Army during World War II. He was a prolific artist who made signs for the town and its vehicles, taught art classes, and commemorated most of the important events in Newport with paintings. Piper is also remembered for his 32 years of friendly service as a Newport postal carrier. He poses in front of the high school in this 1934 photograph. (Courtesy of Linda Boyd.)

Judson Jude was a prominent figure in town affairs. For years, his office was located in the old bank block on Main Street. The son of a lawyer, he eventually became a judge in the district court that was established on Main Street in Newport in the 1950s.

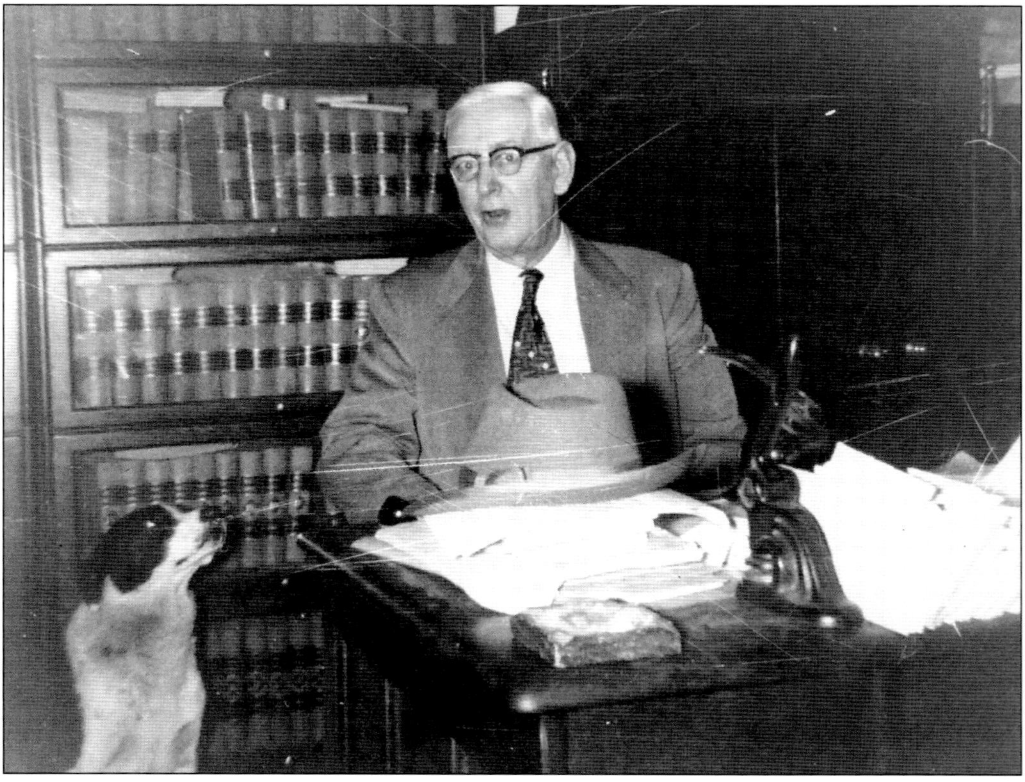

Pfc. Omar Perry served with the U.S. Army in World War II. A Newport native, Omar lived a quiet life in town. Upon his death in 2002, he bequeathed funds to many nonprofit organizations around town. The money that he left to the Newport Public Library and the Newport Historical Society became the seed money for the capital campaign for the Newport Cultural Center, which opened in 2009.

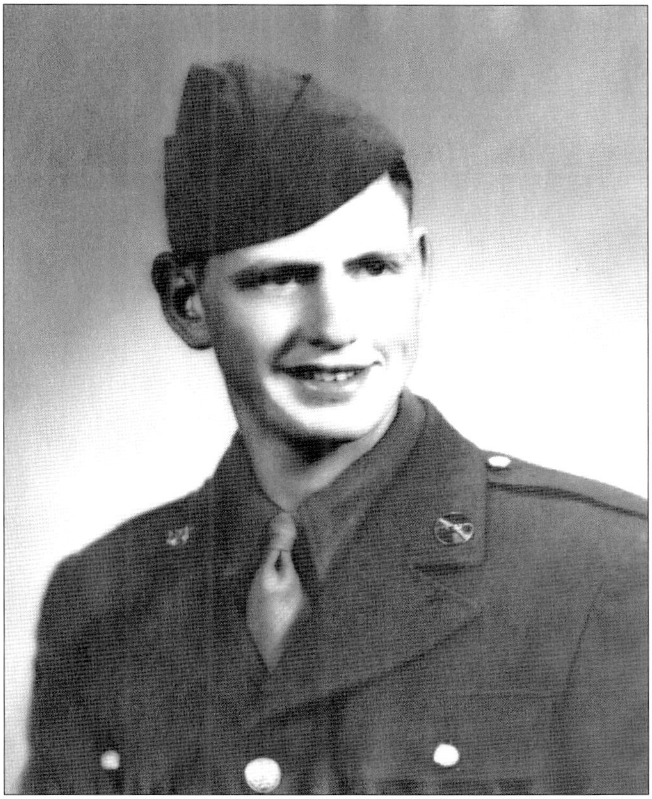

Newport physician Paul W. Burke served the nation as a lieutenant commander in the Navy during World War II. He is pictured (center) in the operating room of the USS *Bushnell* in the South Pacific. After the war ended, Dr. Burke lived and practiced in the former Ellis Jones home on High Street.

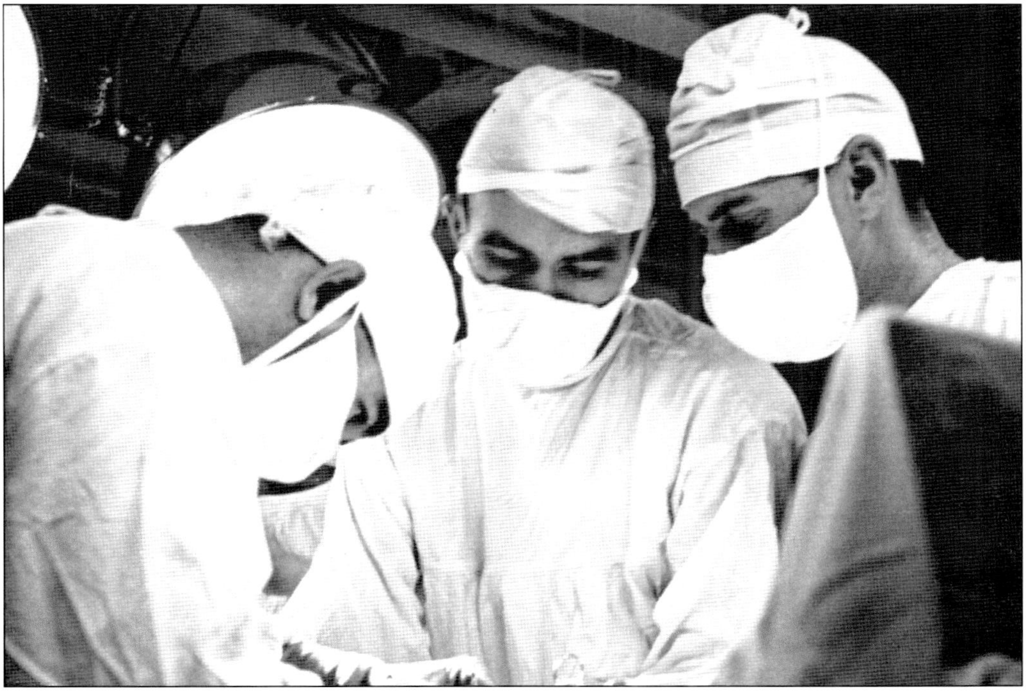

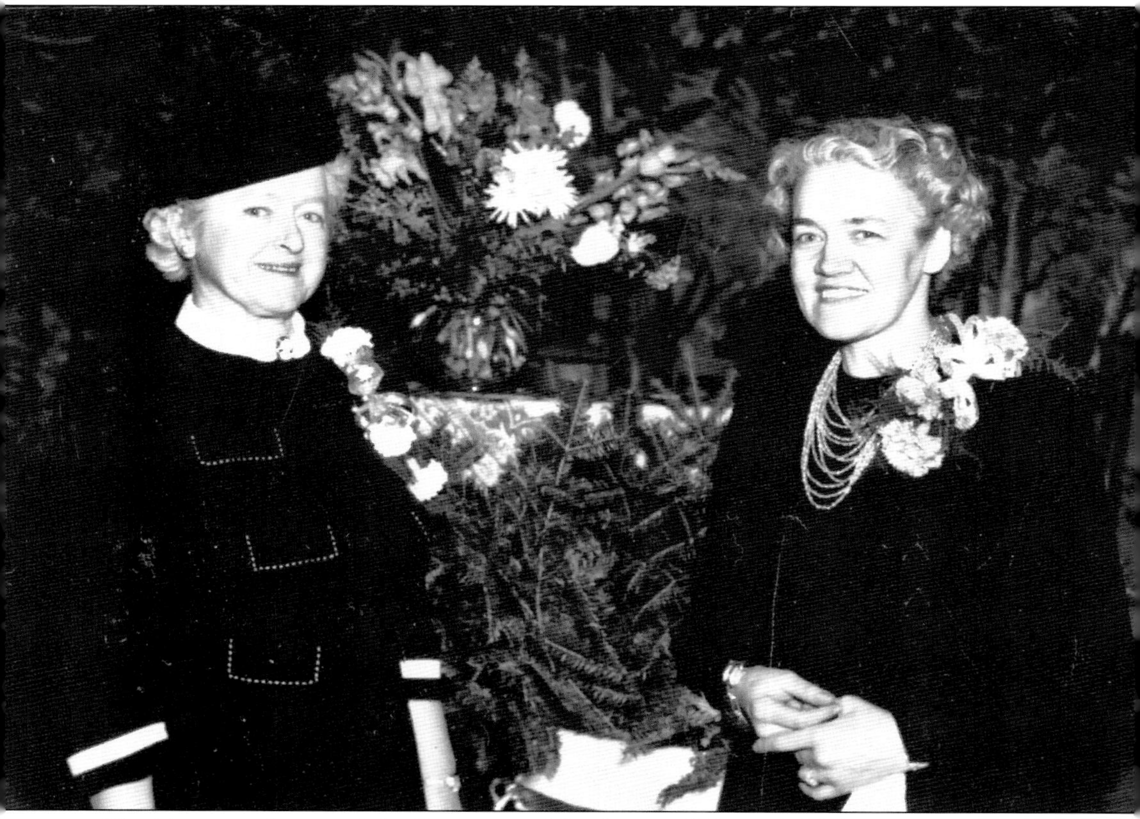

The Newport chapter of the Business and Professional Women's Club was organized in 1947 by Anne Keyes, who became the group's first president. She is shown here in January 1948 with US congresswoman Margaret Chase Smith, a Skowhegan, Maine, native. The Newport club organized a banquet for her at the Jones Inn, followed by a public address at the Grange hall. The club organized events to help launch Smith's successful 1948 campaign for the US Senate, where she served until 1973. Smith was the first woman to serve in both houses of the US Congress. In addition to its political work, the Newport Business and Professional Women's Club organized on-the-job training for female students, offered scholarships, sponsored local students in the state program, and contributed to various state and local charities.

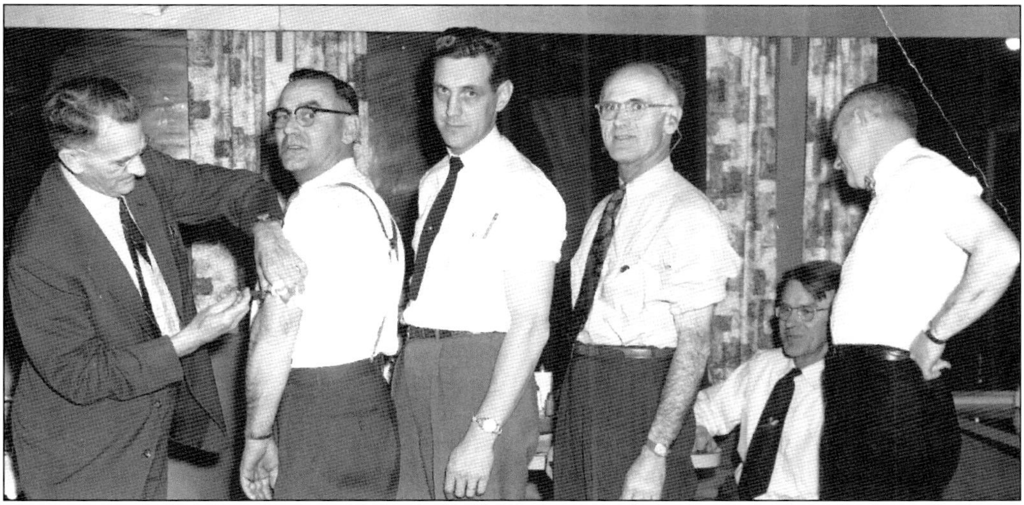

Shown here in 1957, physician George I. Higgins administers the polio vaccine at a public polio clinic in Newport. Higgins practiced medicine in Newport and surrounding towns from 1922 until 1968. Lined up to receive vaccinations are members of the Newport Kiwanis Club, from left to right: John Farnham, Paul Witham Jr., Gerald Clark, Joseph Morton (seated), and Homer Woodard. (Photograph by William Shea.)

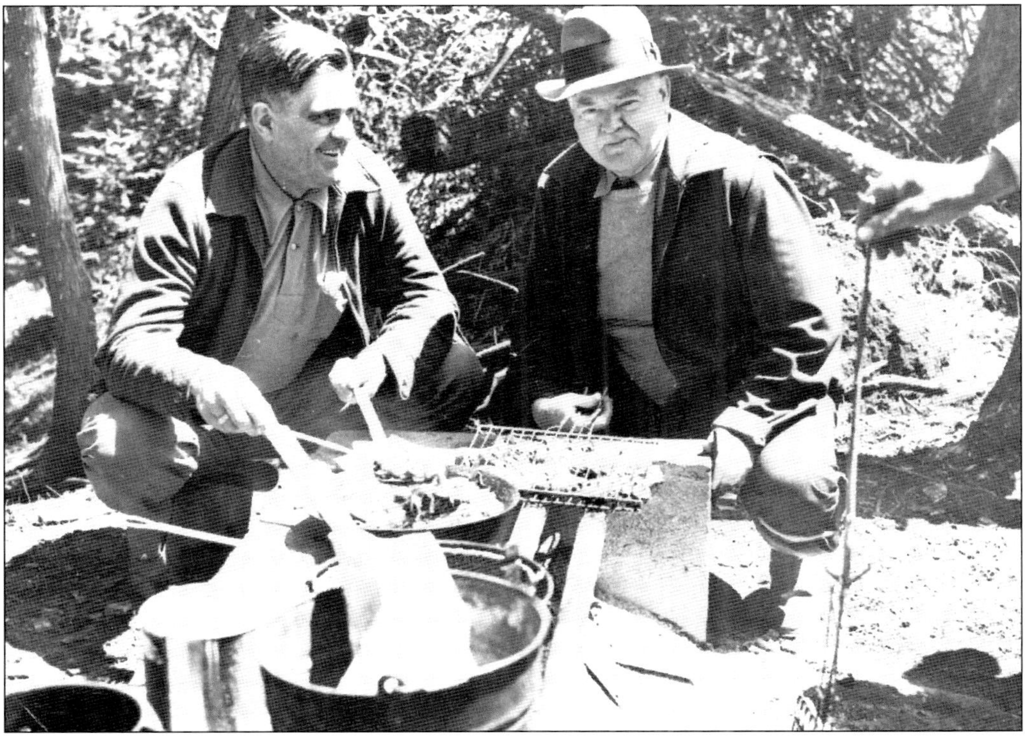

Lewis Barrows was born in 1893 in Newport, graduated from the University of Maine, and joined his father in the family's pharmacy. He was the governor of Maine from 1937 to 1941. His son Edward lost his life during the invasion of Normandy in June 1944. In this photograph taken at Moosehead Lake, Barrows appears with Pres. Herbert Hoover. Barrows died in 1967.

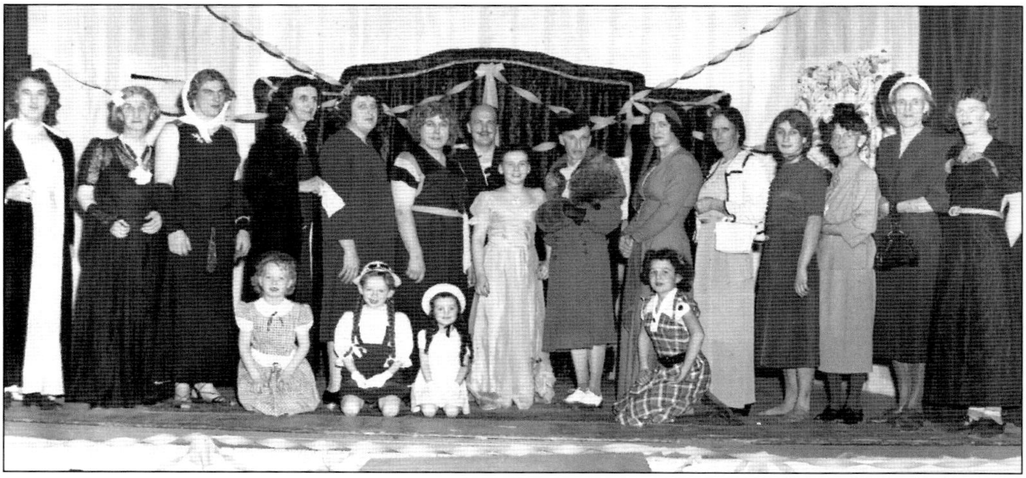

Newport men of the mid-20th century were up to any challenge. Posing in 1950 onstage at the old town hall are members of the Couples Club of the Methodist Church. The stage was the scene for many local events. There were bleachers on the second floor, and basketball games were played there until the armory was built in 1942. Pictured are, from left to right, (kneeling) Ricky Nelson, Bobby Simpson, Freddy Sequist, and unidentified; (standing) Rev. Homer Hughey, J.O. Gilman, George McKenney, Lewman Soper, Dr. Charles Simpson, Liston Goodrich, John L. Doucett, Aubrey Jahmet, David Farnham, Mutt Sweat, Raymond Spooner, Richard Brown, Percy Williams, Dana Banton, and Fred Cormier.

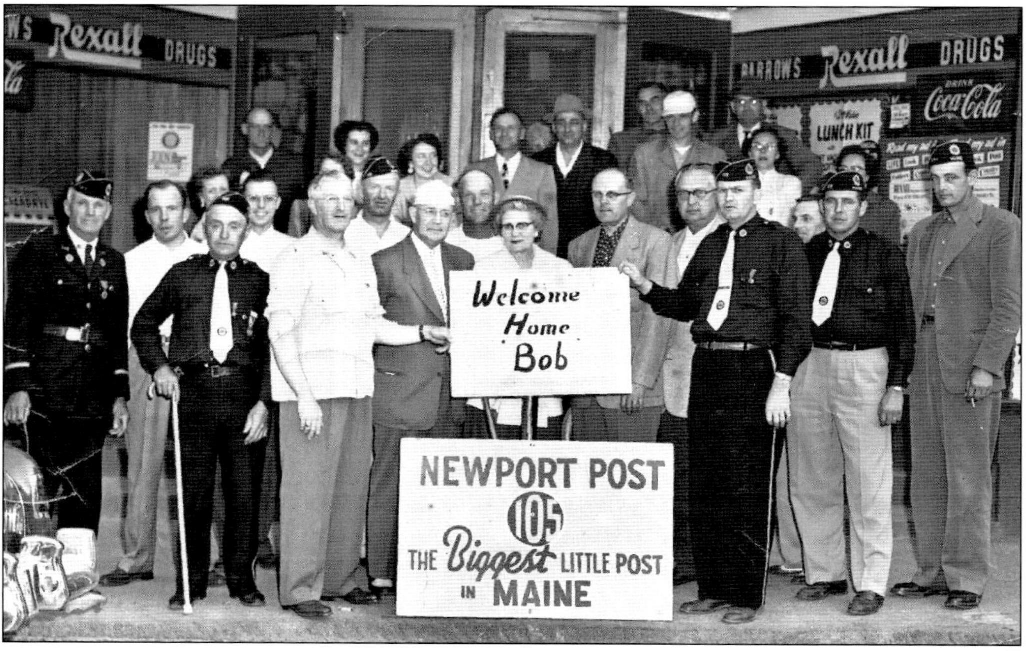

Photographed in the late 1950s, pharmacist Ralph Merrow had been elected state commander of the American Legion and is shown returning from the convention in Rockland. The first row is identified from left to right as Hartland commander Hughes Smith, Joseph Burke, Harold Fraser, Mr. and Mrs. Ralph Merrow, C. Austin Barrett, Norris Friend, Erwin Webber, Everett Anderson, and Peg Hamilton. The photograph was taken in front of Barrows Pharmacy on Main Street.

From the late 1800s until 1949, Newport's police force consisted of a nightwatch officer. In 1949, James G. Gray became the first day officer. In 1953, he organized Newport's first police department and was police chief from 1955 until 1962. The department moved to the newly constructed municipal building in 1958. Other improvements soon followed, including the implementation of car radios in 1960 and the arrival of the first town police cruiser in 1964.

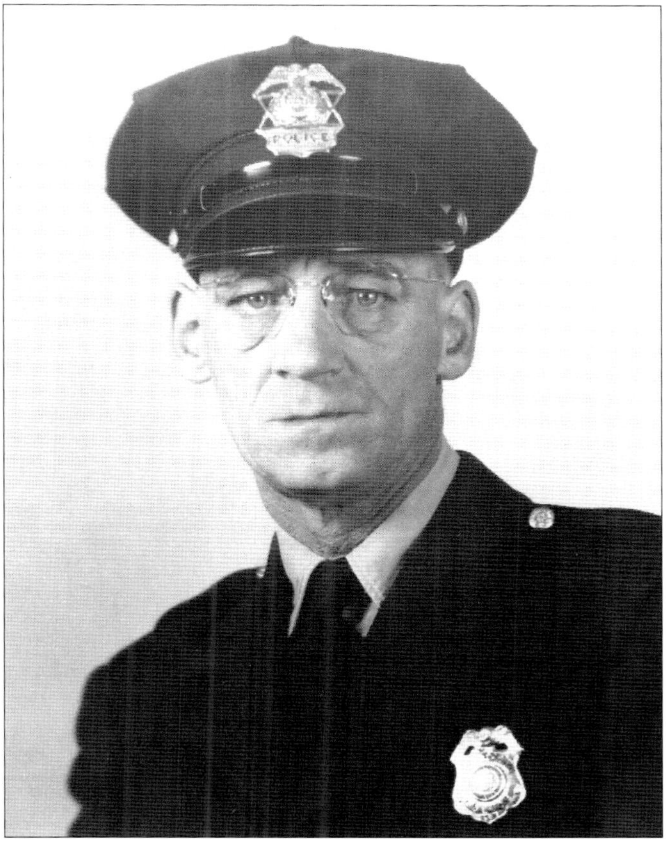

Herbert Towne was a 1949 graduate of Newport High School, served in the Navy, and became a Newport police officer in 1964. Later that year, he was killed in the line of duty pursuing two speeding cars on Route 2, driving Newport's first police car. (Courtesy of Maude Smith.)

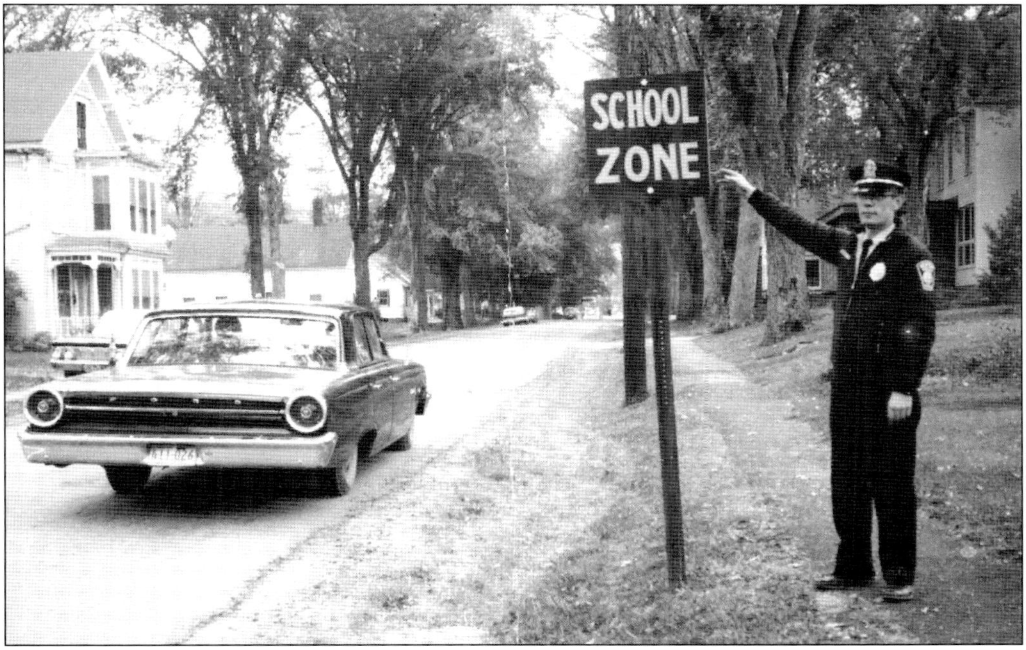

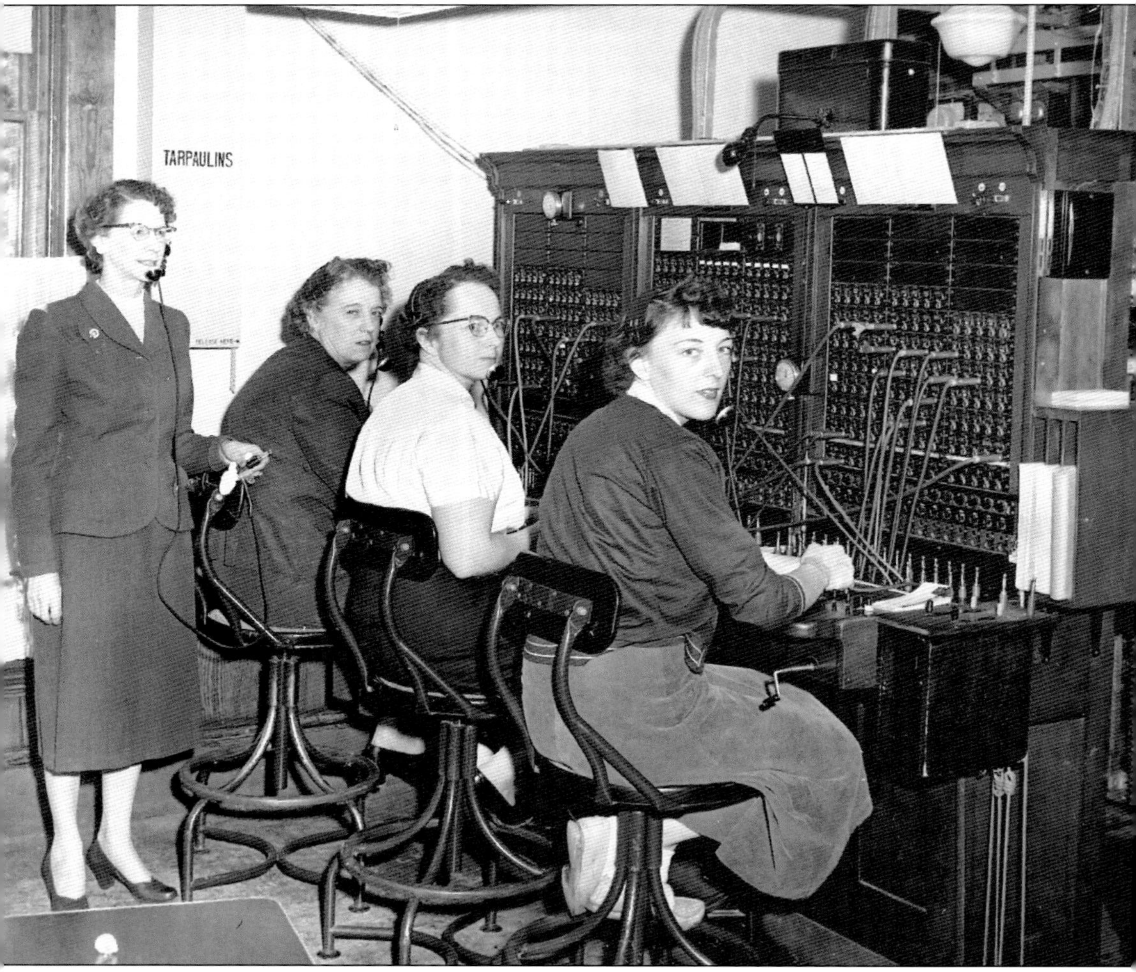

For many years, Dolly (Smith) Croxford was the chief operator at the Newport Telephone Company, located on the second floor of the Croxford building on Water Street. She is photographed here, standing, with operators, from left to right, Ora Franklin, Connie Parent, and Beverly (Seavey) Oldenburg in 1953. This image depicts the end of an era, as the Newport telephone system converted to dial-up in October 1955. The 1902 building held retail businesses downstairs and offices upstairs well into the 1970s. Later, the upper floors were converted into apartments, while various businesses operated on the ground floor. (Courtesy of Maude Smith.)

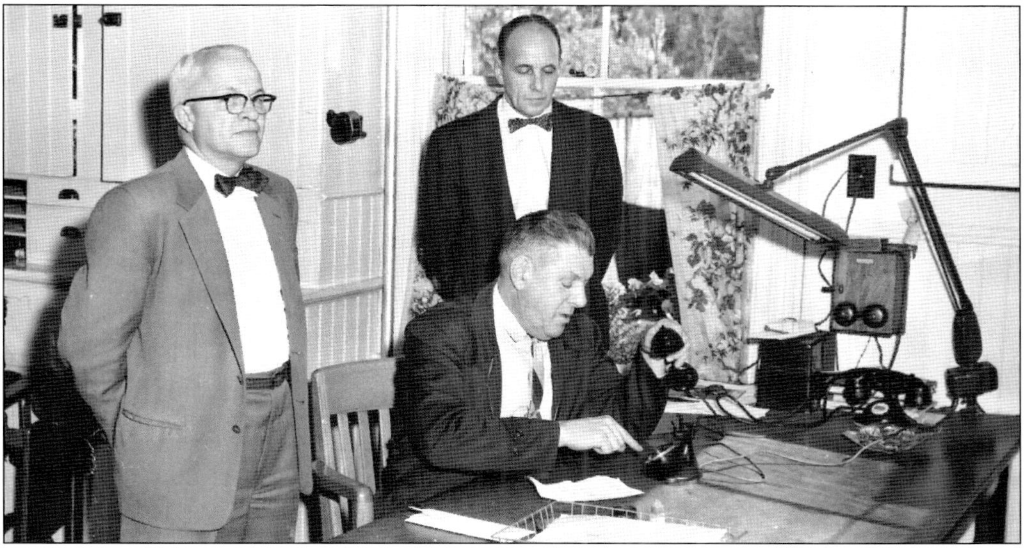

The installation of dial-up telephones ushered in a new era of technological independence for users. This image captures the moment Paul V. Witham (chair of Newport's selectmen and town manager) received the first call on the new phone in the selectmen's office in the late 1950s. Looking on are E.L Merriman, New England Telephone Company Bangor manager (left), and Guy L. Thurston, supervising switchman (right).

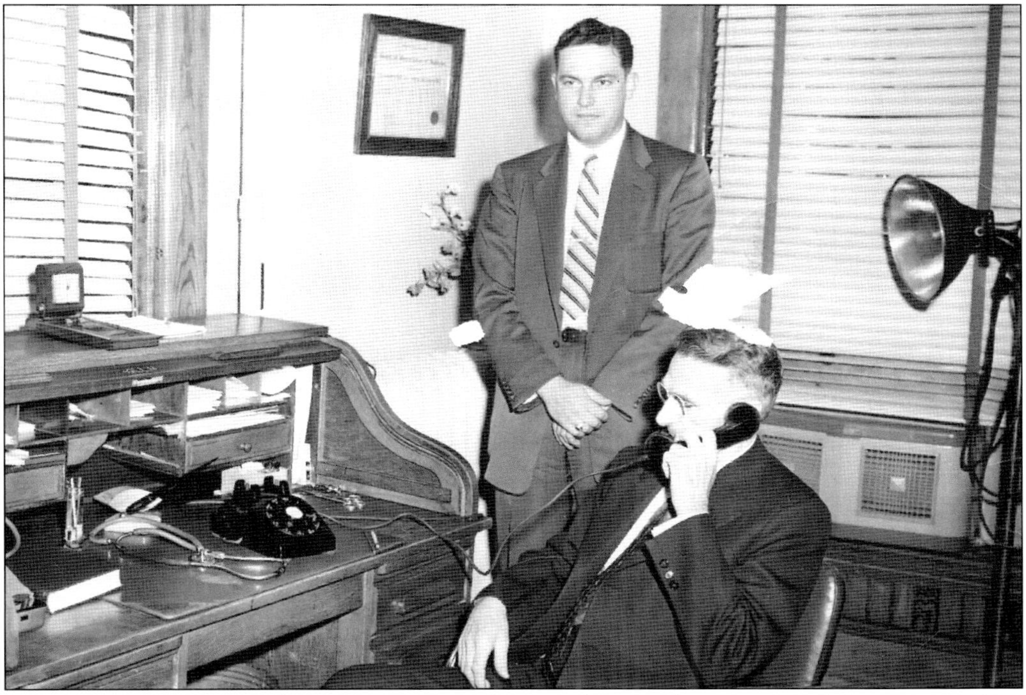

Dr. George Higgins (seated) was the "country doctor" who served Newport and many surrounding towns for nearly 60 years. He is shown making the first dial-up telephone call from his medical office in the Croxford building. Higgins made house calls in all weather and gained local notoriety in the 1920s for driving a Model A Ford fitted with skis. He died in 1968.

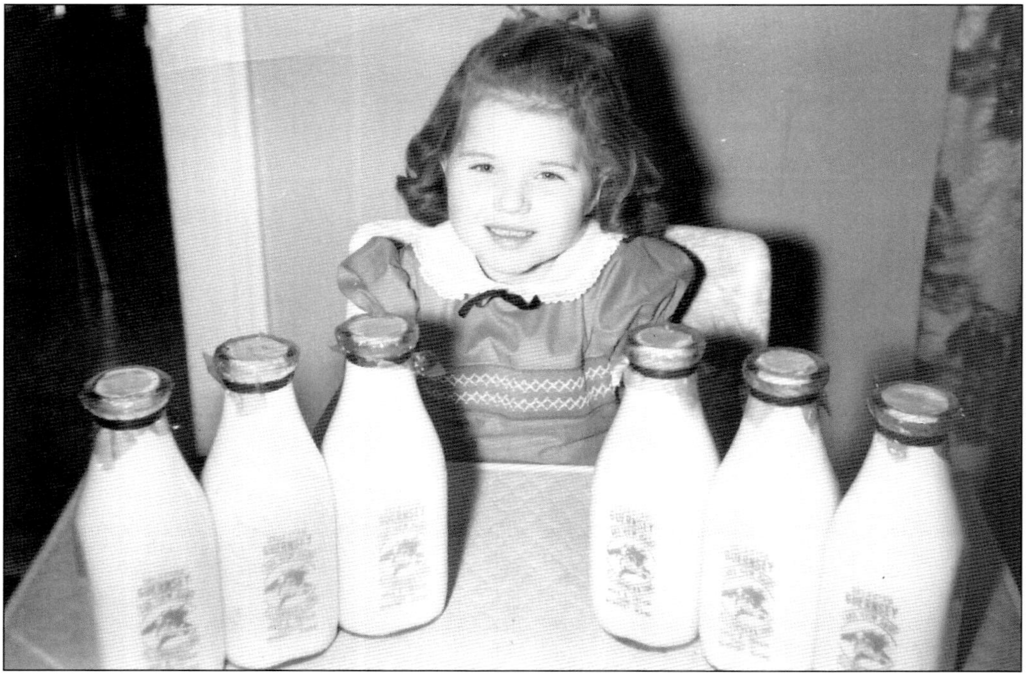

Pam (Turner) Sewall's grandfather, Herbert Turner, owned the Lakeview Dairy. Here, she is pictured with six milk bottles, celebrating her sixth birthday in 1957. The dairy was located on Route 7. (Courtesy of Errald Turner.)

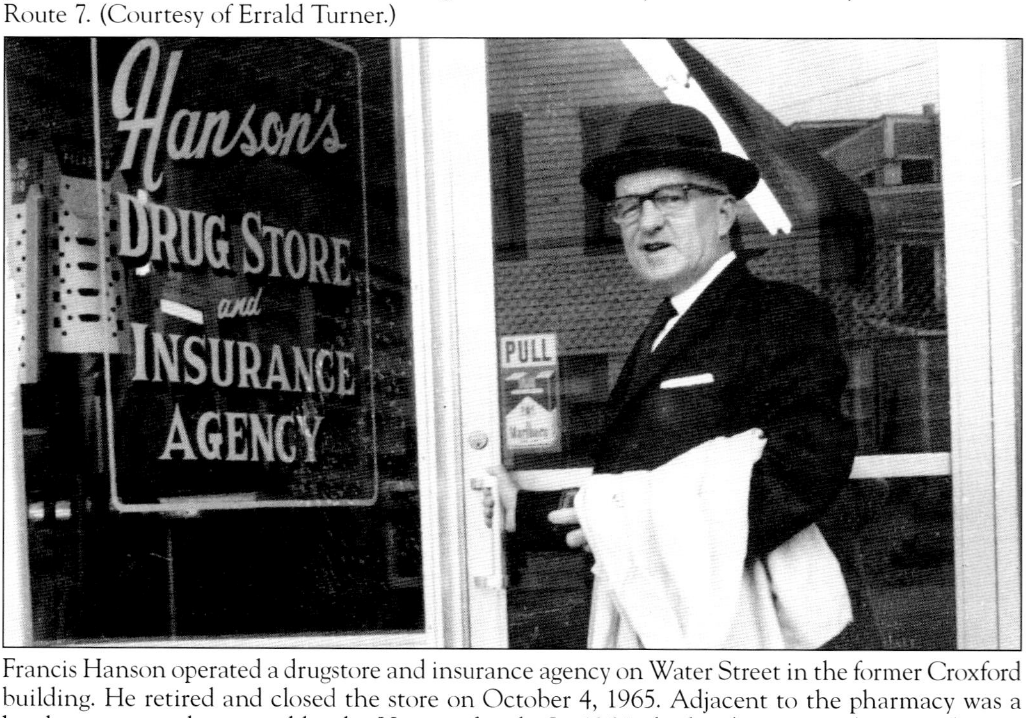

Francis Hanson operated a drugstore and insurance agency on Water Street in the former Croxford building. He retired and closed the store on October 4, 1965. Adjacent to the pharmacy was a hardware store, also owned by the Hanson family. In 1964, the hardware store became the site of Lovley's television shop. (Courtesy of Maude Smith.)

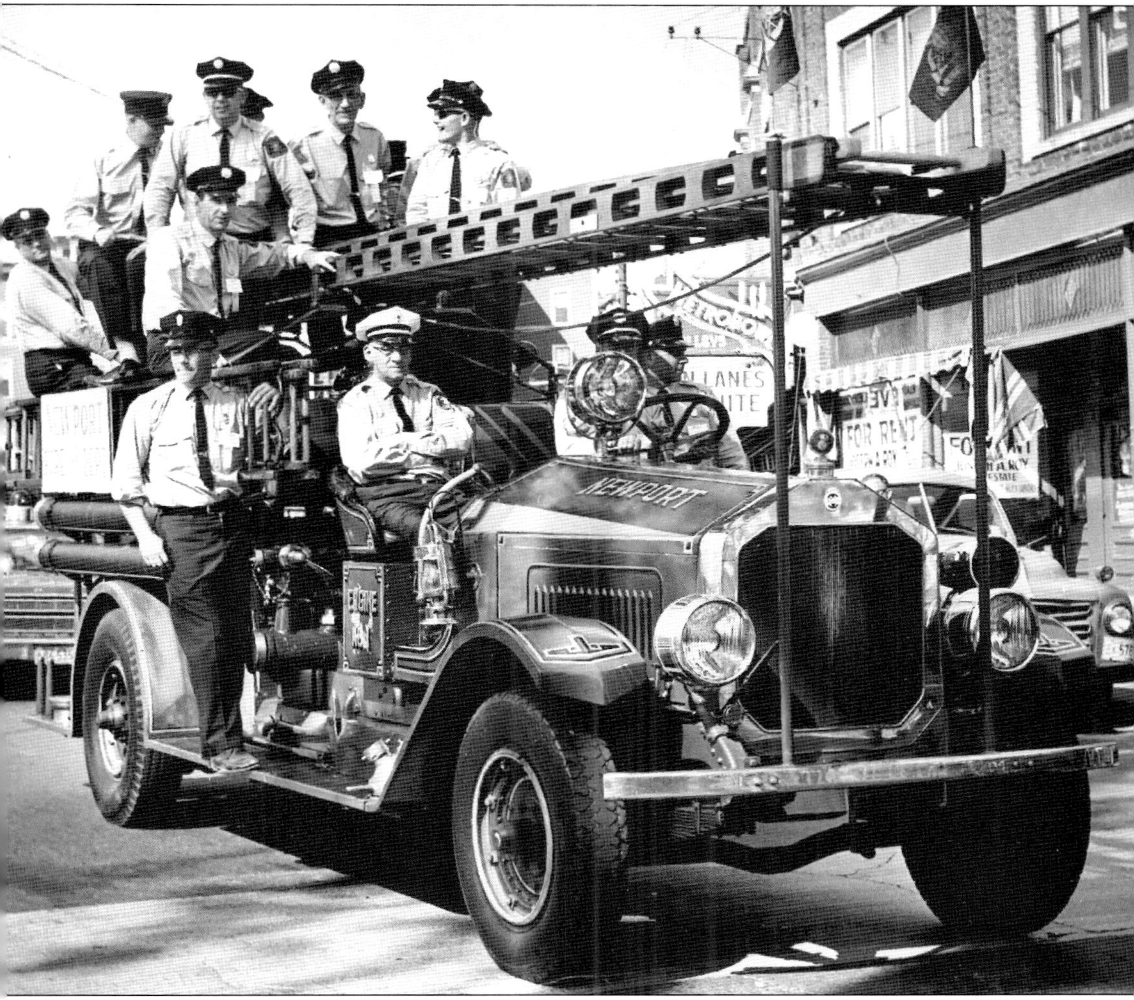

The Newport Fire Department was officially organized in 1904 but had been practicing since 1886 when rudimentary firefighting equipment was purchased. In the early 1900s, the Newport Fire Department played a major role in the Fourth of July celebrations, which was an important fundraising event for them, at Camp Benson. After the 1905 holiday, a newspaper reported, "The fire laddies, with a fat wad of greenbacks in the treasury, are assured of many modern appliances and conveniences in the way of equipment useful in fighting fires of the future." When this 1929 pumper truck was new, it was the first motor-driven truck in the area. In September 1966, the department won a trophy for the pumper truck, affectionately known as "Clancy," in a Waterville parade. Pictured are James Gray, George Gray, Keith Shorey, Charles Peterman, Louis Tuttle, Milton Thompson, Donald Brawn, J.H. Seavey, Donald White, Ernest Paradis, Sidney Gray, John Hanson, Lloyd Ludden, and Francis McKenzie. Clancy still appears in local parades.

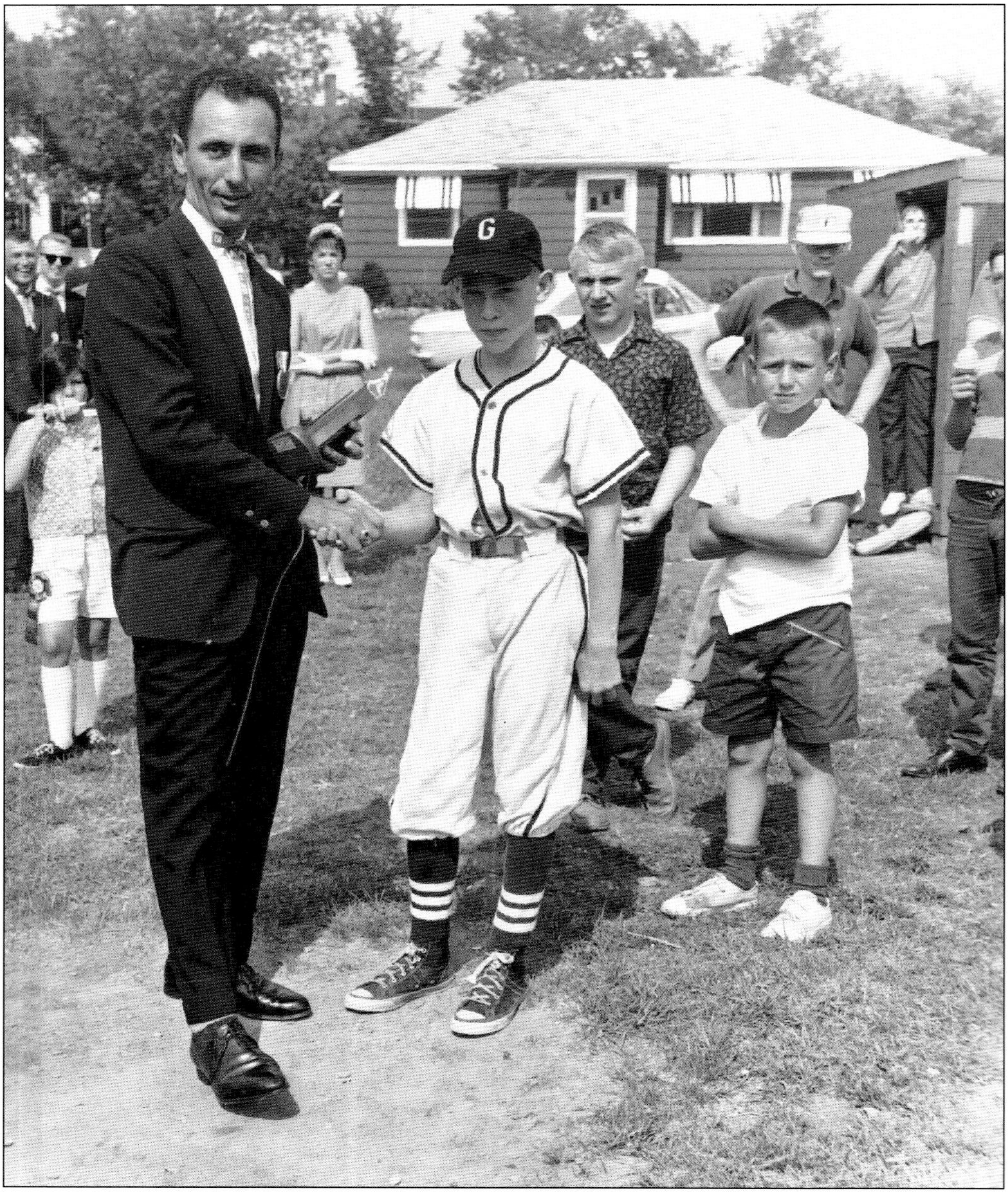

Former Boston Celtic Bob Cousy was the guest of honor at Newport's 1964 Sesquicentennial Youth Day. Cousy was met at the Bangor International Airport by a welcoming committee comprising former Maine governor Lewis Barrows, Richard Banton, Goodie Gilman, Charles Tryder, Judson Jude, Maude Smith, and sesquicentennial queen Jo Ann Tardy. While in Newport, Cousy conducted a basketball clinic at the armory for local high school players. After a special luncheon by the lake, he threw out the first pitch at a Little League championship game at the town ballpark. He is shown here presenting a home run trophy to Aaron Hawthorne. Cousy's visit to Newport was sponsored by the H.P. Hood Company, for which he was a spokesman at the time.

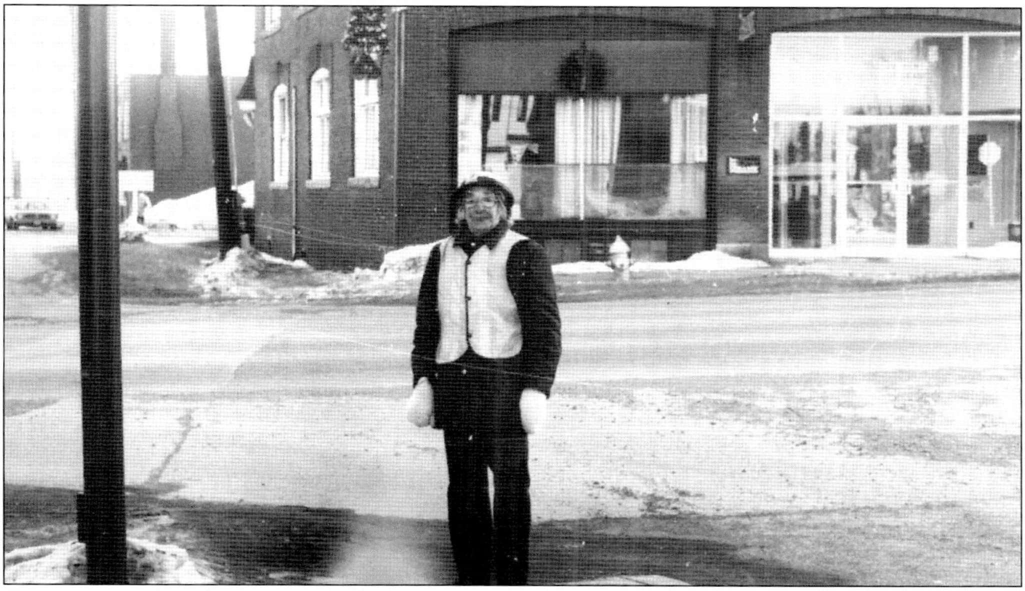

Crossing guard Violet King was a familiar friend to hundreds of Newport schoolchildren over the years as she ushered them through the intersection at Main and Water Streets. (Photograph by Renee Ordway; courtesy of the *Bangor Daily News*.)

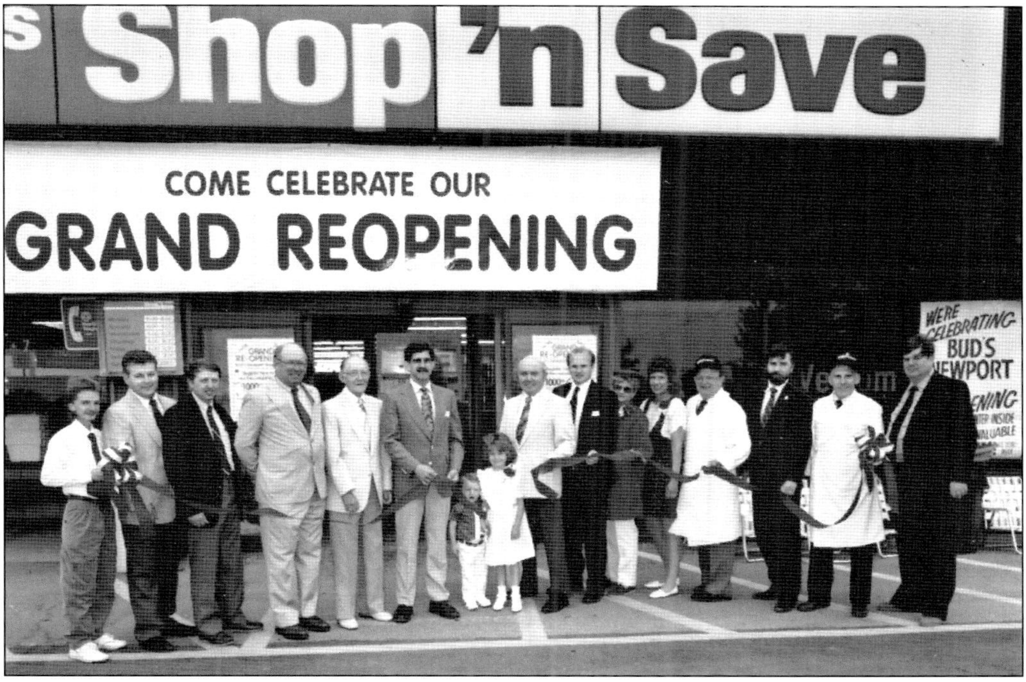

Thirty years after the first Bud's opened in Newport, the family opened a much larger store at the Triangle intersection shopping area on April 13, 1983. Located on the site of the former Andrew Towle farm, Bud's is a town anchor, and it is also patronized by tourists on their way to hunting and skiing adventures farther north. The store, currently owned by Dean Homstead, will celebrate its 60th anniversary in 2013. (Courtesy of Dean Homstead.)

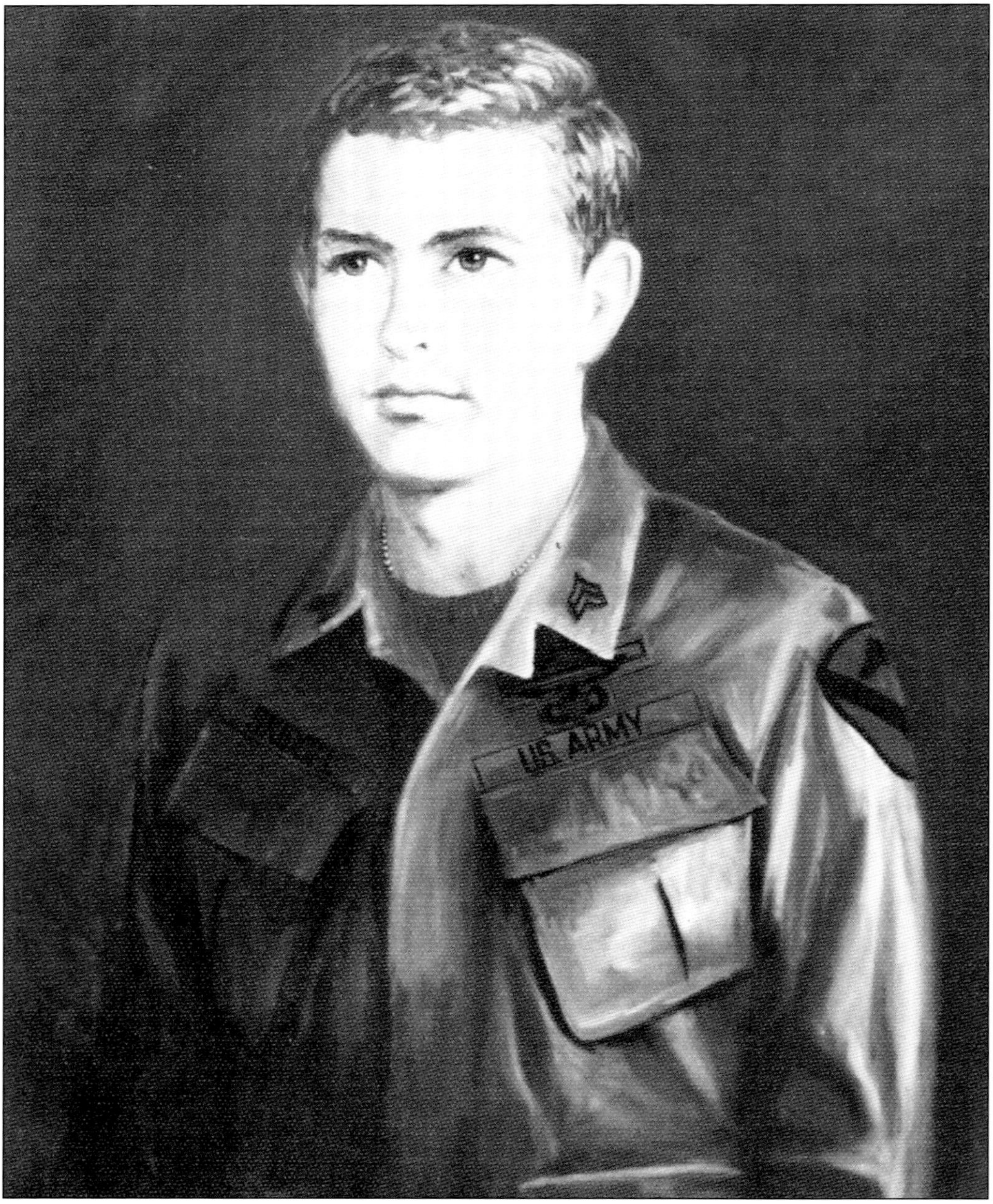

A graduate of Nokomis High School, Sgt. Donald Sidney Skidgel was killed in battle in Vietnam on September 14, 1969. He died while helping comrades in battle and was posthumously awarded the Congressional Medal of Honor for "conspicuous gallantry and intrepidity in action at the risk of his life above and beyond the call of duty." In addition to the Medal of Honor, Skidgel was awarded two Bronze Star Medals and a Purple Heart. In 2011, a new bridge across the East Branch of the Sebasticook River in Newport was named the Donald Sidney Skidgel Memorial Bridge in his honor, by an act of the 125th Maine Legislature. The dedication ceremony took place on October 15, 2011, and was attended by nearly 150 people, including Sen. Susan Collins and Rep. Michael Michaud.

Seven

CENTENNIAL CELEBRATION 1914

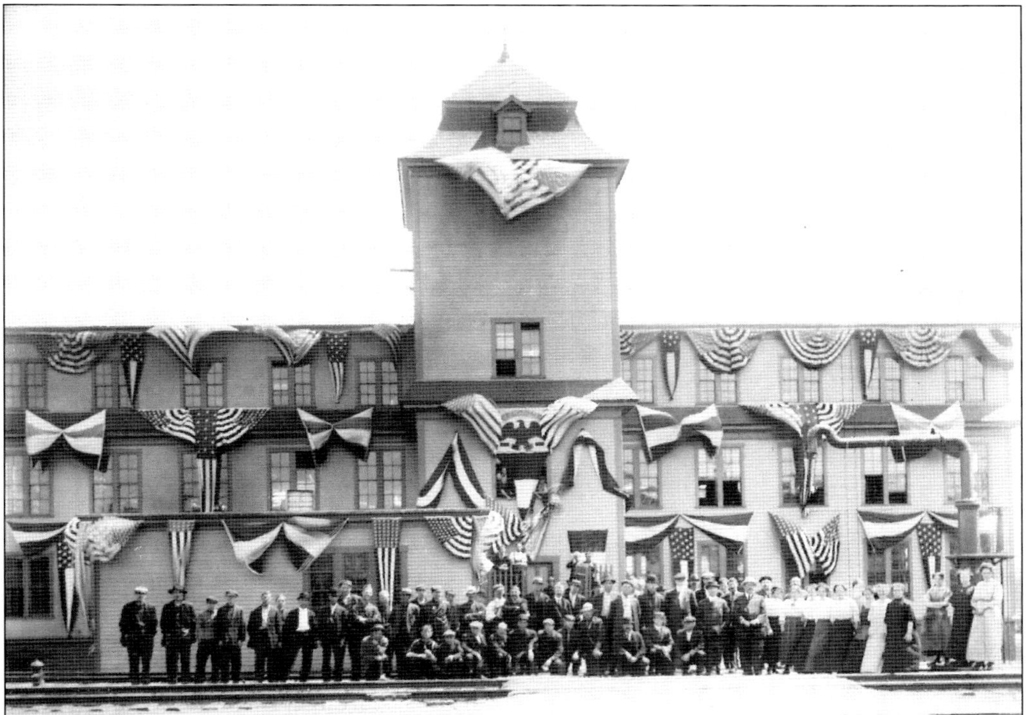

In honor of the town's 100th birthday, the town of Newport staged a celebration on June 13 and June 14, 1914. Events included parades, sports competitions, a concert, a boat parade, and an antiques exhibit at the town hall. Enthusiasm and participation were high. Professional photographers were on hand to document the proceedings, leaving a rich visual record of the celebration. Here, the workers of the Newport Woolen Mill pose outside the facility during the festivities.

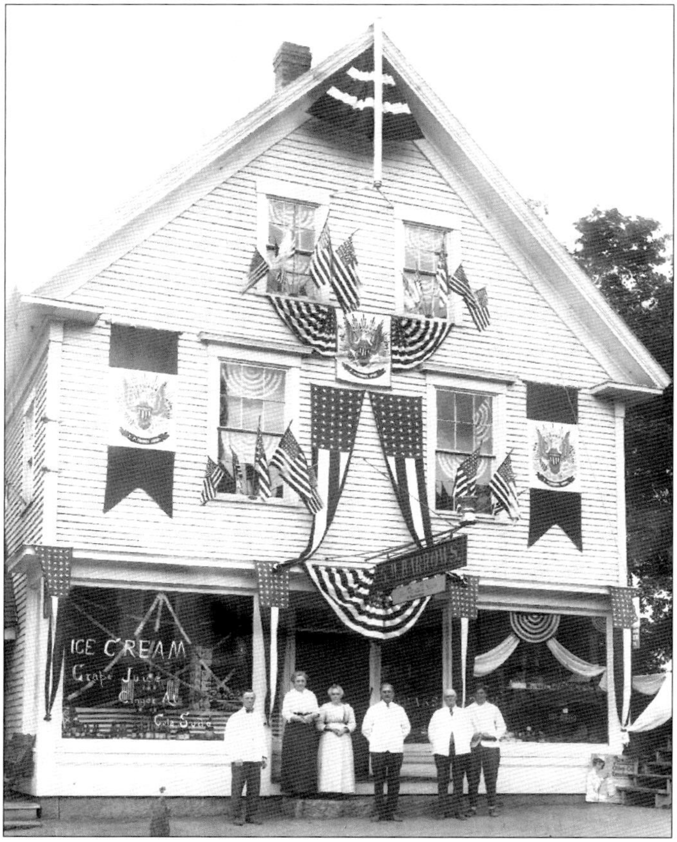

George M. Barrows opened a drugstore in 1892 on Main Street next to the brick bank block. In addition to medicine, the establishment also offered sporting goods, wallpaper, newspapers, and fire insurance. Later, a soda fountain was installed. The building remains today, with a different facade. (Courtesy of the John Dyer family.)

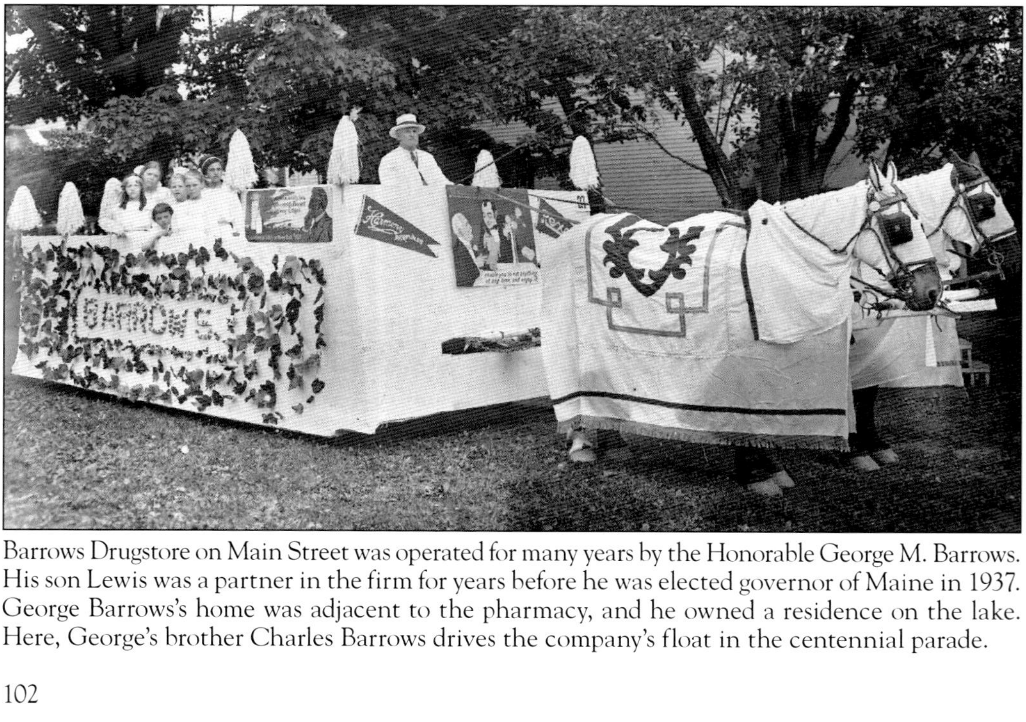

Barrows Drugstore on Main Street was operated for many years by the Honorable George M. Barrows. His son Lewis was a partner in the firm for years before he was elected governor of Maine in 1937. George Barrows's home was adjacent to the pharmacy, and he owned a residence on the lake. Here, George's brother Charles Barrows drives the company's float in the centennial parade.

The Sebasticook Grange was organized in 1889, and the hall on Main Street was built in 1892. Its heyday was in the 1930s and 1940s. Like many Grange buildings, the Sebasticook Grange featured a stage in its second-floor hall and was the site of many community events. After years of declining membership, the Grange hall was sold and is now a privately owned apartment building. (Courtesy of the John Dyer family.)

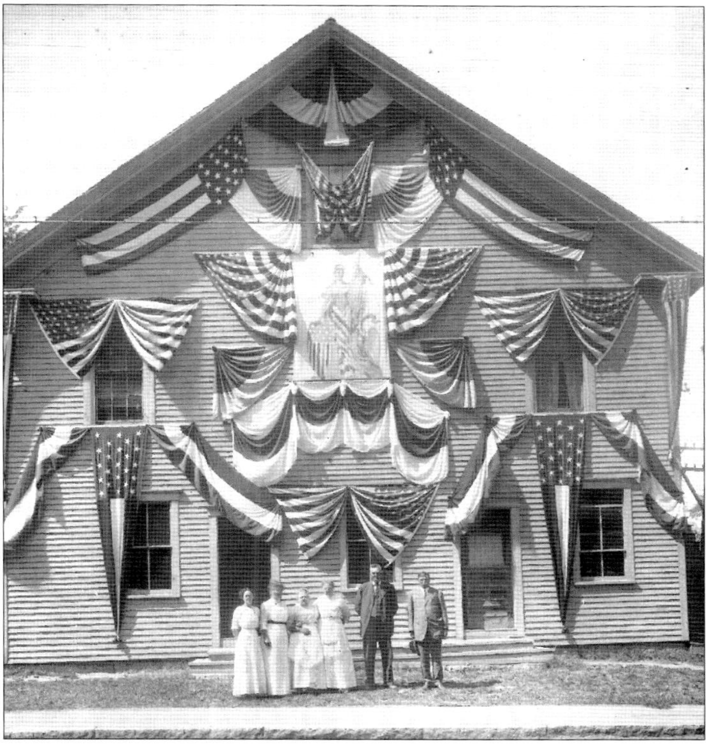

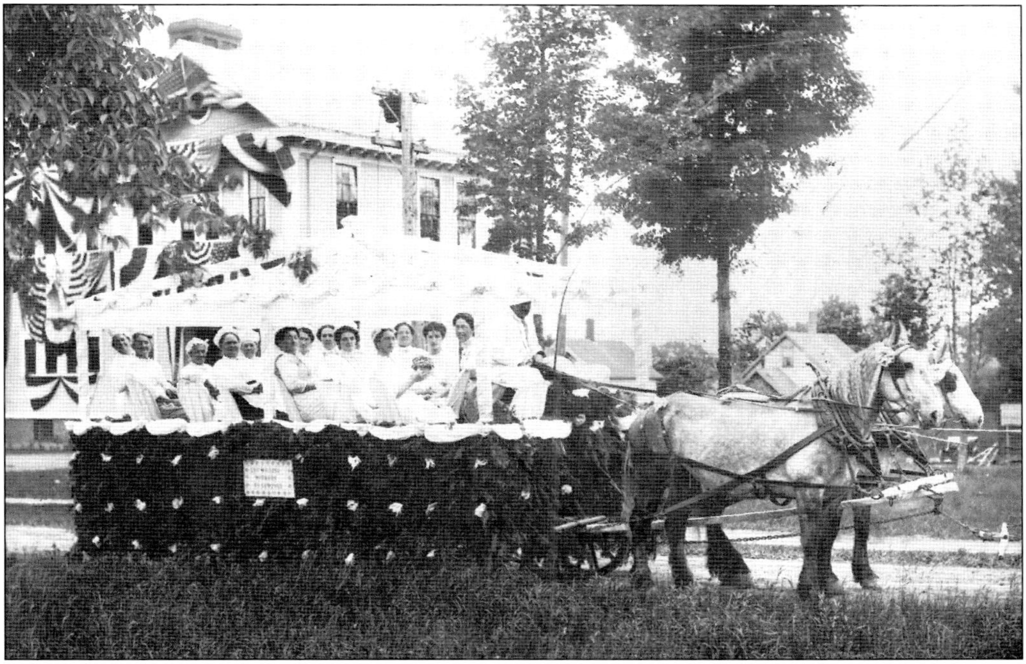

Another float entered in the centennial parade from North Newport was that of the Willing Workers from North Newport Church. The group formed in 1897 to help maintain and improve church facilities and to help with the needs of the community. (Courtesy of Dody Duplisea.)

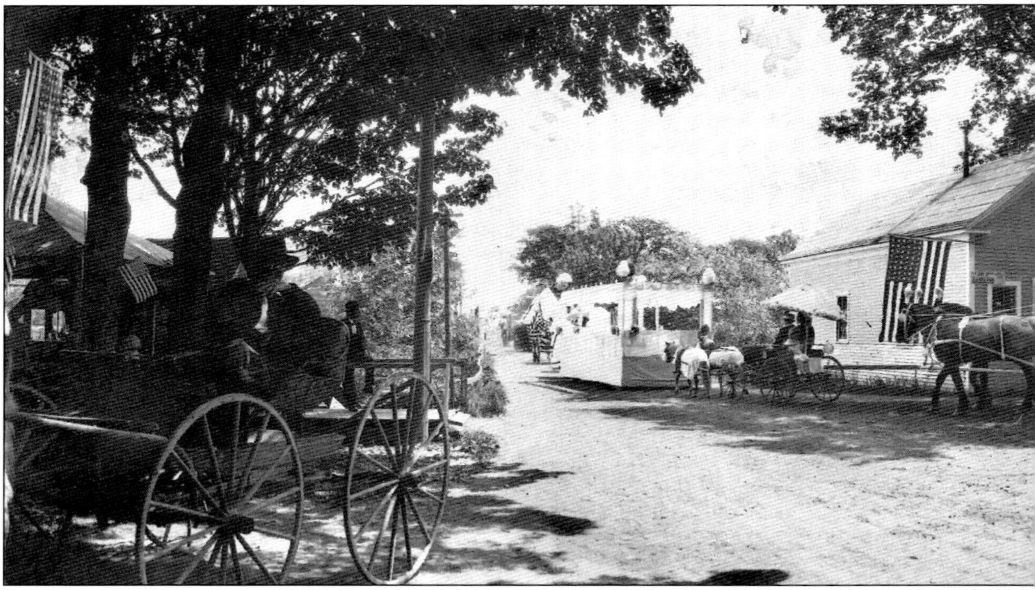

In this photograph, the float of the Ladies Aid of the Methodist Episcopal Church makes a tight corner from Water Street heading across the upper bridge on North Street. Like the Willing Workers of the North Newport Church, the Ladies Aid Society of the Methodist Episcopal Church did work and fundraising for the church and community. Their counterparts at the High Street Union Church were the Union Church Busy Bee Society. All three churches and ladies'

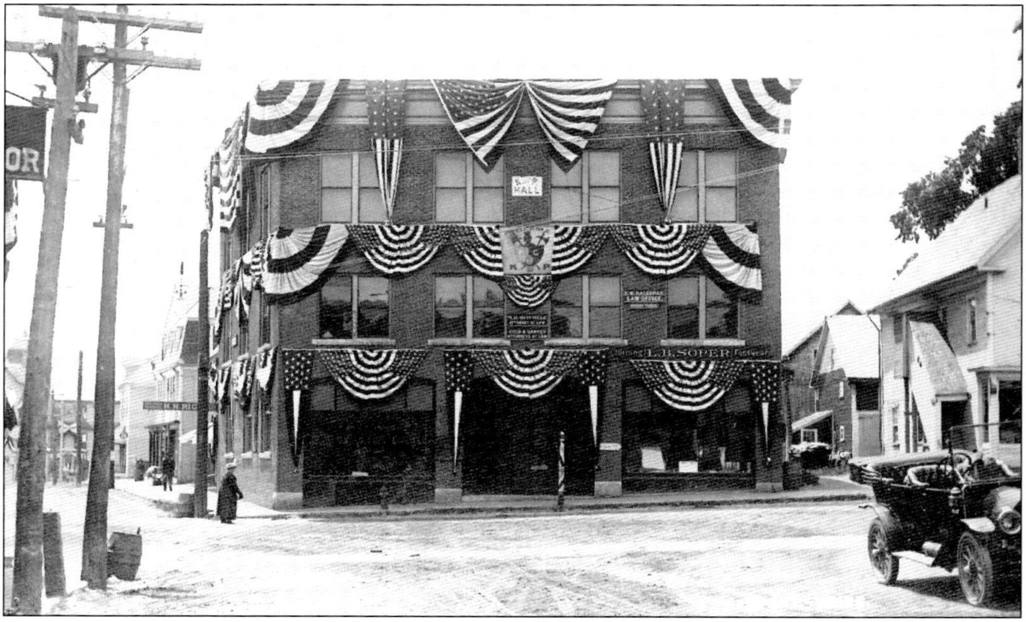

Formerly the home of the Newport branch of the Waterville Trust Company, the bank on Main Street changed affiliations several times in the early part of the 20th century. In 1914, it was known as the Kenduskeag Trust Company, and in 1917, it became the Newport Trust Company. For the centennial, the bank was festooned with bunting up to the third floor.

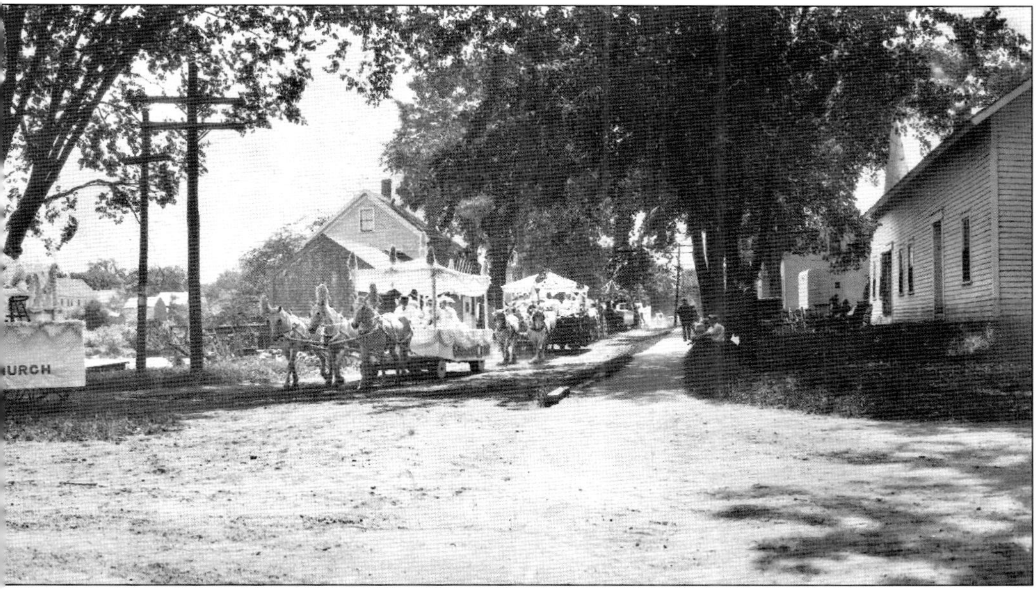

organizations participated in celebrating Newport's 100th birthday. Centennial celebrations in 1914 took place over the course of Saturday, June 13 and Sunday, June 14, exactly 100 years after the incorporation of the town. There was much to celebrate, with the wool and dairy canning factories booming, other businesses thriving, and a growing summer tourism industry to enhance the attractiveness and property values of the town.

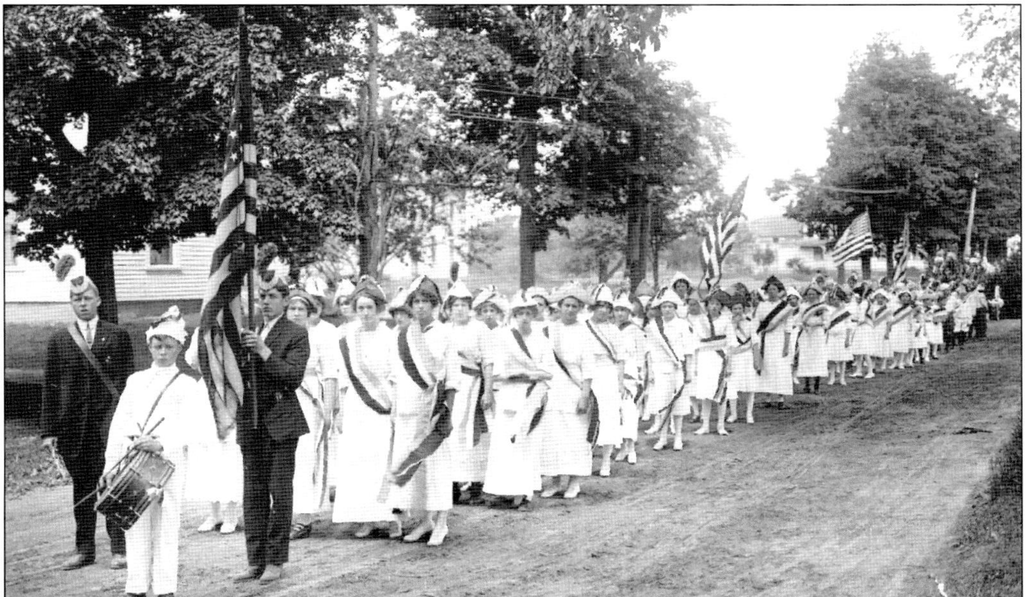

Schoolchildren process down Shaw Street in front of the schools. At 2:00 on the Saturday afternoon of the grand centennial celebrations, the students sang the "Star Spangled Banner." The children and adults in this picture may be arrayed patriotically for that event.

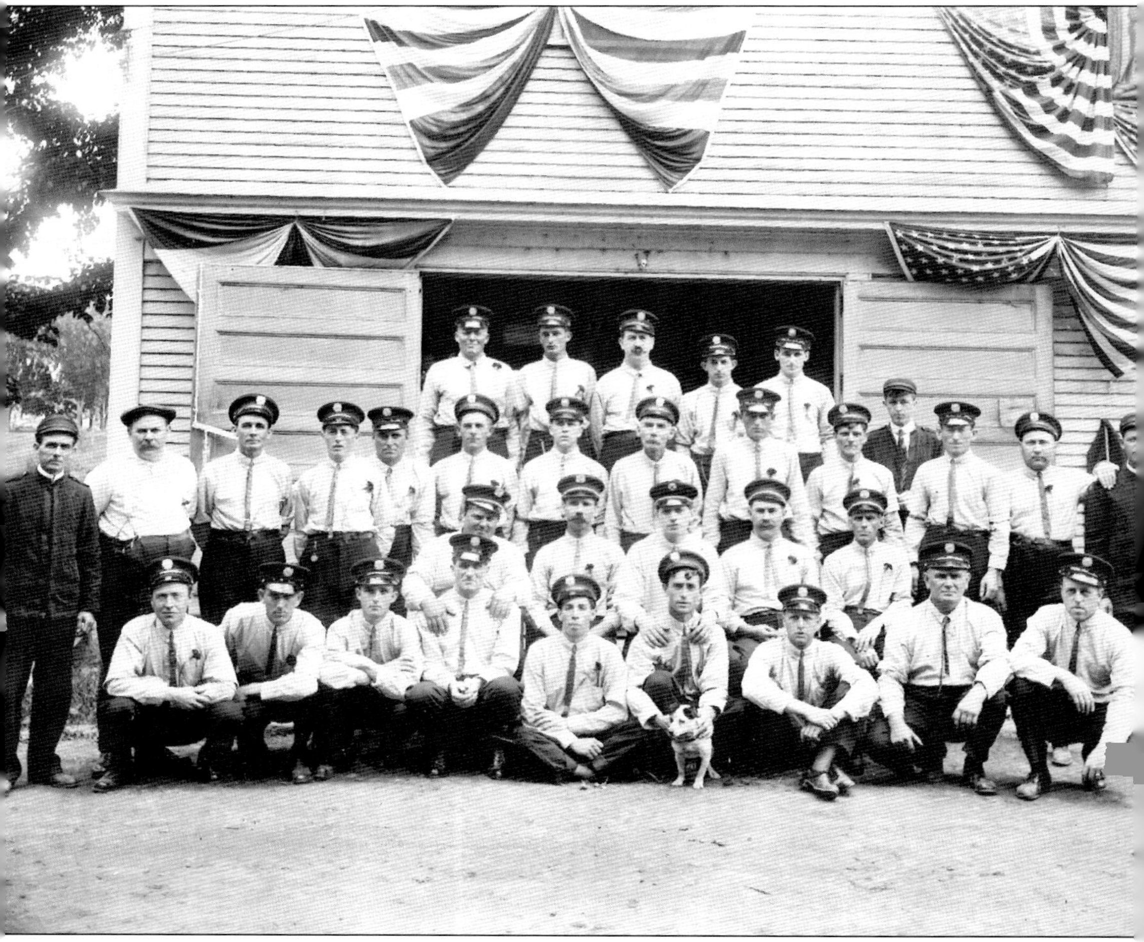

Fire control was of vital importance in densely built-up communities like Newport. The Newport Fire Department was organized in 1886, with the primary equipment a hose carriage. In 1909, the department purchased a gas-powered fire engine. Here, the Newport Fire Department poses in front of the old municipal building on Water Street. The firemen did much of their own fundraising and were proud to be one of the larger uniformed fire departments in the state. Photographed from left to right are (first row) Charles Croxford, Percy York, Allie Newcomb, Bill Barnes, Louis Cook, Carroll Pratt, Harold Millett, Mark Wentworth, and Harry Smith; (second row, seated) Arthur Getchell, Earl Ellis, Jack Heffren, Charles Brann, and Tim Davis; (third row) George Newton, Bert Perham, Charles Moore, Wallace Stuart, Fred Pushor, Cliff Wheeler, Dean Reynolds, Thack Nason, Ossian Soule, Will Towne, Charles Spratt, ? McGowan, and Charles Sheridan; (fourth row) Alvah Woodman, Perley Soule, Win Tolton, John Sanborn, and Sam Leavitt. Other members not pictured included Ross Gilman, Robie Young, and Dan Cram.

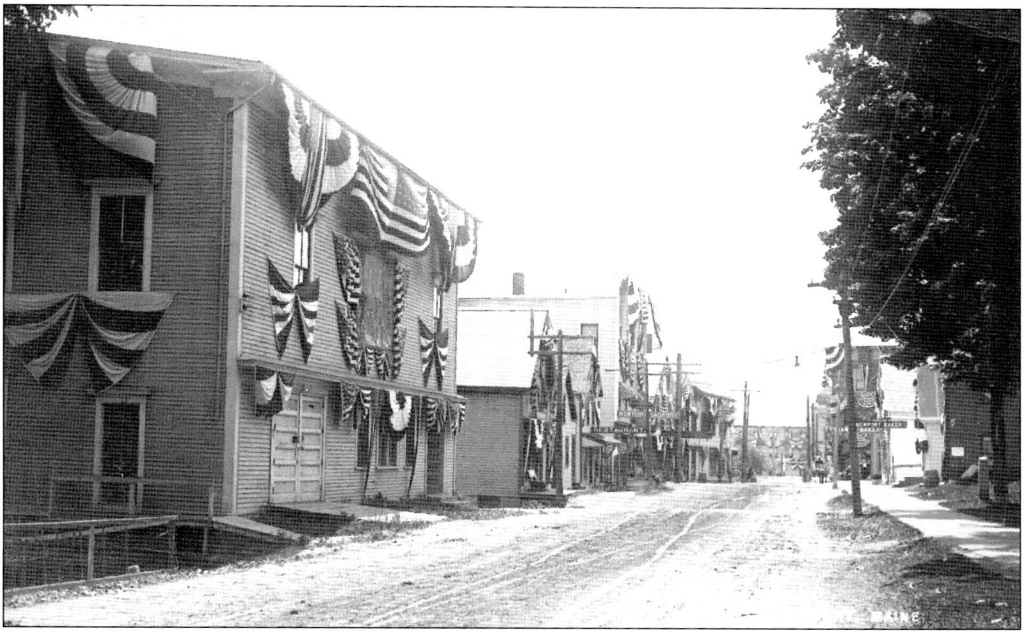

The old town hall was located on Water Street, roughly where the Public Works yard is today. Through the first half of the century, the town's library was located downstairs. Various meetings were held in the large upstairs space, which was also where the high school basketball team practiced, in notoriously tight quarters. The building was razed in 1959, and new facilities were constructed nearby for the police and fire departments.

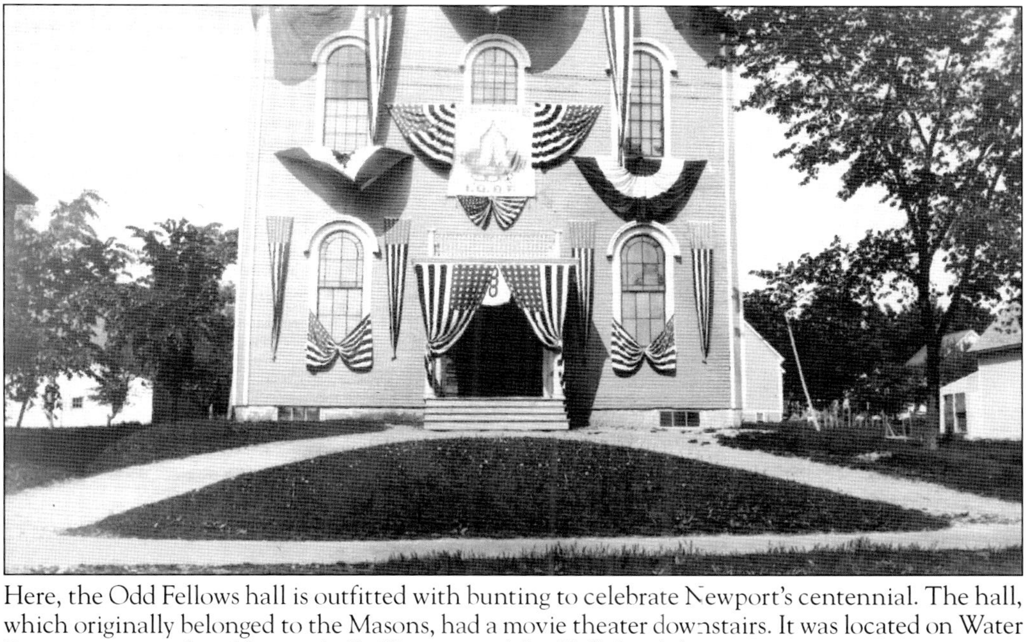

Here, the Odd Fellows hall is outfitted with bunting to celebrate Newport's centennial. The hall, which originally belonged to the Masons, had a movie theater downstairs. It was located on Water Street, opposite the old town hall. (Courtesy of the Hall family.)

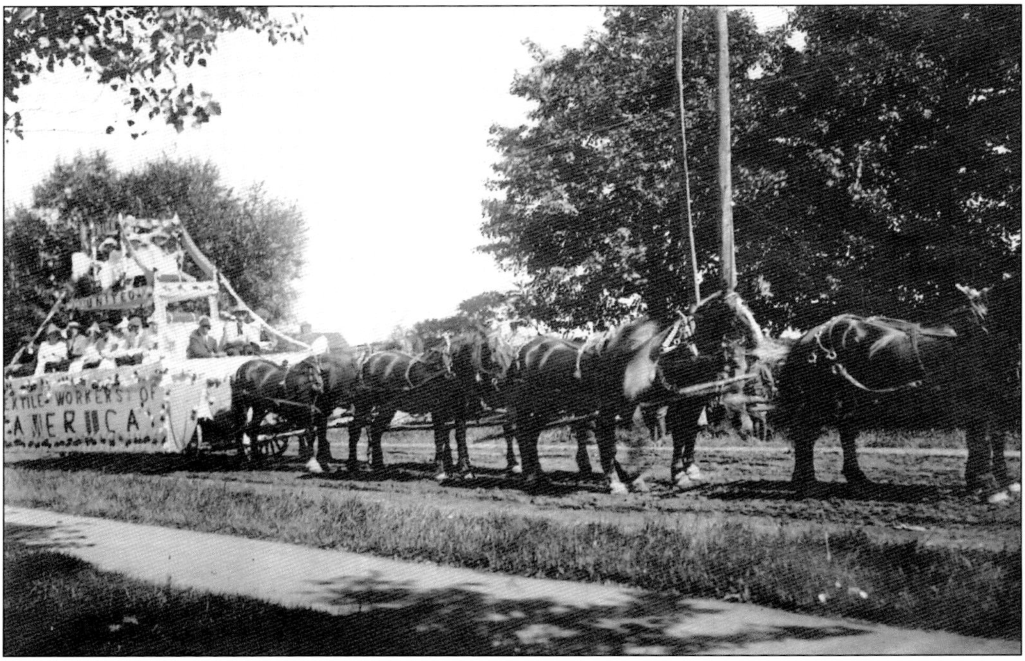

Businesses and organizations of all sorts were proud to enter floats in Newport's 1914 centennial parade. This United Textile Workers of America float was driven by Otis Bowen, who was noted for his horse-handling skills. Here, Bowen is driving a team of eight horses. (Courtesy of Dale Carsley.)

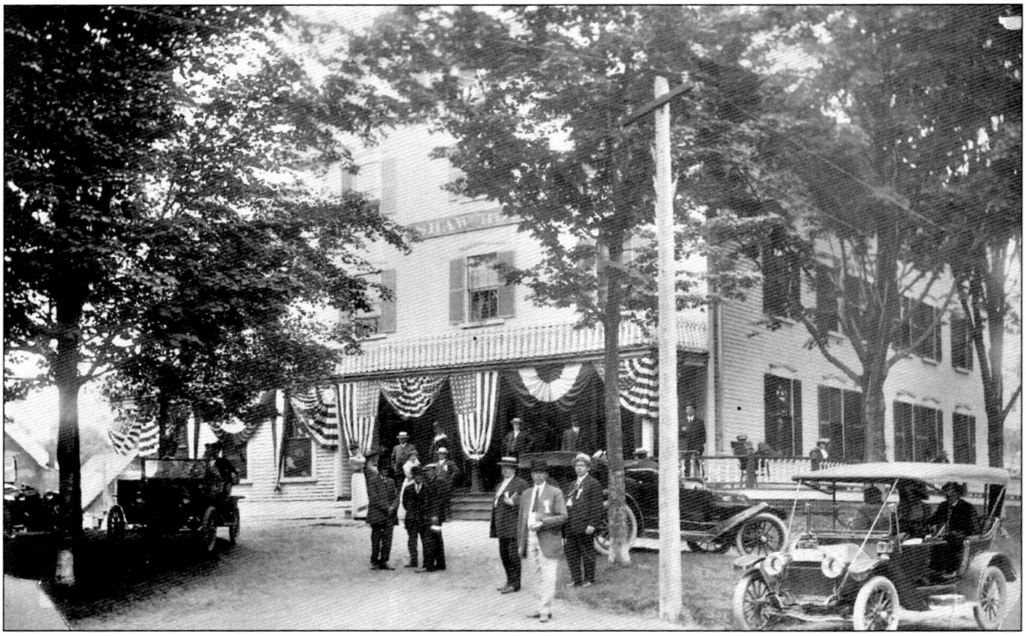

Built in 1860, the Shaw House was conveniently located midway between the towns of Skowhegan, Bangor, and Dexter. First by stagecoach, then by train, and finally by auto, travelers passed through Newport, and many stayed at the Shaw House. In this picture, autos abound, though the stables can still be seen in the left background. It is now a senior housing center called the Newport Inn.

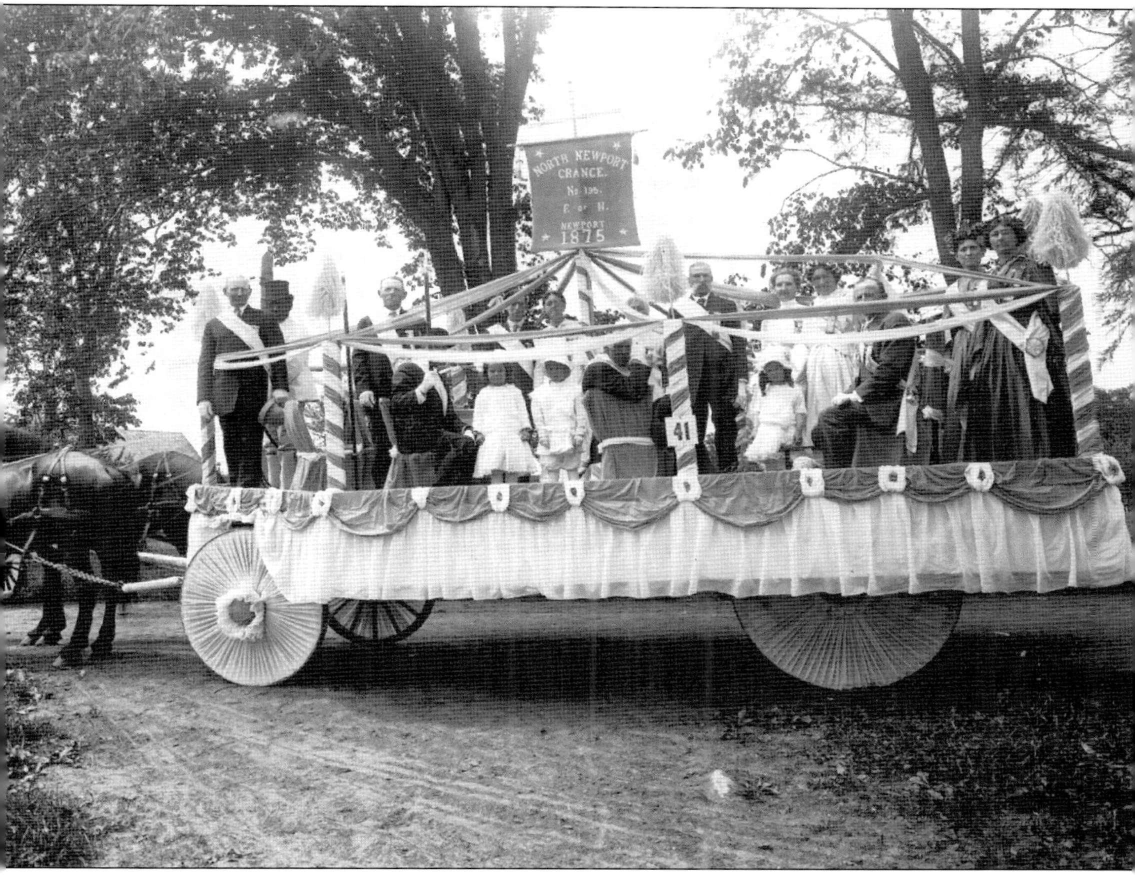

The Grange in North Newport received its charter January 14, 1876. The first meetings were held at the Good Templars hall a half-mile north of the North Newport Church. They bought land diagonally across the road from the church to build a store in 1880. Eventually the store closed, but after renovations were made, the building became their permanent home. In 1914, Grange members posed with their centennial parade float. The North Newport Grange gave up its charter in the 1950s and merged with other Granges in the area. James H. Mullen is the driver. (Courtesy of the John Dyer family; caption provided by Dody Duplisea.)

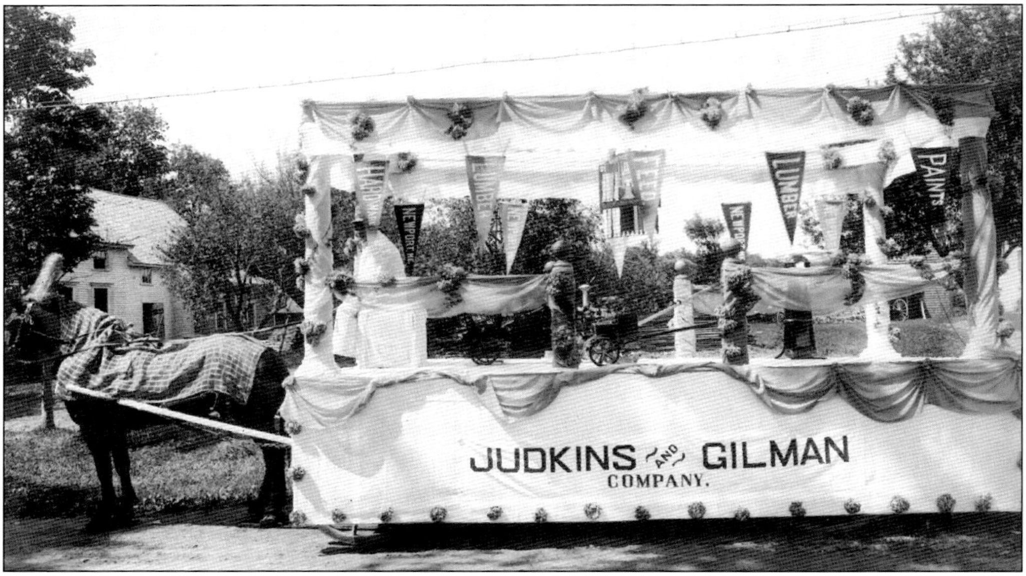

Prominently located on Main Street, Judkins and Gilman sold hardware, paint, coal, lumber, feed, sporting goods, and grocery items. The multilevel store opened for business in the 1860s and became a town fixture. Eventually the company had several storehouses, including one adjacent to the railroad. O.H. Judkins was from Palmyra, and J.O. Gilman was from Newport. The company's float in the centennial parade exhibited some of its wares.

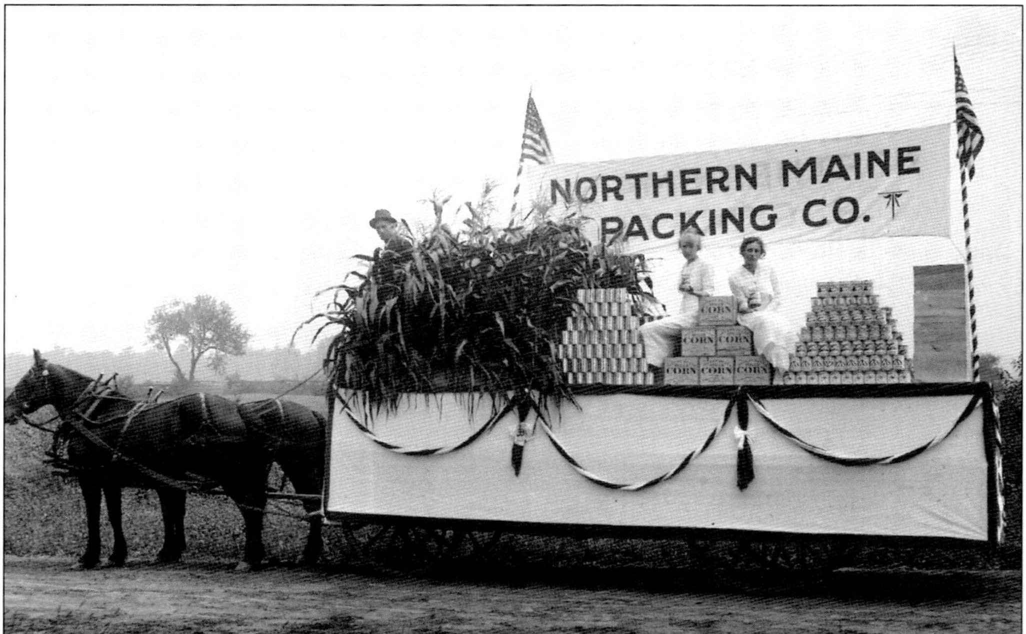

This Northern Maine Packing Company float highlights corn, which, along with apples and potatoes, was a very important crop in the 19th and early 20th centuries. Many of the old fields are now forested. The Northern Maine Packing Company was owned by Charles Moses of Corinna. The float is driven by Frank Coburn and his horses. Seated are Inez Mullen (left) and Myrtle Clark.

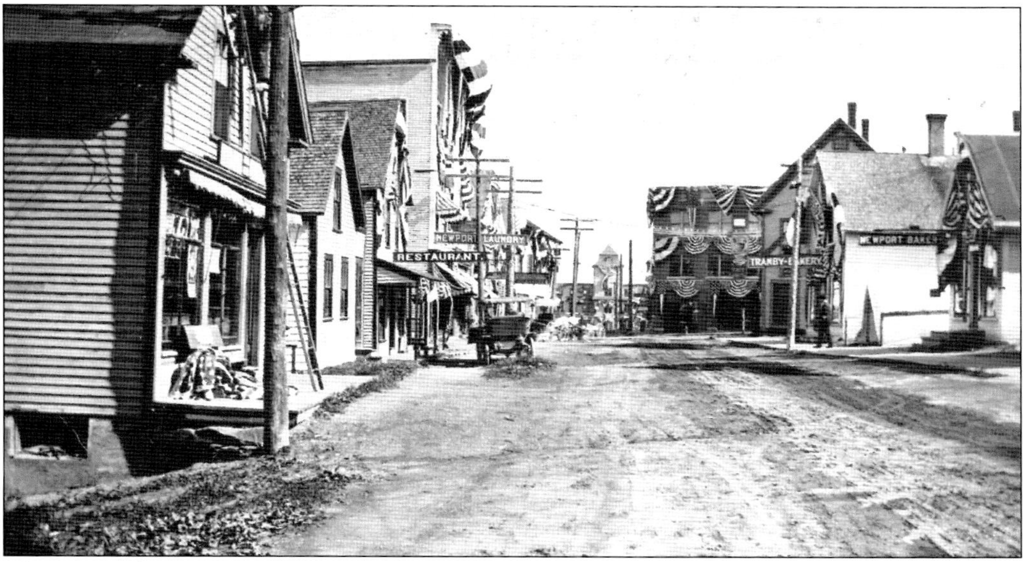

This view of Water Street indicates how many businesses operated in downtown Newport in 1914. This block alone contained two bakeries, a restaurant, and a number of shops and offices. Water Street connected the two vital modes of transportation in the town—the lake and the railroad—and was consequently a prominent roadway.

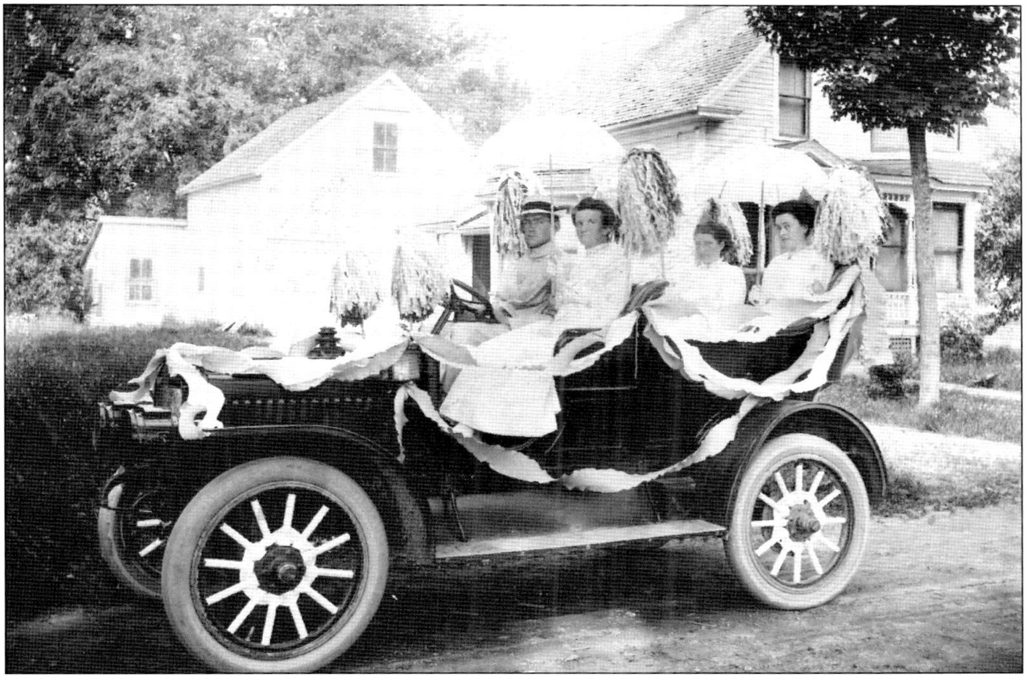

One of the few automobiles in the centennial parade was driven by W.R. Morill. In the car are Ida Morrill, Minnie Morrill, and Mary Dyer. The centennial parade route processed down Main Street, turned left onto Water Street, and then turned right to head up Elm Street. Photographers were poised along the route to take commemorative photographs, which were then sold to many townspeople.

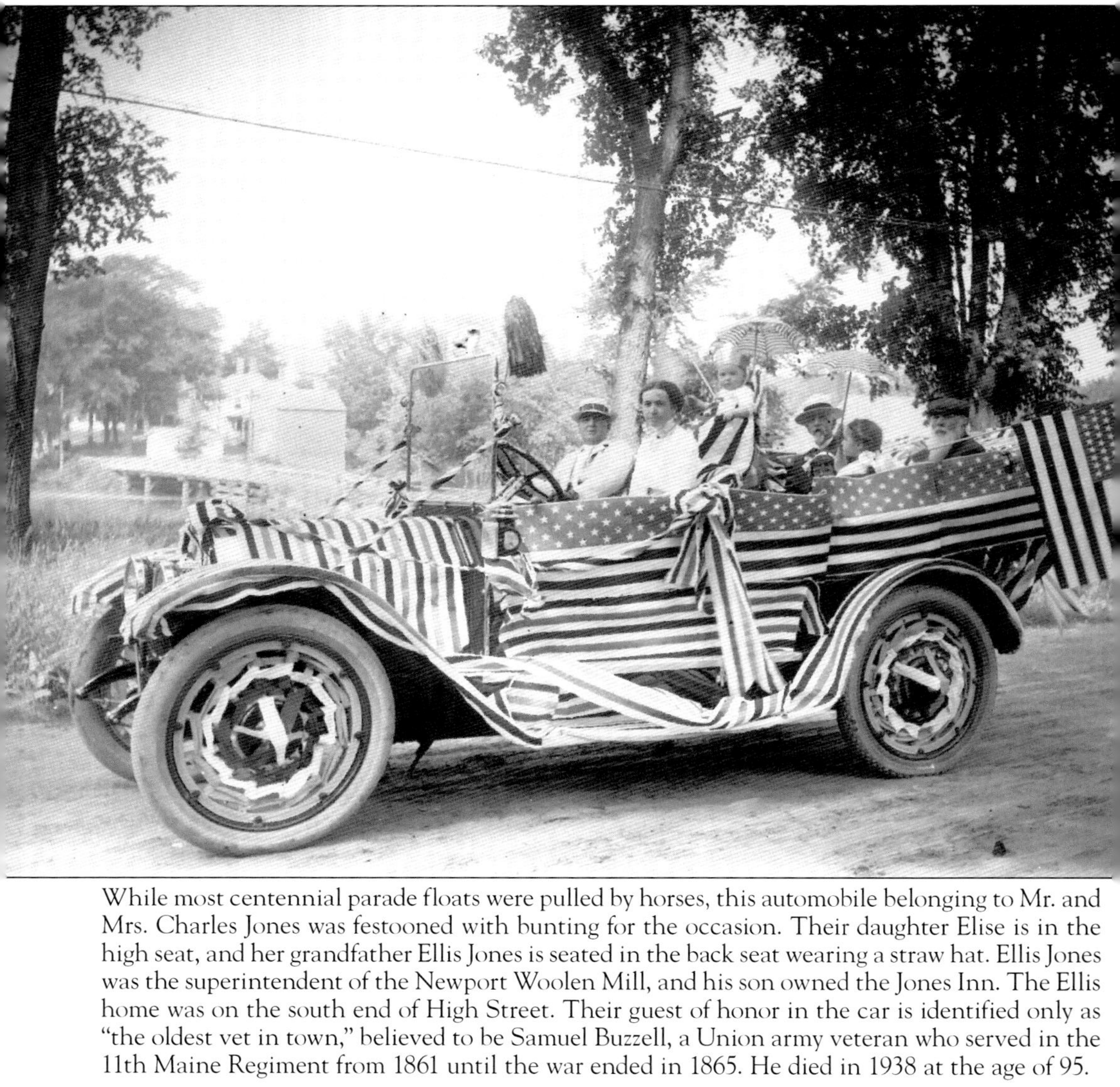

While most centennial parade floats were pulled by horses, this automobile belonging to Mr. and Mrs. Charles Jones was festooned with bunting for the occasion. Their daughter Elise is in the high seat, and her grandfather Ellis Jones is seated in the back seat wearing a straw hat. Ellis Jones was the superintendent of the Newport Woolen Mill, and his son owned the Jones Inn. The Ellis home was on the south end of High Street. Their guest of honor in the car is identified only as "the oldest vet in town," believed to be Samuel Buzzell, a Union army veteran who served in the 11th Maine Regiment from 1861 until the war ended in 1865. He died in 1938 at the age of 95.

Eight

The Sesquicentennial of 1964

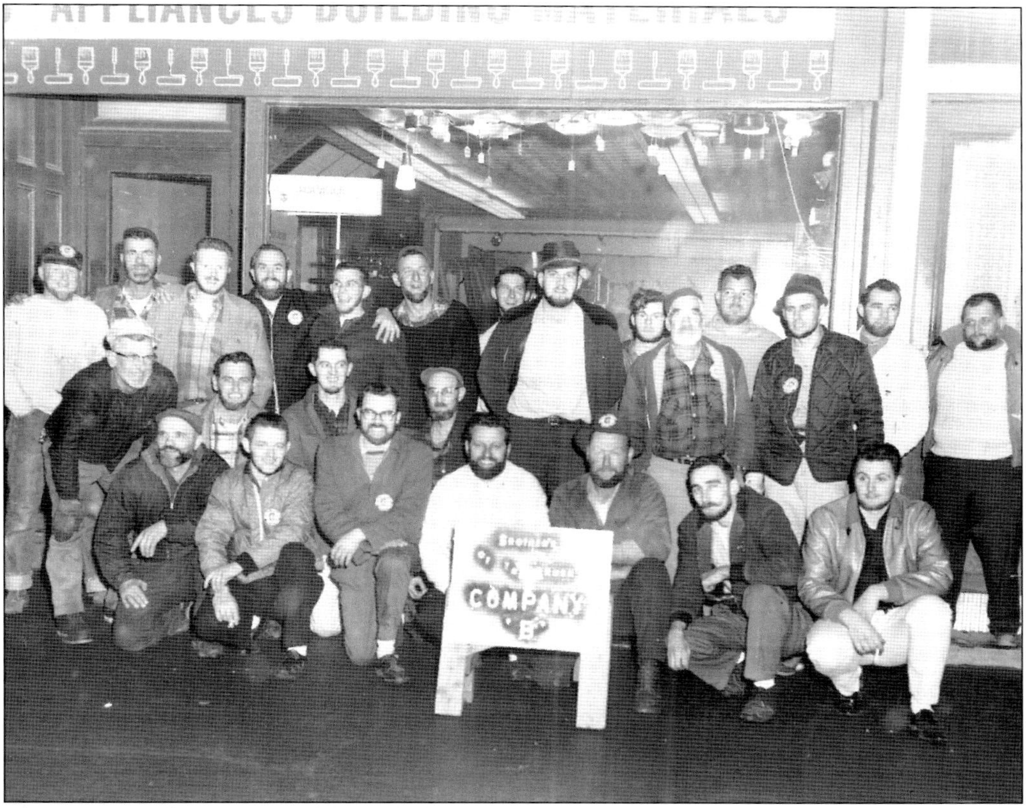

The citizens of Newport celebrated the town's 150th birthday with as much gusto as their predecessors had celebrated the centennial. As part of the celebrations, many men stopped shaving on Lincoln's birthday, February 12, 1964. The planned "Whisker Rebellion" required them to grow out traditional beards to celebrate the 150th anniversary of the town's founding. There were many prizes for the best beards as well as threats of "jail" for those who chose not to participate.

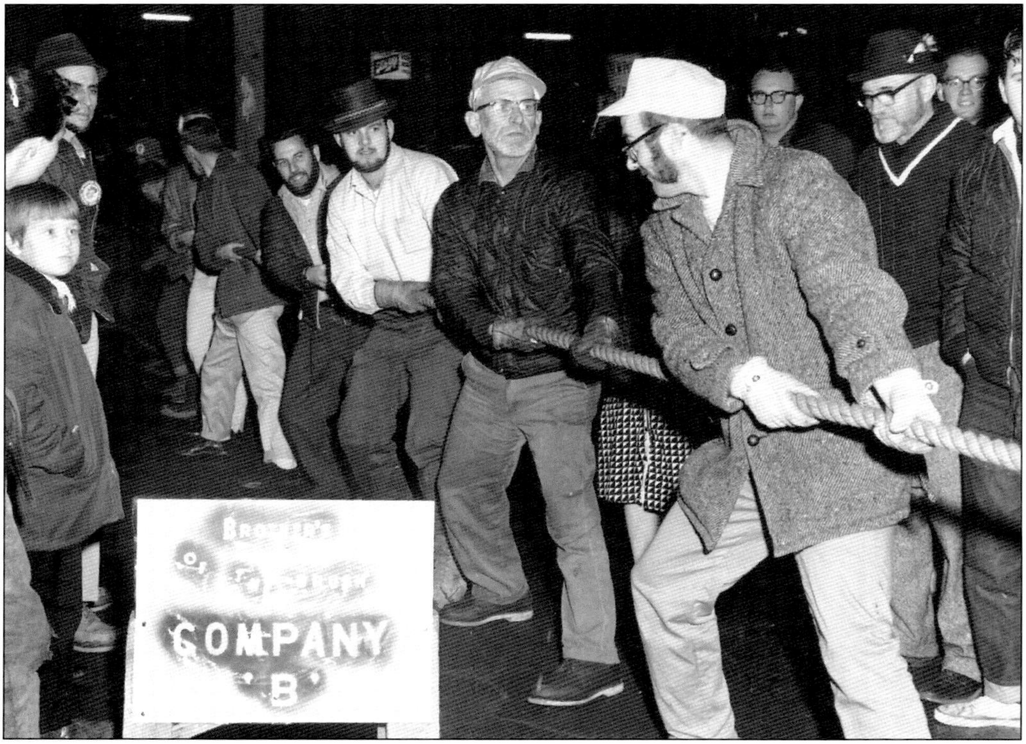

As part of the "Whisker Rebellion," various competitions were staged, such as this tug-of-war. Companies in the rebellion met throughout the spring and early summer for social and competitive events. Men who did not grow beards risked arrest and fines from Keystone Kops. Most men gamely played along.

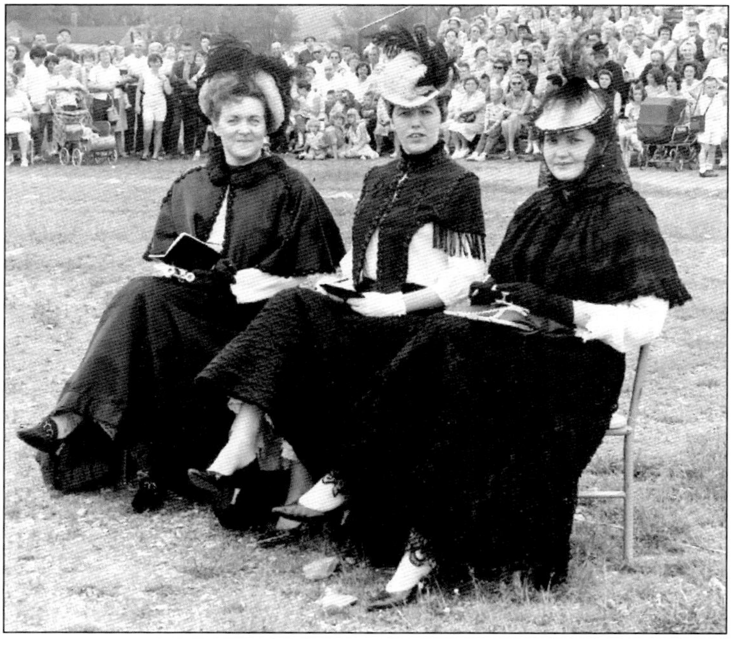

The ladies of the town took pains to outfit themselves with vintage-style dresses to celebrate Newport's heritage. Many sewed their outfits themselves and participated in sewing bees to mentor those lacking sewing skills. The Belles organized themselves into chapters, such as Corset Corvettes, Sisters of the Swish, Polka-Dot Belles, and Petticoat Promenaders. Pictured here are, from left to right, Bev Murray, Sandra Creighton, and Angela Moore.

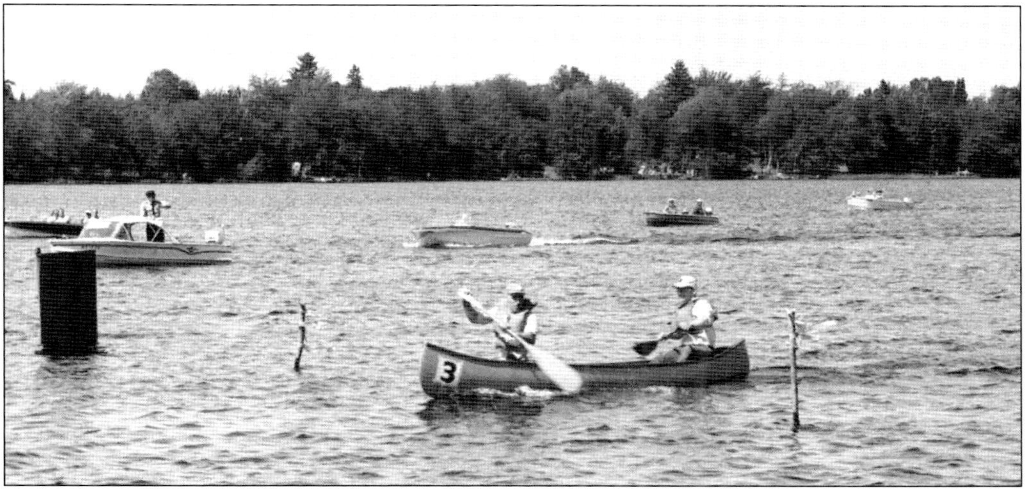

A major event in the summer celebration was a seven-mile canoe race that began at the Durham Bridge. Ten teams competed for the $100 top prize, and hundreds of spectators lined the shore. Shown here are Earl Nelson (front) and Bruce Gould (back) crossing the finish line in the 16-foot Chestnut canoe, with no other teams in sight. Maine game warden Hennessey checks his watch in the background.

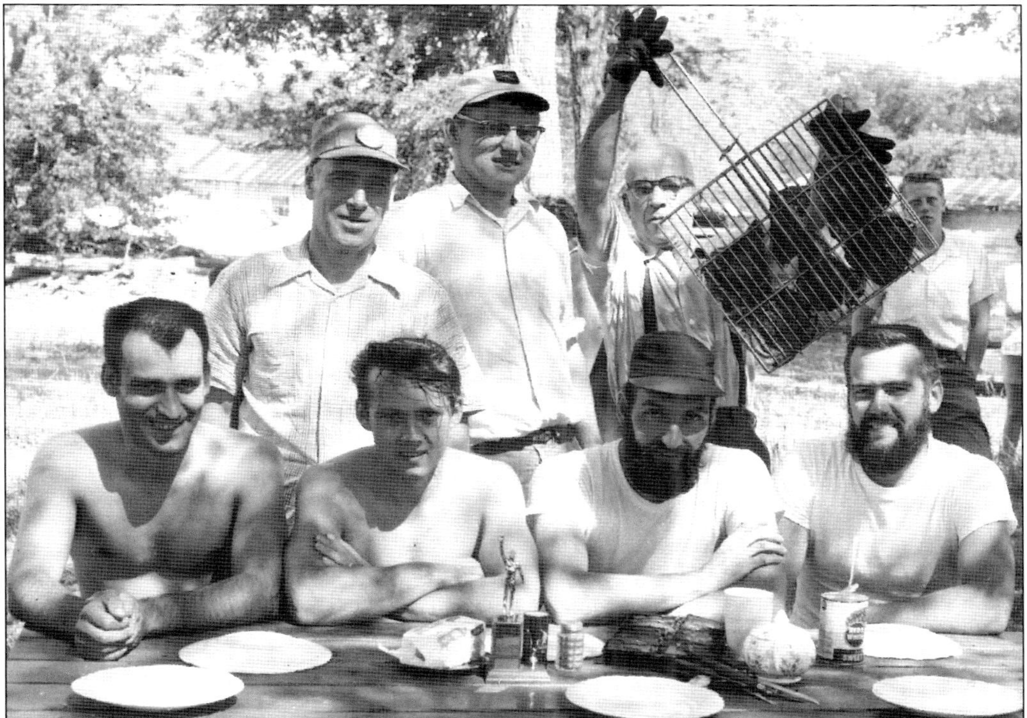

The three fastest teams in the race won a steak dinner cooked up by famed Bangor guide Charlie Miller (rear, holding steaks). About to enjoy their steaks are, from left to right, (seated) Merlon Reynolds and Leroy Humphrey (second place winners), Louis Tuttle and Keith Shorey (third place winners), and (standing) Earl Nelson and Bruce Gould (first place winners).

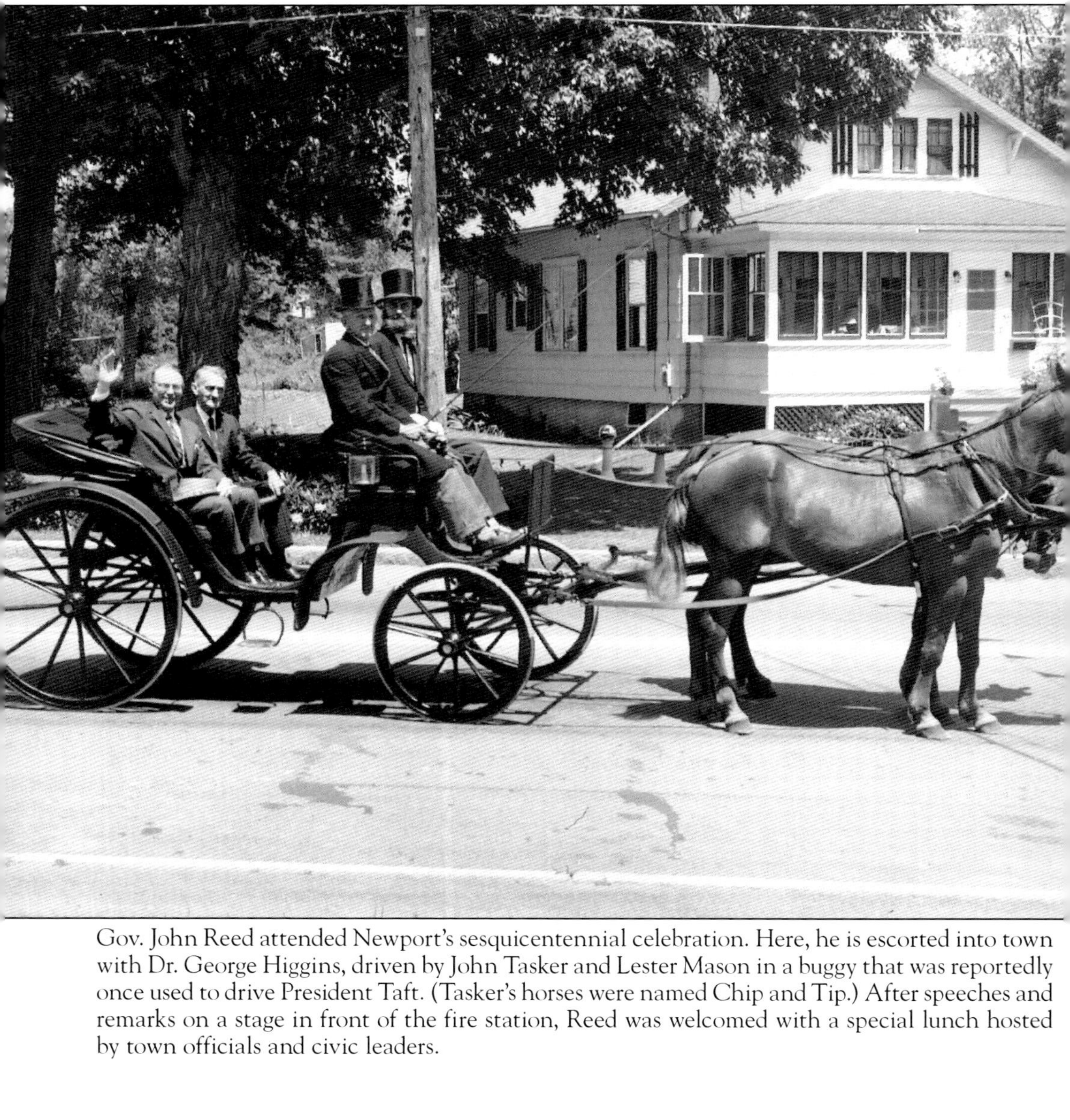

Gov. John Reed attended Newport's sesquicentennial celebration. Here, he is escorted into town with Dr. George Higgins, driven by John Tasker and Lester Mason in a buggy that was reportedly once used to drive President Taft. (Tasker's horses were named Chip and Tip.) After speeches and remarks on a stage in front of the fire station, Reed was welcomed with a special lunch hosted by town officials and civic leaders.

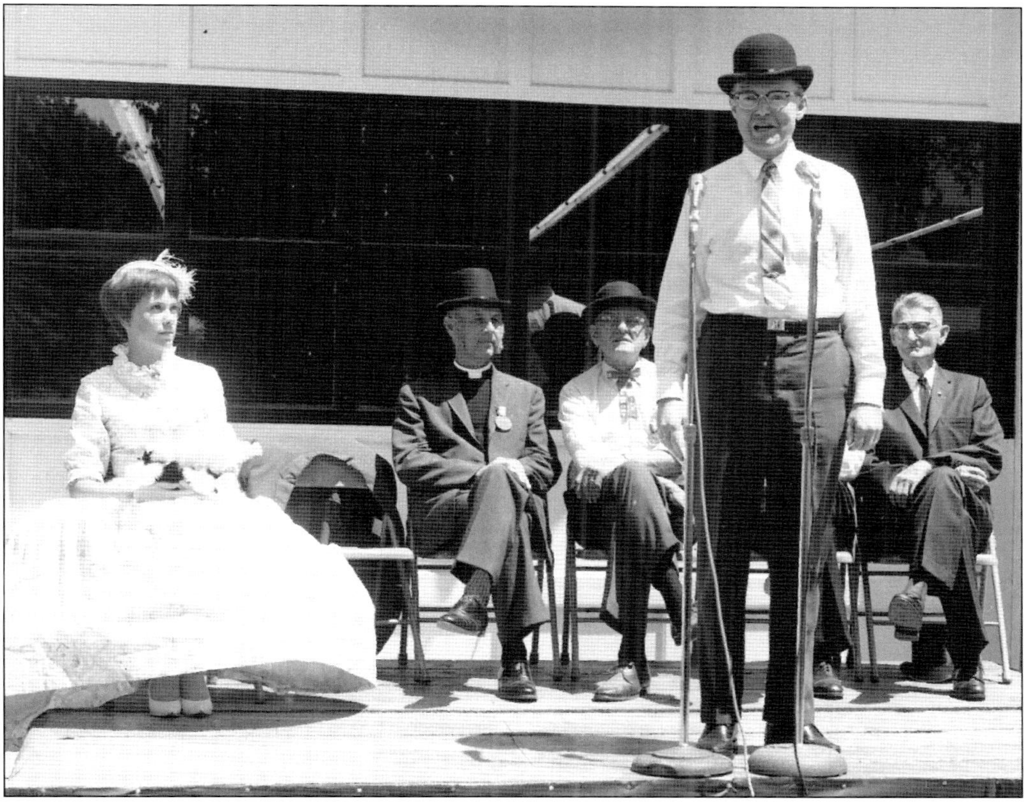

Jo Ann Tardy was chosen as the sesquicentennial queen for the celebration. With her on stage is Governor Reed at the microphone. Seated are, from left to right, the Reverend Homer Hughey, former governor Lewis O. Barrows, and Dr. Higgins. Later in the ceremony, Dr. Higgins was honored for his long service to the community. Many participants in the sesquicentennial events dressed in period clothing to commemorate the 1814 incorporation of the town.

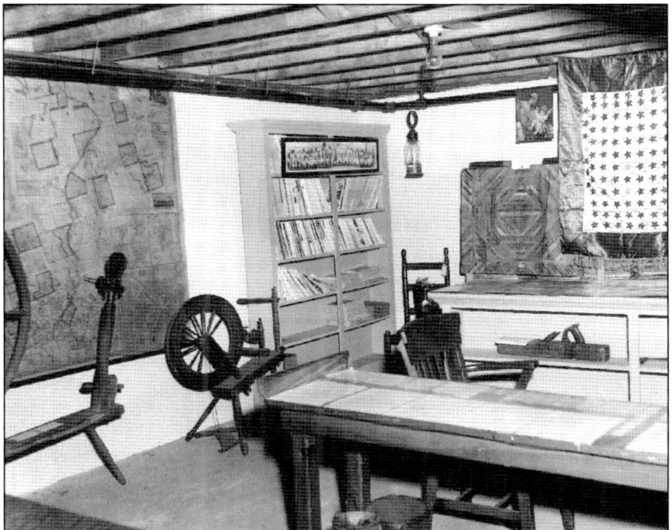

Businesses and organizations around town set up historical displays for the anniversary celebration. Shown here is a display at the Newport Public Library on Main Street created by the newly established Newport Historical Society. Gilman's Inc. displayed old tools. Beverly's Hair Fashions featured an antique doll and other items.

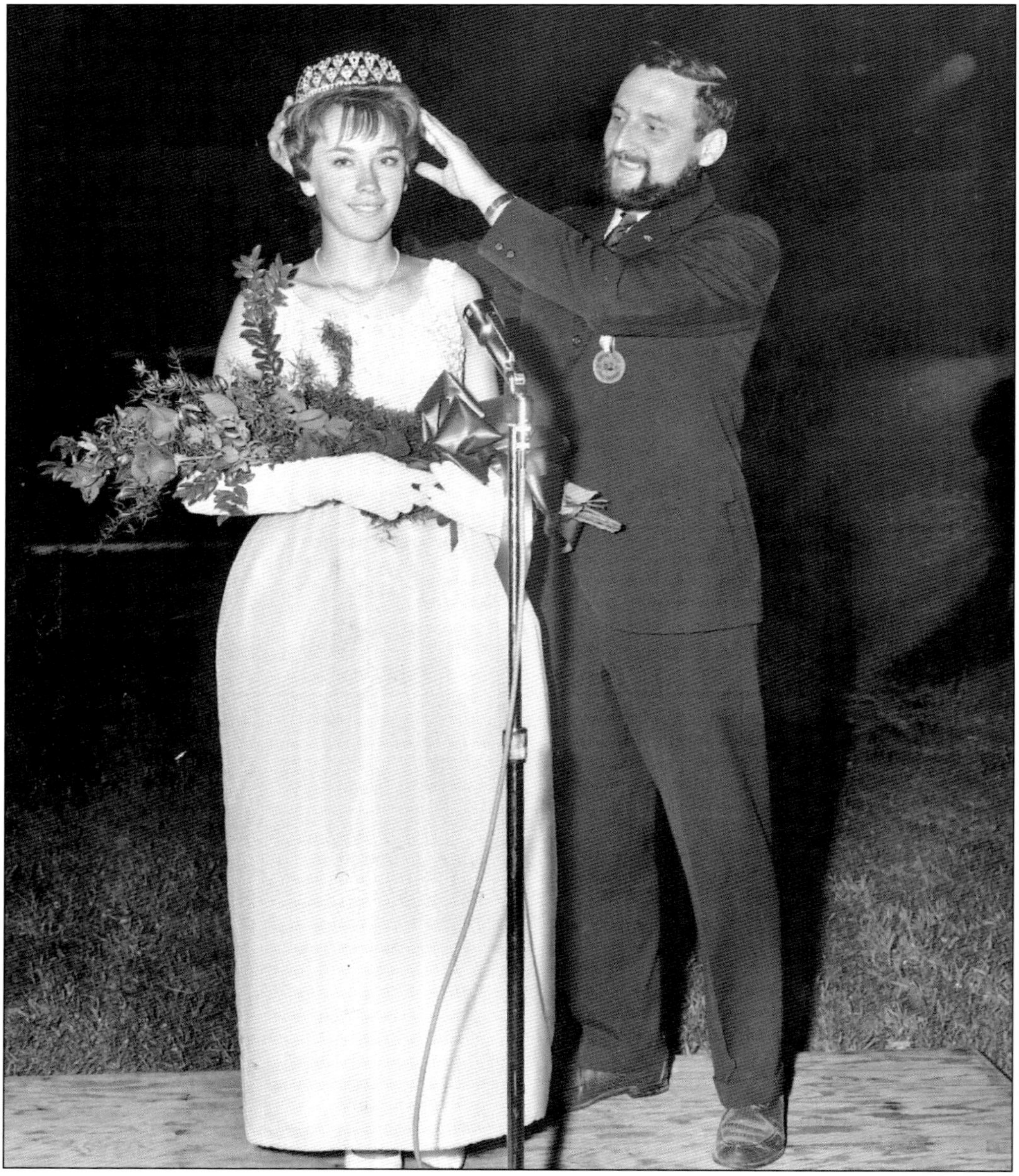

Master of ceremonies Gilman Friend crowns Jo Ann Tardy as the sesquicentennial queen at the sesquicentennial ball, held at the Newport state armory. (Frances Amo was second runner-up, and Barbara Chambers was first runner-up.) One hundred fifty couples attended, and many wore period attire. Tardy was awarded a dozen roses and a trip to the New York World's Fair. The armory was a perfect venue for the sesquicentennial ball. It was built with state funds in 1942 to provide a drill hall, basement shooting range, and other amenities to the Newport army unit. A newspaper article at the time noted, "The drill hall, occupying the entire width of the building, is a real surprise. It is 60 by 88 feet; the floor is of hardwood . . . It can be converted into a wonderful ballroom." Located opposite the swim front and boat landing, the armory has proven to be a good location for town events, including the annual town meeting each March. The building is now privately owned but leased to the town.

This float was arranged by the H.G. Women's Relief Corps. The group, founded in 1894, was named after Hollis Gardiner Libby, a 17-year-old from Newport who volunteered to serve in the Civil War in 1861. Libby took part in the first Battle of Bull Run then was fatally wounded at the second Battle of Bull Run. He died September 17, 1861. The group's float in the sesquicentennial parade emphasized the values of fraternity, charity, and loyalty.

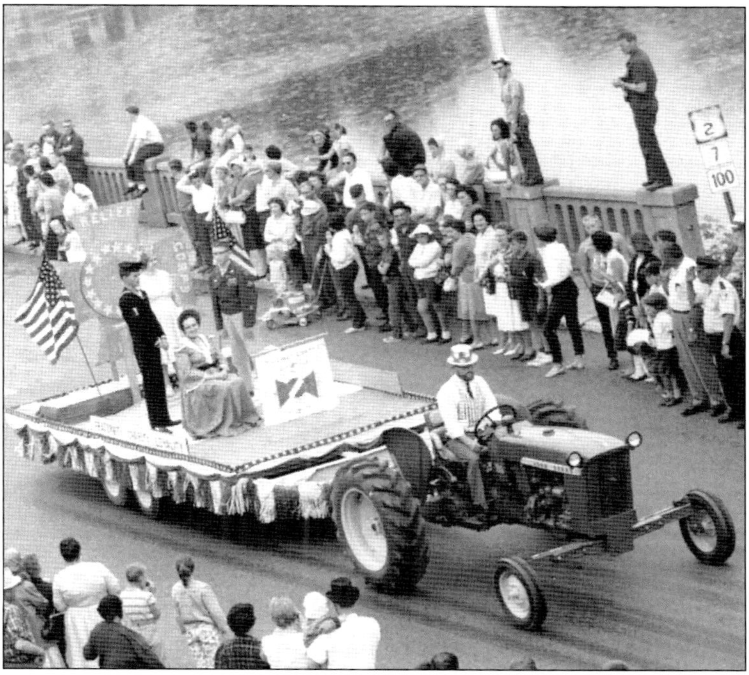

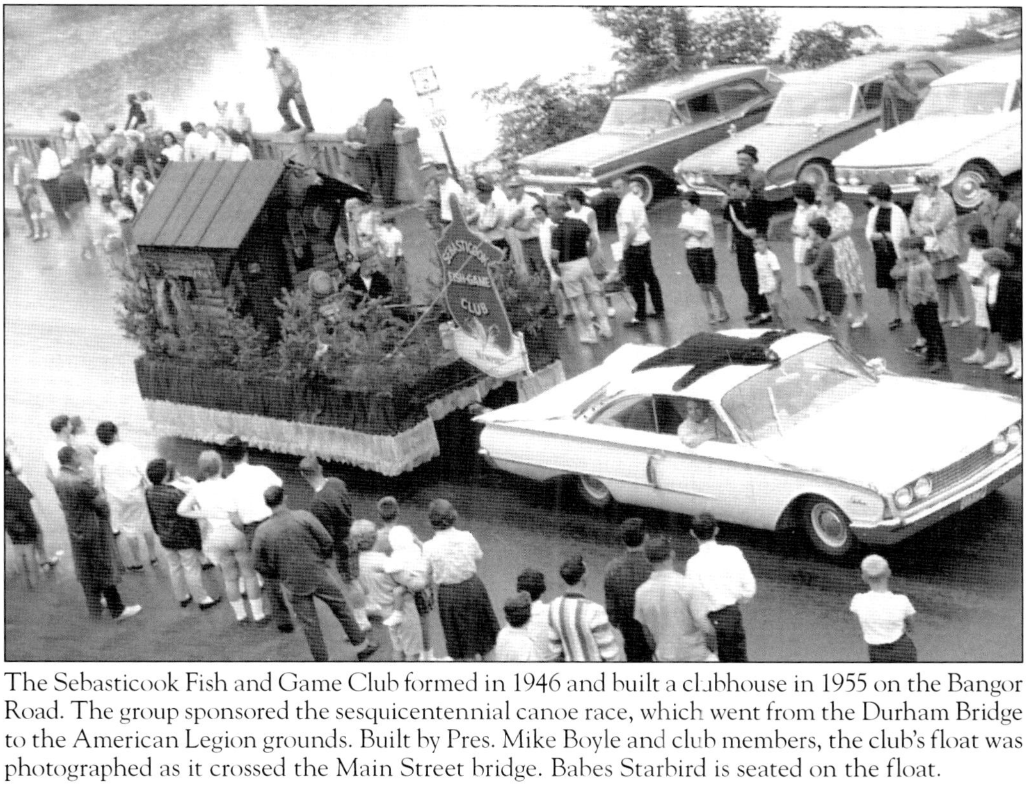

The Sebasticook Fish and Game Club formed in 1946 and built a clubhouse in 1955 on the Bangor Road. The group sponsored the sesquicentennial canoe race, which went from the Durham Bridge to the American Legion grounds. Built by Pres. Mike Boyle and club members, the club's float was photographed as it crossed the Main Street bridge. Babes Starbird is seated on the float.

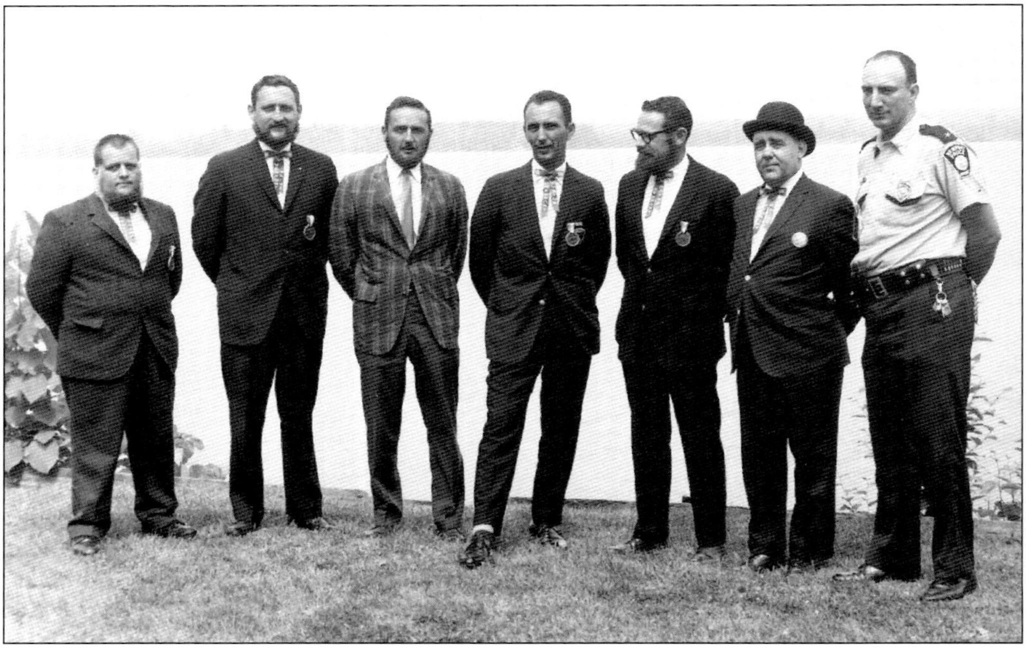

Former Boston Celtic Bob (Cooz) Cousy, sponsored by the H.P. Hood Company, flew in to Bangor and was driven to Newport to attend some of the sesquicentennial events. A luncheon was held in his honor, and guests included, from left to right, Spike King, Gilman ("Gillie") Friend, Peter Friend, Bob Cousy, Rick Banton, Judson Jude, and Howard Seavey.

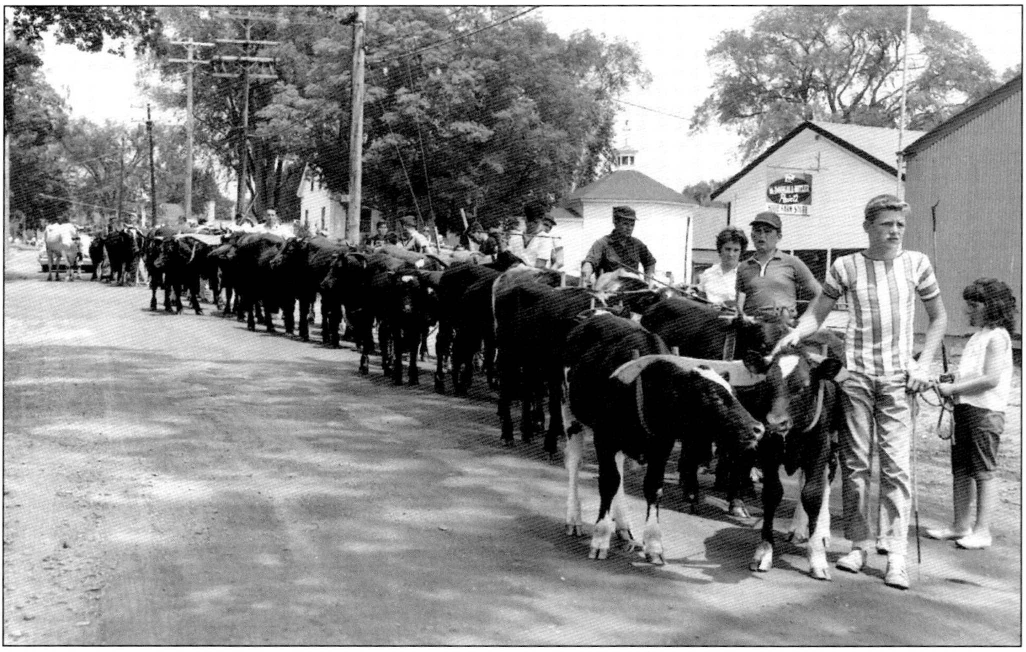

In this photograph, the 4-H Club drives oxen down Spring Street (past the noteworthy hexagonal barn of the former P.L. Bennett estate) during the sesquicentennial Homecoming Day. Agriculture is still an important part of the local economy, though fewer young people are involved.

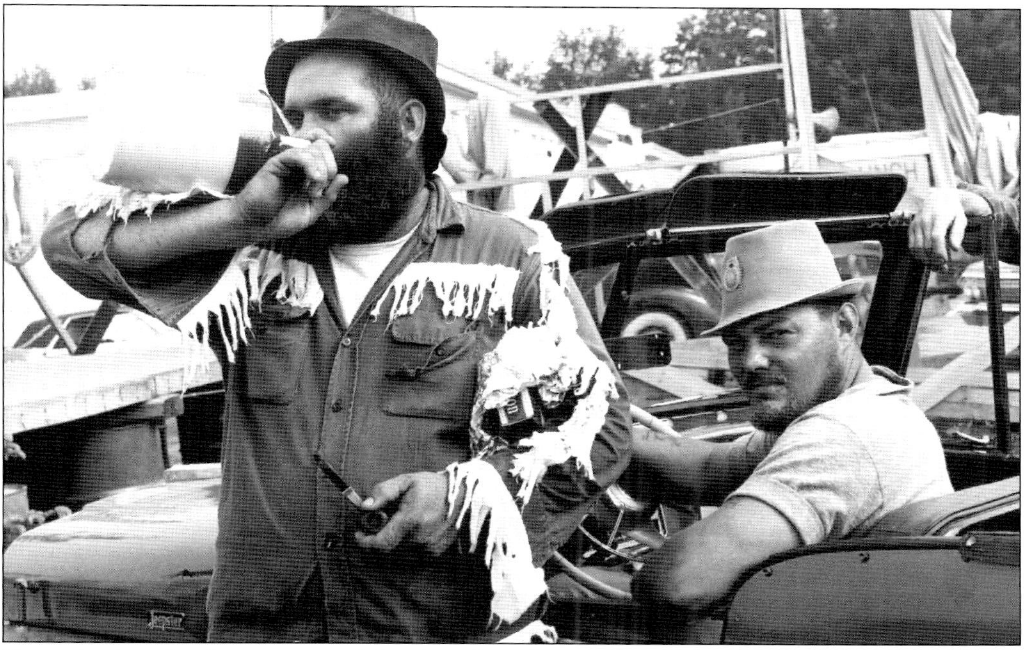

Hamming it up for the camera are John Ayer, first place winner in the whisker contest, and Edward "Sonny" Caruso. Participants in the "Whisker Rebellion" and members of the Sesquicentennial Belles formed a "caravan" to travel to several area towns. Members of the caravan, dressed in vintage costumes, visited town dignitaries and passed out handbills inviting people to Newport's celebration.

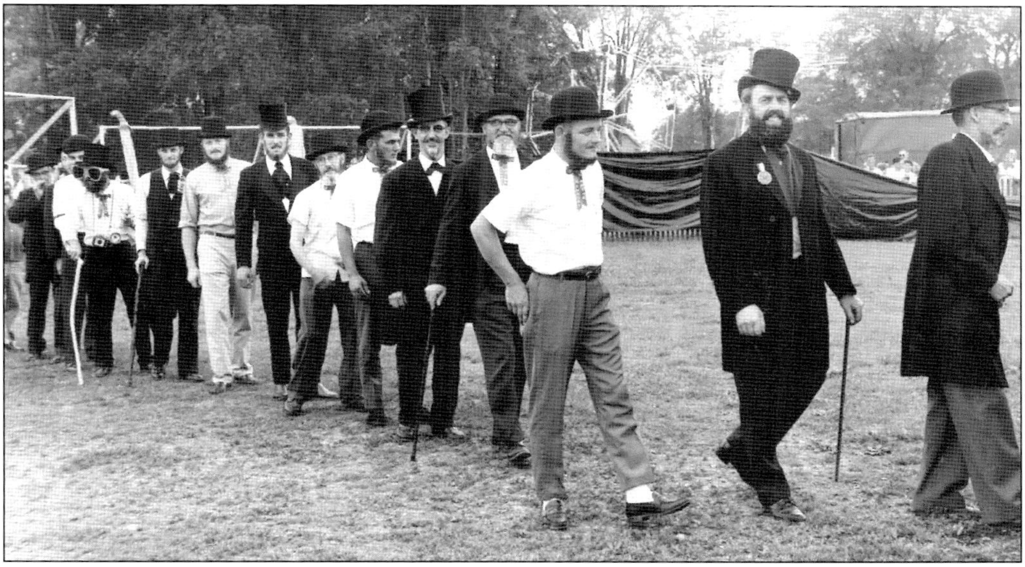

Participants in the whisker contest parade at the waterfront near the American Legion Hall. Members of the "Whisker Rebellion" (the bearded men) and the Belles attended events in costume throughout the area in the weeks leading up to the celebration. Although Newport was formally incorporated June 14, the sesquicentennial was celebrated over the Independence Day holiday, so more people would be able to participate.

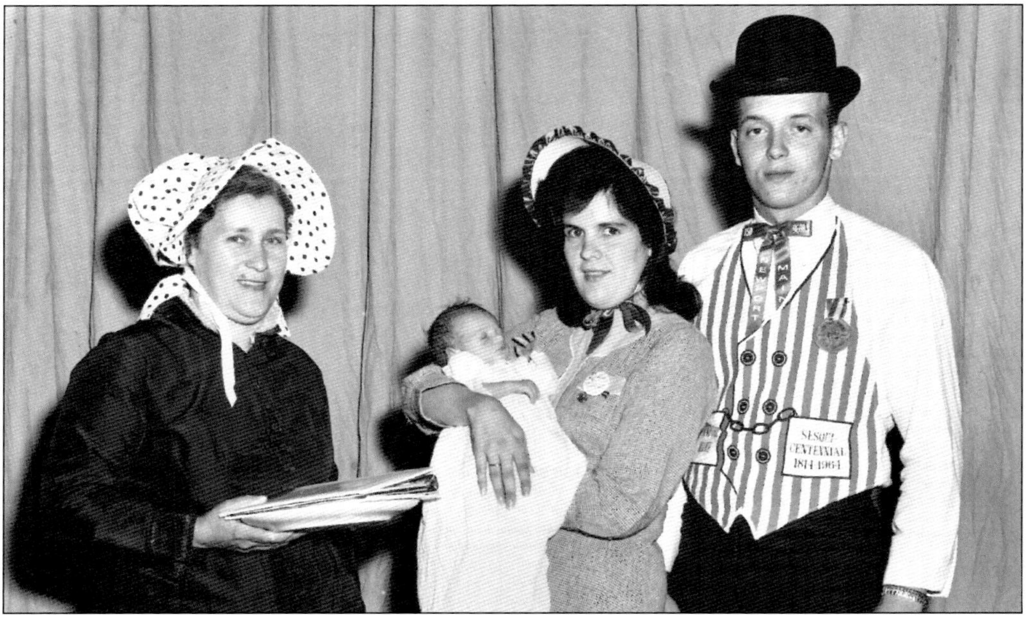

The sesquicentennial prince, Scott Testa, receives a gift from a Belle in vintage togs, Norma Garnett. Testa, the son of Mr. and Mrs. Raymond Testa, was born four weeks earlier, June 16.

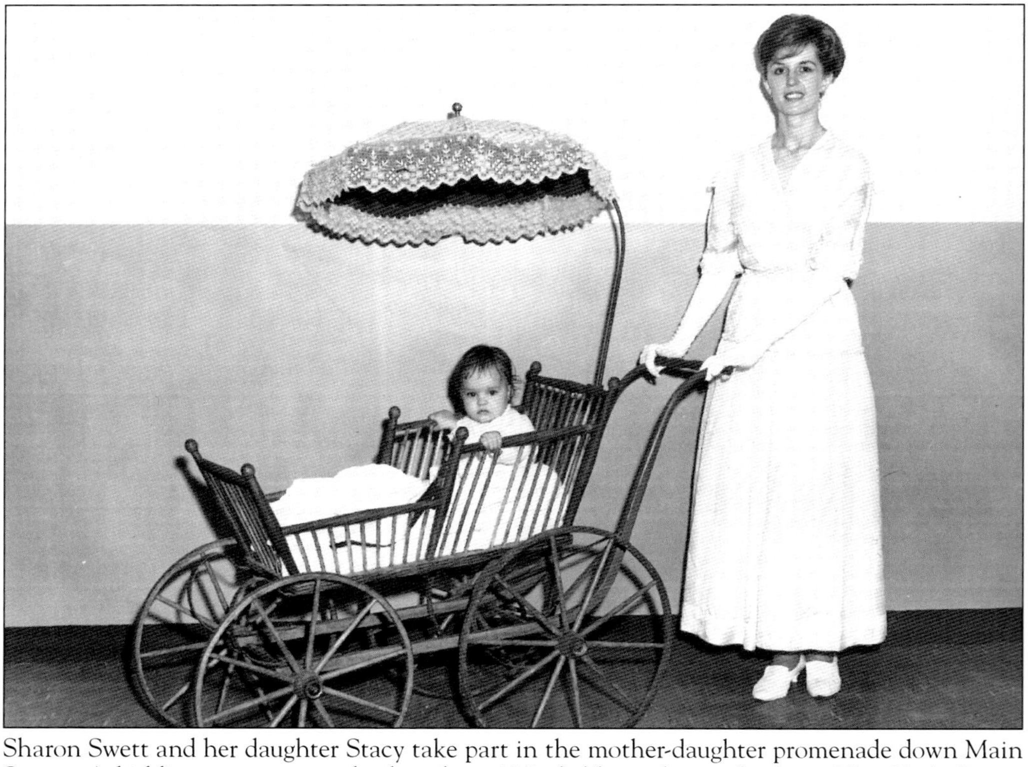

Sharon Swett and her daughter Stacy take part in the mother-daughter promenade down Main Street. A kiddie costume parade that drew 100 children also took place. The High Street Congregational Church hosted a baby contest, and all 40 entries took home prizes.

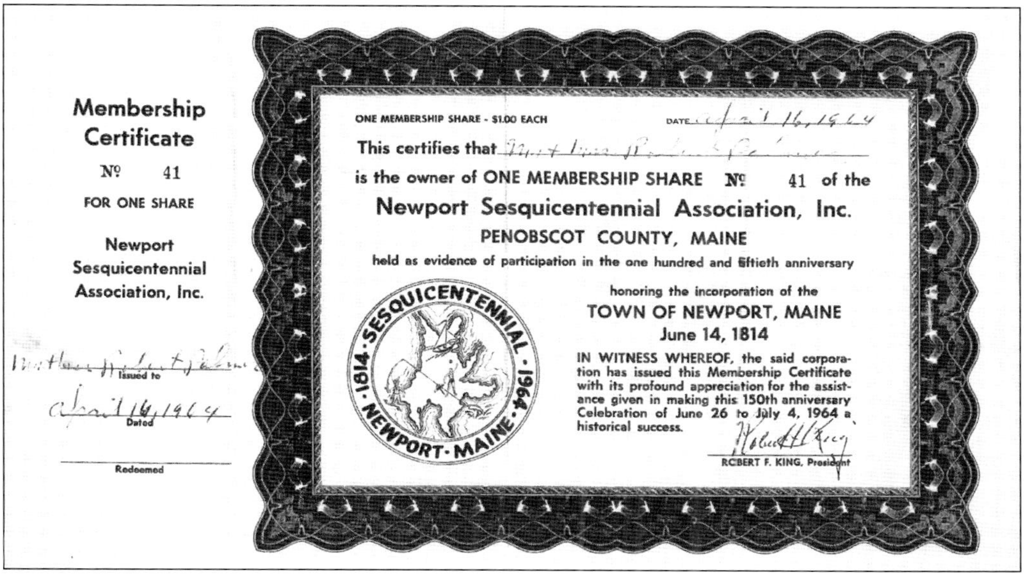

Membership Certificate

№ 41

FOR ONE SHARE

Newport Sesquicentennial Association, Inc.

Issued to

April 16, 1964

Dated

Redeemed

ONE MEMBERSHIP SHARE - $1.00 EACH

DATE April 16, 1964

This certifies that

is the owner of ONE MEMBERSHIP SHARE № 41 of the

Newport Sesquicentennial Association, Inc.

PENOBSCOT COUNTY, MAINE

held as evidence of participation in the one hundred and fiftieth anniversary

honoring the incorporation of the

TOWN OF NEWPORT, MAINE

June 14, 1814

IN WITNESS WHEREOF, the said corporation has issued this Membership Certificate with its profound appreciation for the assistance given in making this 150th anniversary Celebration of June 26 to July 4, 1964 a historical success.

ROBERT F. KING, President

To raise money for the festivities, sesquicentennial planners sold stock certificates. Most people kept their certificates as mementos, making it a particularly effective fundraiser. Committees met throughout the spring of 1964 to plan the events. Fundraising ideas were creative and plentiful.

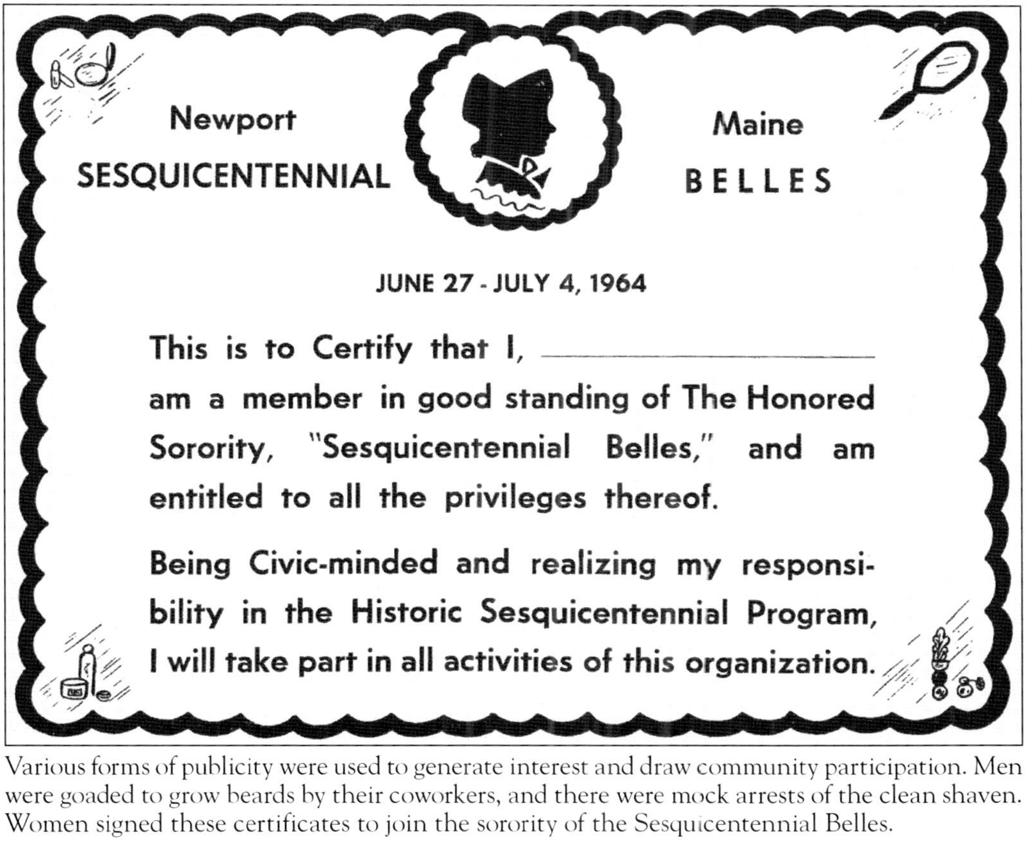

Newport Maine

SESQUICENTENNIAL BELLES

JUNE 27 - JULY 4, 1964

This is to Certify that I, ____________

am a member in good standing of The Honored Sorority, "Sesquicentennial Belles," and am entitled to all the privileges thereof.

Being Civic-minded and realizing my responsibility in the Historic Sesquicentennial Program, I will take part in all activities of this organization.

Various forms of publicity were used to generate interest and draw community participation. Men were goaded to grow beards by their coworkers, and there were mock arrests of the clean shaven. Women signed these certificates to join the sorority of the Sesquicentennial Belles.

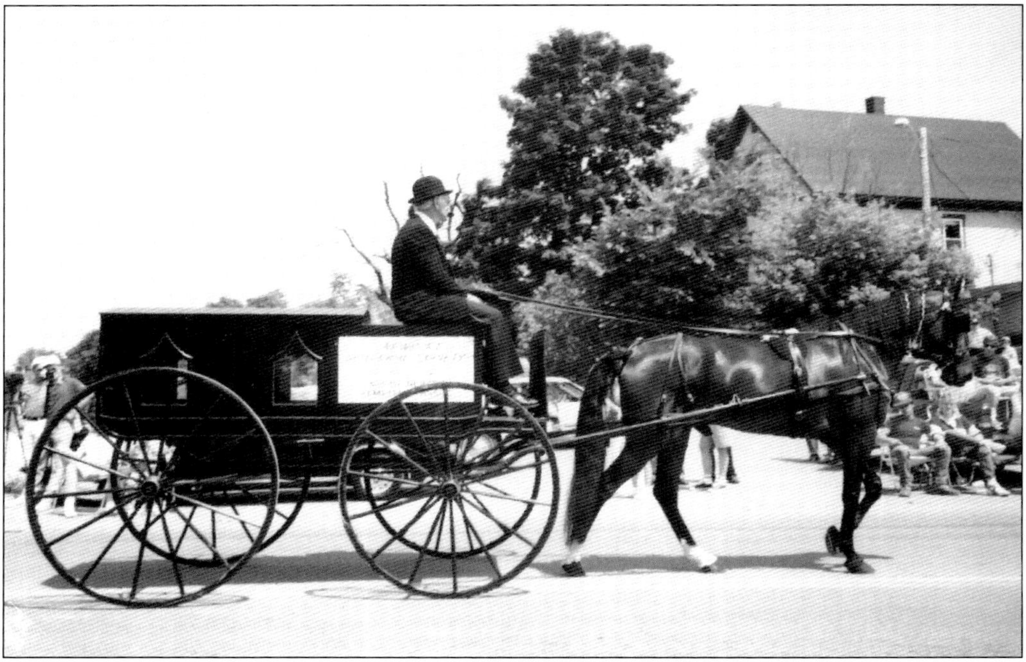

In 1987, the town planned events to commemorate its 175th anniversary celebration. While not as elaborate as the sesquicentennial, it featured a parade with more than 175 entries. Shown here is the North Newport Cemetery Association's antique hearse, one of the oldest in New England.

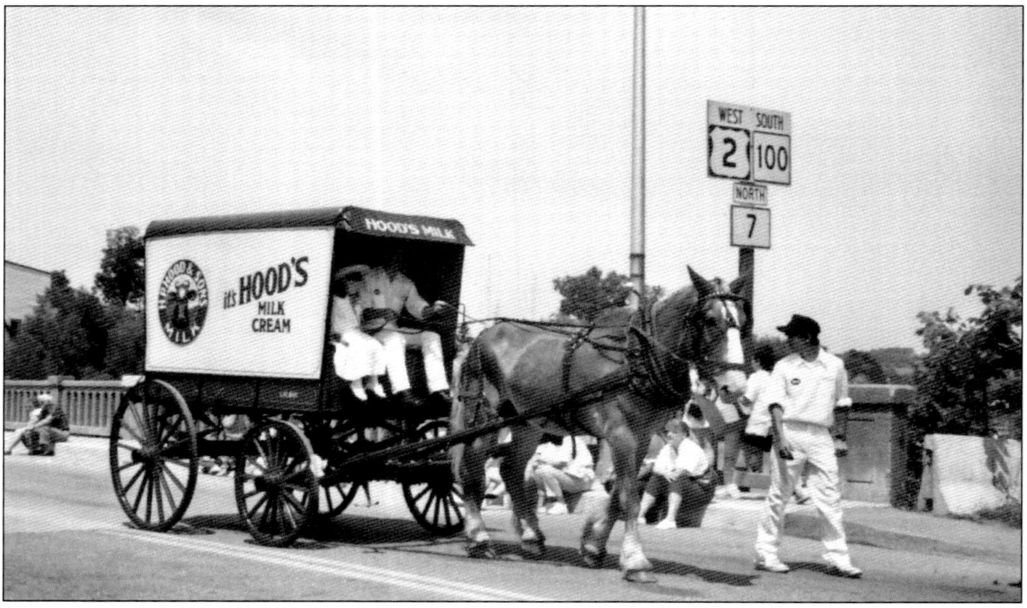

Newport's 175th birthday was celebrated the week of June 30, 1989. Long a major employer in the town, H.P. Hood provided a vintage milk wagon for the parade, as it had for the sesquicentennial. The dairy processing plant that eventually became Hood's opened in 1891. Located adjacent to the railroad tracks, the plant pumped condensed milk into special insulated train cars for transport until the 1950s. The Hood plant closed permanently in 1990.

Local businessman Goody Gilman was arrested by the Keystone Kops as part of the day's festivities. Lakefront events included a fire muster, a concert by the National Guard band, and a barbecue. A beard contest, fashion show, street dance, canoe race, and fireworks display were part of the five-day celebration.

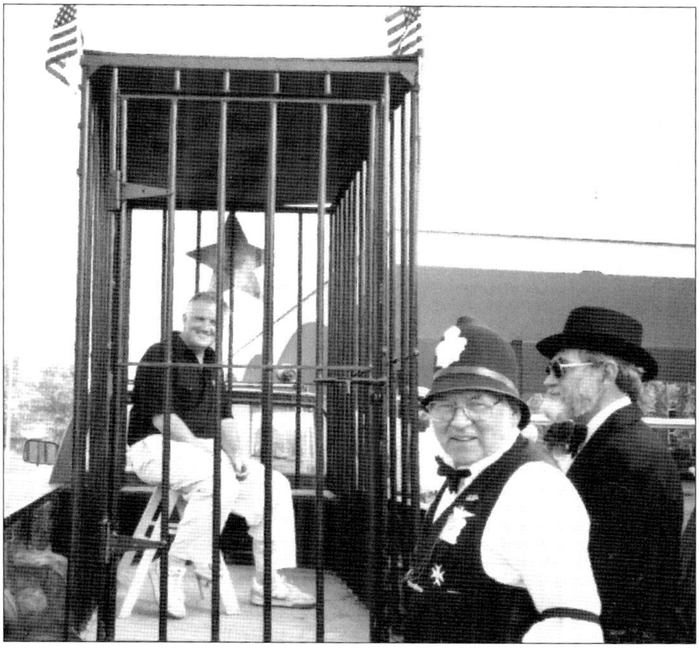

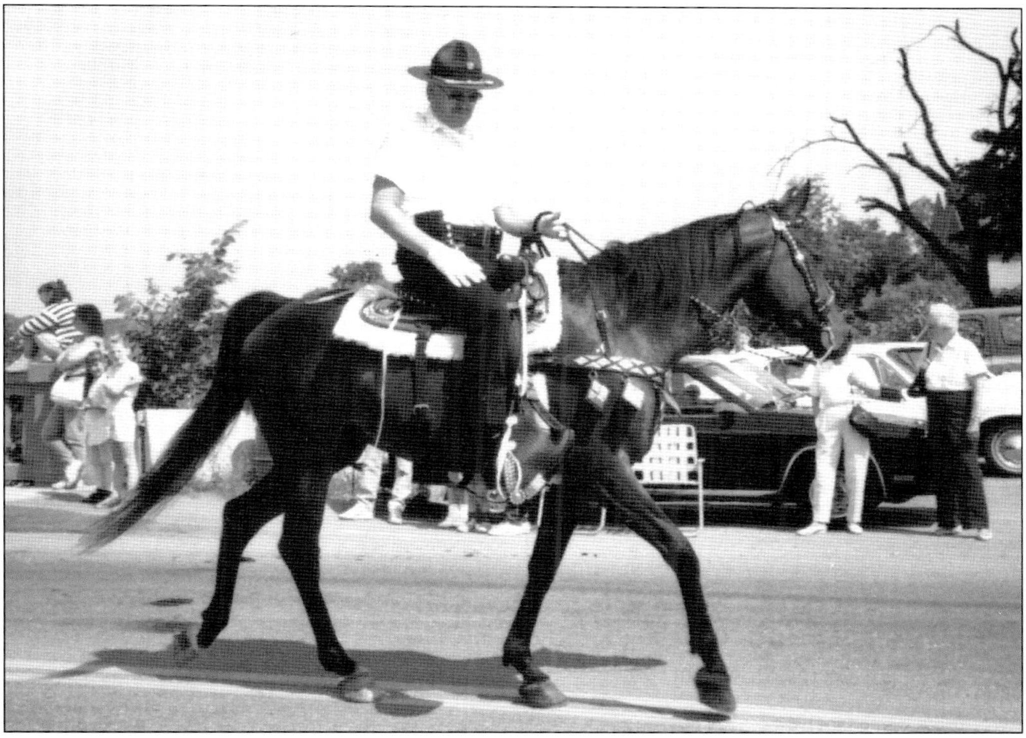

Newport's police chief (and later town manager) rode his horse, Nick, in the parade. Here, they are shown crossing the Main Street bridge. Newport's three-year revitalization campaign had been completed just in time for the 175th anniversary. Near the bridge, a small park and new gazebo were dedicated to Dr. Paul Burke.

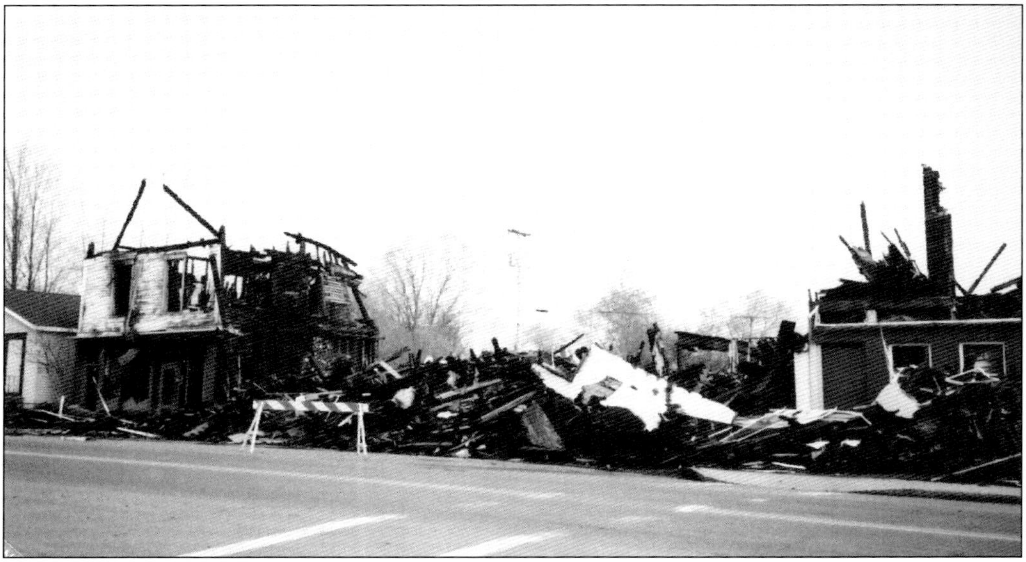

After the celebrations of 1989, there followed a difficult year for the town with a number of tragedies that affected the entire community. This photograph shows the aftermath of the May 1990 fire that razed the Gilman block (long the site of the Judkins and Gilman business) on Main Street. An entire block burned down and remained vacant for more than 15 years. (Courtesy of Goody Gilman.)

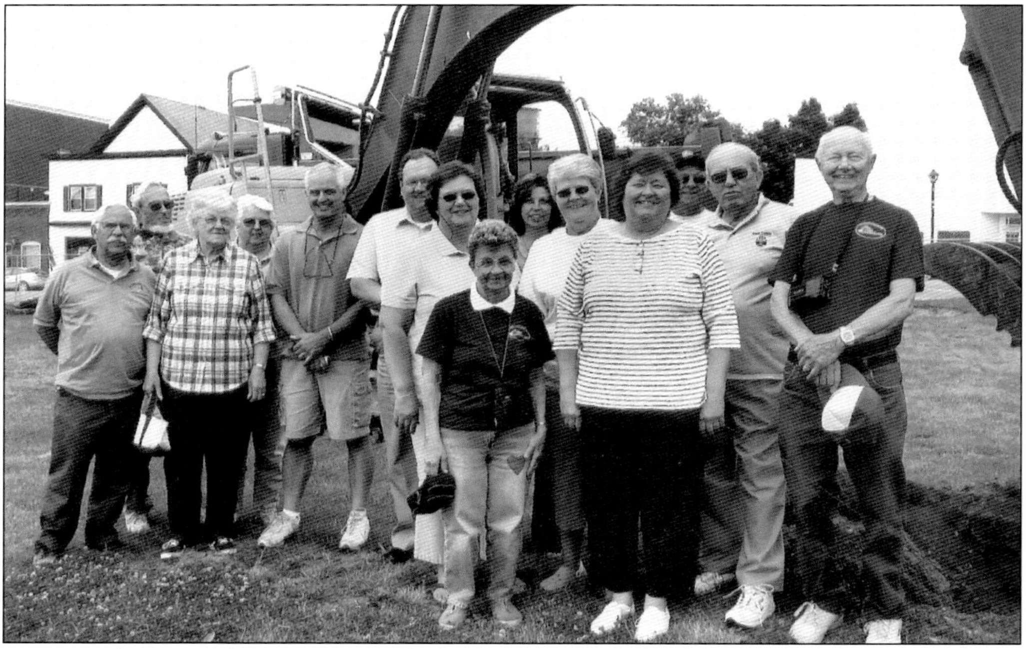

In 2007, after more than two years of meetings and fundraising efforts, the Newport Cultural Center broke ground at the Main Street site of the 1990 fire. Shown are some of the residents who helped make the Newport Cultural Center a reality: Ron Hopkins, Roland Petersen, Dot Landry, Alma Petersen, Jim Miller, Phil Brown, Sandra Brown, Gwen Emery, Paula Scott, Polly Michaud, Eileen Bemis, John Michaud, Dick Parlee, and Don Emery. (Courtesy of Polly Michaud.)

About the Newport Cultural Center

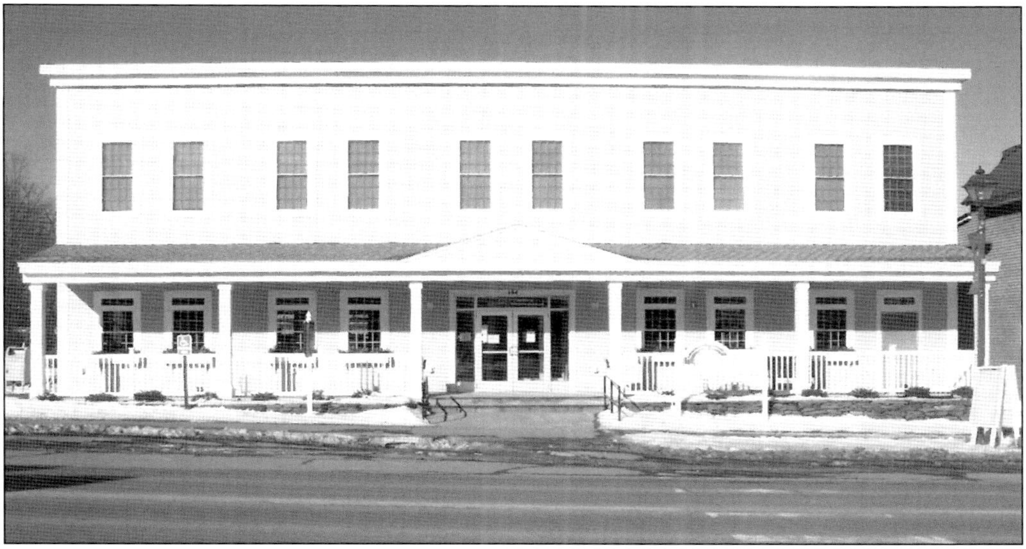

Opened in 2009, the Newport Cultural Center is the creation of a group of visionary local residents, officials, and business leaders. In addition to offering public library services and historical exhibits, the center offers a range of programming, including concerts, art exhibits, conferences, classes, concerts, and extensive programming for children. There are local history exhibits throughout the library book stacks and display areas as well as an extensive display of local Native American stone tool artifacts. Upstairs there is an archive and genealogy research room as well as a large storage area to safely house the artifacts and records documenting local history. There are two meeting spaces on the second floor, including the large community room and the Kasey Lander Children's Activity Room. The Newport Cultural Center is a nonprofit organization and depends upon the generous support of the community to continue offering its services. (Courtesy of Jan Laux.)